FISKE GUIDE TO GETTING INTO THE RIGHT COLLEGE

FOURTH EDITION

EDWARD B. FISKE & BRUCE G. HAMMOND

Published by Sourcebooks, Inc.
P.O. Box 4410
Naperville, Illinois 60567-4410
(630) 961-3900
Fax: (630) 961-2168
www.sourcebooks.com

Your comments and corrections are welcome. Please send them to:

Fiske Guide to Colleges
P.O. Box 287
Alstead, NH 03602
Fax: (603) 835-7859
Email: editor@fiskeguide.com

Printed and bound in the United States of America
DR 10 9 8 7 6 5 4 3 2 1

FISKE
GUIDE TO
GETTING INTO
THE RIGHT
COLLEGE

FOURTH EDITION

To our parents

Also by Edward B. Fiske

Fiske Guide to Colleges

Fiske Countdown to College with Bruce G. Hammond

Fiske Real College Essays That Work with Bruce G. Hammond

Fiske Nailing the New SAT with Bruce G. Hammond

Fiske WordPower with Jane Mallison and Margery Mandell

Fiske 250 Words Every High School Freshman Needs to Know
with Jane Mallison and David Hatcher

Fiske 250 Words Every High School Graduate Needs to Know
with Jane Mallison and David Hatcher

Smart Schools, Smart Kids: Why Do Some Schools Work?

Using Both Hands: Women and Education in Cambodia

Decentralization of Education: Politics and Consensus

When Schools Compete: A Cautionary Tale with Helen F. Ladd

Elusive Equity: Education Reform in Post-Apartheid South Africa
with Helen F. Ladd

Handbook of Research in Education Finance and Policy,
ed. with Helen F. Ladd

Contents

Part One:

Finding the Right College

1. The Search Begins
(or, What to Do When You Don't Have a Clue)

The college advising office in your high school can be a pretty intimidating place, especially on your first visit. An eerie silence pervades the room. As you cross the threshold and survey the scene, your eye catches the twelfth-grade boy who used to flick spitballs into your hair from the back of the bus when you were in middle school. He's still wearing the same flea-bitten Nine Inch Nails T-shirt, but now his nose is buried in a college guide as he scribbles feverishly in a spiral notebook. On the other side of the room, the girl from down the street with the doting mother and the 4.0 grade point average is staring purposefully into a computer screen, clacking the keyboard every few seconds as she calls up a new file. Suddenly, you get a sinking feeling that she and all the other kids in the room know exactly what they're doing. You're the only one who doesn't have a clue. Of course, you could always ask Mrs. Stonebreaker for help. That is, if you don't mind the familiar glasses-on-the-end-of-the-nose routine and the icy stare that says you've just asked the stupidest question of her thirty-four-year career. You want to beat a hasty retreat and come back later—much later.

It's no wonder that beginning college applicants often get the strong urge to run away and hide. Talk about an intimidating situation! Many students have barely gotten comfortable in high school before the college search looms ominously on the horizon. Rumblings about "selective colleges" and "the job market" begin to pop up in dinner conversations and guidance office bulletin boards. Friends who used to be party animals suddenly begin to hit the books and talk about "getting the grades for college." Relatives you haven't seen in years marvel about how much you've grown—and then want to know all about your career plans.

As if those storm clouds weren't threatening enough, there is the little matter of finding one college out of about twenty-two hundred four-year schools in the nation. They come in more flavors than Baskin-Robbins or Ben and Jerry ever dreamed of making—large, small, middle-sized, rural, urban, and a thousand permutations. If colleges were ice cream, a student could sample four or five flavors and make a choice. Unfortunately, college applicants must get it right the first time or go through the same agony again when they transfer. How can you figure out what sort of college is right for you?

One place you won't find the answer is your mailbox, which, if you have blackened a certain oval on your PSAT exam, has become a direct pipeline to the propaganda factories of colleges coast to coast. Though the deluge of college mail can be highly entertaining, every school from Harvard to Ho Hum U. advertises a similar bill of goods. If you were confused before, try figuring out the difference between two colleges by reading the glossy viewbooks. The scenes in their pages are always the same: eager hordes of racially diverse undergraduates thinking deep thoughts or frolicking in a perpetual spring against a backdrop of white columns and grassy lawns. Let's see now...College X offers "academic excellence" and "rich diversity." On the other hand, College Y offers "rich diversity" and "academic excellence." Still can't tell the difference?

Meanwhile, all the adults in your life (and a few you've never seen before) offer their two cents about where you should go to school. From your grandfather, you get the latest updates on colleges and the job market from *U.S. News & World Report*. Mom says that you can choose any school you want—as long as you stay within fifty miles of home. Even your great uncle Pete, whom you barely know, takes you under his wing and says he has the perfect college for you based on his wonderful experience in the early 1960s.

If you're confused by conflicting advice, if you're put off by college propaganda, if you're eager to get started but don't know where to begin, this book is your ticket to a successful college search. We'll take you on a guided tour of the entire process: how to find the right college for you, how to get in, and how to pay for it. Along the way, we'll help you focus your thoughts and figure out what you're really looking for. We'll tell you how to cut through the college search nonsense and then give you insider sketches of hundreds of colleges in dozens of categories. We'll reveal the secrets of the highly selective admissions game and how you can play it to win. And finally, we'll delve into the shadowy world of college financial aid—how to get your hands on it and how your need for it may affect your chances for admission.

Before we begin plotting strategy, let's step back for a minute and remind ourselves of what the college search is all about. Amid all the anxiety about getting in, it helps to keep the big picture in mind.

Why College?

That may seem like a stupid question, but there is more to the answer than meets the eye. Practicality says that people go to college to get a good job after graduation and there is plenty of research to show that college is a sound economic investment. On average, college graduates can expect to earn more than twice as much as those with a high school diploma over a working lifetime and the gap is widening.

There are two schools of thought about how to get the most out of your college experience. Many educators stress the value of exposure to a broad spectrum of human knowledge. The phrase "liberal arts education" connotes learning that "liberates" the mind to think new thoughts. A liberal arts education is an introduction to the great events and ideas of the past, as well as the most recent discoveries of today. It can include history, art, astronomy, zoology, and everything in between. It doesn't prepare you for any particular job, but instead equips you with the basic skills—reading, writing, thinking—to meet any challenge that comes down the pike. In other words, it means "learning to learn."

The alternative to a liberal arts education is to use college to prepare for a particular career. This approach places less emphasis on a well-rounded general education than the acquisition of knowledge related to a particular job or subset of jobs. Some careers, such as engineering and architecture, require concentrated training beginning in the freshman year that leaves little time for smelling the roses. Facing the uncertainties of the job market, nervous undergraduates often feel strong pressure to "major in something practical."

Nervous undergraduates often feel strong pressure to "major in something practical."

Nearly as important as what you study in the classroom will be the things you do outside of class. In recent years, the possibilities have multiplied dramatically. Study abroad once meant a handful of students doing a semester in Europe. Today, opportunities are available to the distant corners of the globe, during both the academic year and the summer. Internships, which will allow you to sample the world of work while in college, are also more plentiful than ever before. Traditional extracurriculars such as newspaper or community service also provide outlets for hands-on learning.

In addition to the many opportunities it provides, college attendance also provides a high school graduate with the first public measure of his or her academic and personal success. Admission to a "name" college is like getting an *A* in growing up and comes with the presumption of future success to follow. The ego of anyone—especially an eighteen-year-old—is fragile. Who wouldn't want a stamp of approval from one of the world's most respected institutions?

With all the practical reasons to attend, let us not forget that college is also a once-in-a-lifetime experience. You can test your limits, try new things, and make some incredibly stupid mistakes—all without the responsibility of having to make a living. The friendships you form will last a lifetime and so, too, will the memories. Decades from now, when you're rocking away the retirement years on the front porch, college will probably rank high on the list of things that made life worth living.

Taking A Year Off

More and more of today's brightest students are deciding that they want to go to college—but not right away. From hiking in the Alps to working on an assembly line, year-off experiences give students a chance to see the world, make some money, and recharge their batteries before plunging ahead with four more years of school. The possibilities are endless; just make sure you have a well thought out plan that will expand your horizons. If you're contemplating a year off, we recommend that you go through the college admission process as a high school senior and then ask to defer enrollment at the college of your choice. Most will be happy to oblige.

There is no perfect way to categorize everything a college experience can give you, but these are the basics: (1) a liberal arts education, (2) career training, (3) a prestigious affiliation, and (4) enduring friendships and a once-in-a-lifetime experience. Which of them seems most important to you? Are there other benefits that you think are just as crucial? Don't feel pressure to answer right away because your choice will probably dictate the shape of your college search. Most applicants will be looking for a combination of some or all, but the process of examining priorities is still useful. If a liberal arts education ranks high, you'll definitely want to look at institutions where teaching is a priority. Those interested in career training should focus less on institution-wide characteristics than on the programs in their field of interest. Interest in a prestigious affiliation means playing the highly selective admissions game. If friendships and experiences are a high priority, you may be the kind of person who marches to his or her own drummer or at least the type who is less interested in high-powered academics than a healthy balance between work and play.

Only you can decide what is important in a college, but we would like to help you avoid two major pitfalls.

First, many applicants mistakenly think that prestige automatically equals academic quality. Call it the brand-name syndrome: the idea that if you haven't heard of a college, it can't be any good. Many big-name schools do deliver educational excellence, but others are overcrowded, overrated, and coasting on reputation. There are scores of comparatively little-known colleges, most of them small, that offer an education every bit as good.

But you're probably thinking, Don't all the best jobs go to Ivy League graduates? Not by a long shot. They get their share, but so do graduates of countless other schools that aren't household names. In a landmark study of colleges with the highest percentage of graduates earning a PhD degree, the top finisher wasn't Harvard, but Harvey Mudd College. Harvard placed thirty-seventh, behind liberal arts colleges such as Eckerd, Wabash, and Kalamazoo, which continue to produce excellent graduates with much less fanfare.

Famous Liberal Arts Graduates	Major
Mitch Albom	Sociology
Katie Couric	American Studies
Hilary Clinton	Political Science
Matt Groening	Philosophy
Eric Holder	History
Barack Obama	Political Science
Conan O'Brien	Literature and U.S. History
Regis Philbin	Sociology
Colin Powell	Geology
Maria Shriver	American Studies
Jon Stewart	Psychology
Source: Current Biography	

Our second pitfall is also caused by career jitters. In the name of practicality, too many students get stampeded into career preparation and lose the once-in-a-lifetime chance to get an education. If you've wanted to be an accountant since age six, don't hesitate. But if you plan to major in accounting just because you think that's where the jobs are, think again. What's the point of using your college years to prepare for a career you might not enjoy? And how are you going to know unless you sample different things? In the working world, nothing is less practical than devoting fifty or sixty hours a week to a job you don't like. That is why so many high-priced lawyers and investment bankers are quitting their jobs today. They have a few extra dollars in their pockets, but they are also miserable.

> **Getting a Clue about Your Major**
>
> For a sneak peek at the choices you'll face in college, browse the academic catalog of a college or university, either printed or online. Which departments offer the most courses that seem interesting?

College career preparation may help you land that first job, but it may also leave you stranded there when other people have moved on to bigger and better things. The Bureau of Labor Statistics says that current college graduates will go through half a dozen careers on average. Even for those who stay in the same industry, a liberal arts education offers the flexibility to make lateral moves on the way to the top. As any corporate president will tell you, the people who get to the executive suite are the ones who see the big picture and, more often than not, got a liberal arts education. You can always go back later for that business or law degree when the time is right.

Despite all we have said, anyone contemplating the liberal arts should keep at least one eye on the job market. Technology can create new opportunities almost overnight, as it did with the Internet in the 1990s. Entire industries are now thriving in cyberspace that were not even imagined twenty years ago. But in other sectors, corporate downsizing and mergers have taken a heavy toll on entry-level positions. The ups and downs of the national economy can drastically change the hiring picture from year to year and competition for the most desirable positions is always tough.

So what should you do? Grab your bean counter and head for an accounting class? We think not, unless accounting happens to be your passion. Our blanket recommendation is simple: follow your interests. And follow them. And follow them. The person who succeeds in tomorrow's job market isn't going to be the one who majors in something "practical"—or, for that matter, the one with the highest grade point average. Rather, it will be the person who pursues an interest—any interest—wherever it may lead.

When you find an academic subject that appeals to you, talk to the professor after class. Join an extracurricular group that may have related concerns or find out from the professor about private companies that might be doing related work.

Call those companies. Intern for those companies. Take summer jobs at those companies. The students who habitually take that kind of initiative, no matter what their major, are going to be the ones who get the jobs. As one high-ranking executive at B.F. Goodrich told us, "I run a three-hundred-million-dollar-a-year operation and, frankly, I don't care what they study. We hired someone recently because he had been head of Habitat for Humanity at the University of Florida. If a person can talk intelligently about experiences they've had, I listen."

Among other things, your college experience will give you four years to search out at least one thing that you love to do. Once you've found your passion, go after it with everything you've got. You may find that what is the most interesting is also the most practical.

In the final analysis, your college experience is about something even more important than your career: the kind of person you will one day become. In one of his final reports as president of Yale University, Kingman Brewster Jr. described the value of a liberal arts education and we can think of no better way to make the case than to remember his words:

> The most fundamental value of a liberal education is that it makes life more interesting. This is true whether you are fetched up on a desert island or adrift in the impersonal loneliness of the urban hurly-burly. It allows you to see things which the undereducated do not see. It allows you to understand things that the untutored find incomprehensible. It allows you to think things which do not occur to the less learned. In short, it makes it less likely that you will be bored with life. It also makes it less likely that you will be a crashing bore to those whose company you keep.

2. Sizing Yourself Up

In case you haven't noticed, today's world is changing at a pace that would boggle the minds of people in centuries past. The possibilities of 21st century life are endless. We can go almost anywhere, do almost anything, and communicate with virtually anyone instantaneously with texts and tweets. No one knows what the next big thing will be, but we can be sure that it will come sooner rather than later.

With frenetic change all around, society is now asking you to participate in a rite of passage that has been going on for decades and centuries—to pack your bags and head off to college for four years. For better or worse, you'll be arriving at institutions that have changed relatively little in the midst of our societal upheaval. Professors still hold forth in front of students who sit in rows, teaching assistants still conduct discussion sections, and students still hand-write exams on creaky desks. The list of majors available to you is largely unchanged from 50 years ago, as are the requirements for graduation. Weekend social life, with its parties and protests, is not much different than it was a generation ago.

But college life has not been entirely immune to the digital age. The biggest change has been the amount of time that students spend on the Internet, and the related fact that libraries are now mainly study spaces rather than places to get information from books. Classes and majors may be largely the same, but a new array of activities outside the classroom beckons students who have the initiative to take advantage. Students now routinely travel to the remotest corners of the globe—on break, during the summer, or as part of a term abroad. Internships that provide hands-on experience in the business world are now a standard part of the college experience. Today's college students have a wider array of choices than at any other time in the history of higher education.

If the nature of a college education is changing, albeit slowly, the process of getting in is also different from a generation ago, and the change is not for the better. Today's admissions process resembles a high-stakes obstacle course. Many colleges are more interested in making a sale than they are in making a match. Under intense competitive pressure, many won't hesitate to sell you a bill of goods if they can get their hands on your tuition dollars. Guidance counselors generally mean well, but they are often under duress from principals and trustees to steer students toward prestigious schools regardless of whether the fit is right. Your friends won't be shy with advice on where to go, but their knowledge is generally limited to a small group of hot colleges that everyone is talking about. National publications rake in millions by playing on the public's fascination with rankings, but a close look at their criteria reveals distinctions without a difference.

Before you find yourself spinning headlong on this merry-go-round, take a step back. This is your life and your college career. What are you looking for in a college? Think hard and don't answer right away. Before you throw yourself and your life history on the mercy of college admissions officers, you need to take some time to objectively and honestly evaluate your needs, likes and dislikes, strengths and weaknesses. What do you have to offer a college? What can a college do for you?

Unlike the high school selection process, which is usually predetermined by your parents' property lines, income, or religious affiliation, picking a college isn't a procedure you can brush off on dear ol' Mom and Dad. You have to take some initiative. You're the best judge of how well each school fits your personal needs and academic goals.

We encourage you to view the college selection process as the first semester in your higher education. Life's transitions often call forth extra energy and focus. The college search is no exception. For the first time, you'll be contemplating a life away from home that will unfold in any direction you choose. Visions of majors and careers will dance in your head as you sample various institutions of higher learning, each with hundreds of millions of dollars in academic resources; it is hard to imagine a better hands-on seminar in research and matchmaking than the college search. The main impact, however, will be measured by what you learn about yourself. Piqued by new worlds of learning and tested by the competition of the admissions process, you'll be pushed as never before to show your accomplishments, clarify your interests, and chart a course for the future. More than one parent has watched in amazement as an erstwhile teenager suddenly emerged as an adult during the course of a college tour. Be ready when your time comes.

Develop Your Criteria

Setting priorities is crucial to a successful college search. The main problem won't be thinking of qualities to look for—you could probably name dozens—but rather figuring out what criteria should play a defining role in your search. One strategy is to begin with a personal inventory of your own strengths and weaknesses and your

> **Summer Job, Lifetime Career**
>
> If you're interested in a career-oriented major, volunteer during the summer with someone who works in the field to test it out. See your guidance counselor for ideas.

"wish list" for a college. This method tends to work well for compulsive list-makers and other highly organized people. What sorts of things are you especially good at? Do you have a list of skills or interests that you would like to explore further? What sort of personality are you looking for in a college? Mainstream? Conservative? Offbeat? What about extracurriculars? If you are really into riding horses, you might include a strong equestrian program in your criteria.

Serious students should think carefully about the intellectual climate they are seeking. At some schools, students routinely stay up until 3:00 AM talking about topics like the value of deconstructing literary texts or the pros and cons of free trade. These same students would be viewed as geeks or weirdos on less cosmopolitan campuses. Athletes should take a hard look at whether they really want to play college ball and, if so, whether they want to go for an athletic scholarship or play at the less-pressured Division III level. Either way, intercollegiate sports require a huge time commitment.

Young women have an opportunity all to themselves—the chance to study at a women's college. The One-Hour College Finder (Chapter 6) profiles twelve such campuses, a vastly underappreciated resource on today's higher education scene. With small classes and strong encouragement from faculty, students at women's colleges move on to graduate study in significantly higher numbers than their counterparts at coed schools, especially in the natural sciences. Males seeking an all-male experience will find four options in the Finder: Hampden-Sydney College, Morehouse College, Deep Springs College, and Wabash College.

If you want to be a lawyer, don't worry yourself looking for something labeled "prelaw."

Students with a firm career goal will want to look for a course of study that matches their needs. If you want to major in aerospace engineering, your search will be limited to schools that have the program. Outside of specialized areas like this, many applicants overestimate the importance of their anticipated major in choosing a college. If you're interested in a liberal arts field, your expected major may have little to do with your college selection.

A big purpose of college is to develop interests and set goals. Most students change their intentions regarding a major at least two or three times before graduation and, once out in the working world, they often end up in jobs bearing no relation to their academic specialty. Even those with a firm career goal may not need as much specialization as they think at the undergraduate level. If you want to be a lawyer, don't worry yourself looking for something labeled "prelaw." Follow your interests, get the best liberal arts education available, and then apply to law school.

Naturally, it is never a bad idea to check out the department(s) of any likely major and, occasionally, your choice of major will suggest a direction for your search. If you're really into national politics, it may make sense to look at some schools in or near Washington, D.C. If you think you're interested in a relatively specialized field, say, anthropology, then be sure to look for some colleges that are a good match for you and also have good programs in anthropology. But for the most part, rumors about top-ranked departments in this or that should be no more than a tie-breaker between schools you like for more important reasons. There are good professors (and bad ones) in any department. You'll have plenty of time to figure out who is who once you've enrolled.

Being undecided about your career path as a senior in high school is often a sign of intelligence. Don't feel bad if you have absolutely no idea what you're going to do when you "grow up." One of the reasons you'll be paying megabucks to the college of your choice is the prospect that it will open some new doors for you and expand your horizons. Instead of worrying about particular departments, try to keep the focus on big-picture items like, "What's the academic climate?" "How big are the freshman classes?" "Do I like it here?" and "Are these my kind of people?"

As you ponder academic and extracurricular life on various campuses, there is one more question to think about: which campus will best allow me to pursue academic and career interests outside the classroom? Some institutions are much better than others in helping students make the transition from traditional classrooms to the work world. How are opportunities such as internships, study abroad, independent study, and online work woven into the curriculum? Most of the recent innovation in higher education has occurred in these categories. The list of available opportunities at each institution will be a good barometer of how well it is engaging with the needs of today's students.

Keep an Open Mind

The biggest mistake of beginning applicants is hyper-choosiness. At the extreme is the "perfect-school syndrome," which comes in two basic forms.

In one category are the applicants who refuse to consider any school that doesn't have every little thing they want in a college. If you're one who begins the process with a detailed picture of Perfect U. in mind, you may want to remember the oft-quoted advice, "Two out of three ain't bad." If a college seems to have most of the qualities you seek, give it a chance. You may come to realize that some things you thought were absolutely essential are really not that crucial after all.

The other strain of perfect-school syndrome is the applicant who gets stuck on a "dream" school at the beginning and then won't look anywhere else. With twenty-two hundred four-year colleges out there (not counting those in Canada), it is just a bit silly to insist that only one will meet your needs. Having a first choice is okay, but the whole purpose of the search is to consider new options and uncover new possibilities. A student who has only one dream school—especially if it is a highly selective one—could be headed for disappointment.

As you begin the college search, don't expect any quick revelations. The answers will unfold in due time. Our advice? Be patient. Set priorities. Keep an open mind. Reexamine priorities. Be patient.

To get the ball rolling, move on to the Sizing-Yourself-Up Survey.

Fiske's Sizing-Yourself-Up Survey

With apologies to Socrates, knowing thyself is easier said than done. Most high school students can analyze a differential equation or a Shakespearean play with the greatest of ease, but when it comes to cataloging their own strengths, weaknesses, likes, and dislikes, many draw a blank. But self-knowledge is crucial to the matching process at the heart of a successful college search. The thirty-item survey below offers a simple way to get a handle on some crucial issues in college selection—and what sort of college may fit your preferences.

In the space beside each statement, rate your feelings on a scale of 1 to 10, with 10 = Strongly Agree, 1 = Strongly Disagree, and 5 = Not Sure/Don't Have Strong Feelings. (For instance, a rating of 7 would mean that you agree with the statement, but that the issue is a lower priority than those you rated 8, 9, or 10.) After you're done, read on to Grading Yourself to find out what it all means.

Size

_____ 1) I enjoy participating in many activities.

_____ 2) I would like to have a prominent place in my community.

_____ 3) Individual attention from teachers is important to me.

_____ 4) I learn best when I can speak out in class and ask questions.

_____ 5) I am undecided about what I will study.

_____ 6) I want to earn a PhD in my chosen field of study.

_____ 7) I learn best by listening and writing what I hear.

_____ 8) I would like to be in a place where I can be anonymous if I choose.

continued

_____ 9) I prefer devoting my time to one or two activities rather than many.

_____ 10) I want to attend a college that most people have heard of.

_____ 11) I am interested in a career-oriented major.

_____ 12) I like to be on my own.

Location

_____ 13) I prefer a college in a warm or hot climate.

_____ 14) I prefer a college in a cool or cold climate.

_____ 15) I want to be near the mountains.

_____ 16) I want to be near a lake or ocean.

_____ 17) I prefer to attend a college in a particular state or region.

_____ 18) I prefer to attend a college close to home.

_____ 19) I want city life within walking distance of my campus.

_____ 20) I want city life within driving distance of my campus.

_____ 21) I want my campus to be surrounded by natural beauty.

Academics and Extracurriculars

_____ 22) I like to be surrounded by people who are free-thinkers and nonconformists.

_____ 23) I like the idea of joining a fraternity or sorority.

_____ 24) I like rubbing shoulders with people who are bright and talented.

_____ 25) I like being one of the smartest people in my class.

_____ 26) I want to go to a prestigious college.

_____ 27) I want to go to a college where I can get an excellent education.

_____ 28) I want to try for an academic scholarship.

_____ 29) I want a diverse college.

_____ 30) I want a college where the students are serious about ideas.

Grading Yourself

Picking a college is not an exact science. People who are total opposites can be equally happy at the same college. Nevertheless, particular types tend to do better at some colleges than others. Each item in the survey is designed to test your feelings on an important issue related to college selection. On the following page, Sizing Up the Survey offers commentary on each item.

Taken together, your responses may help you construct a tentative blueprint for your college search. Statements 1–12 deal with the issue of size. Would you be happier at a large university or a small college? Here's the trick: add the sum of your responses to questions 1–6. Then make a second tally of your responses to 7–12. If the sum of 1–6 is larger, you may want to consider a small college. If 7–12 is greater, then perhaps a big school would be more to your liking. If the totals are roughly equal, you should probably consider colleges of various sizes.

Statements 13–21 deal with location. The key in this section is the intensity of your feeling. If you replied to No. 13 with a 10, does that mean you are going to look only at schools in warm climates? Think hard. If you consider only schools within a certain region or state, you'll be eliminating hundreds of possibilities. By examining your most intense responses—the 1s, 2s, 9s, and 10s—you'll be able to create a geographic profile of likely options.

Statements 22–30 deal with big-picture issues related to the character and personality of the college that may be in your future. As before, pay attention to your most intense responses. Read on for a look at the significance of each question.

Sizing Up the Survey

1. **I enjoy participating in many activities.** Students at small colleges tend to have more opportunities to be involved in many activities. Fewer students means less competition for spots.

2. **I would like to have a prominent place in my community.** Student council presidents and other would-be leaders take note: it is easier to be a big fish if you're swimming in a small pond.

3. **Individual attention from teachers is important to me.** Small colleges generally offer more one-on-one with faculty both in the classroom and the laboratory.

4. **I learn best when I can speak out in class and ask questions.** Students who learn from interaction and participation would be well-advised to consider a small college.

5. **I am undecided about what I will study.** Small colleges generally offer more guidance and support to students who are undecided. The exception: students who are considering a preprofessional or highly specialized major.

6. **I want to earn a PhD in my chosen field of study.** A higher percentage of students at selective small colleges earn a PhD than those who attend large institutions of similar quality.

7. **I learn best by listening and writing what I hear.** Students who prefer lecture courses will find more of them at large institutions.

8. **I would like to be in a place where I can be anonymous if I choose to be.** At a large university, the supply of new faces is neverending. Students who have the initiative can always reinvent themselves.

9. **I prefer devoting my time to one or two activities rather than many.** Students who are passionate about one activity—say, writing for the college newspaper—will often find higher quality at a bigger school.
10. **I want to attend a college that most people have heard of.** Big schools have more name recognition because they're bigger and have Division I athletic programs. Even the finest small colleges are relatively anonymous among the general public.
11. **I am interested in a career-oriented major.** More large institutions offer business, engineering, nursing, etc., though some excellent small institutions do so as well (depending on the field).
12. **I like to be on my own.** A higher percentage of students live off campus at large schools, which are more likely to be in urban areas than their smaller counterparts.
13. **I prefer a college in a warm or hot climate.** Keep in mind that the Southeast and the Southwest have far different personalities (not to mention humidity levels).
14. **I prefer a college in a cool or cold climate.** Consider the Midwest, where there are many fine schools which are notably less selective than those in the Northeast.
15. **I want to be near the mountains.** You're probably thinking Colorado or Vermont, but don't zero in too quickly. States from Maine to Georgia and Arkansas to Arizona have easy access to mountains.
16. **I want to be near a lake or ocean.** Oceans are only on the coasts, but keep in mind the Great Lakes, the Finger Lakes, etc., etc. Think about whether you want to be on the water or, say, within a two hour drive.

continued

17. **I prefer to attend a college in a particular state or region.** Geographical blinders limit options. Even if you think you want a certain area of the country, consider at least one college located elsewhere just to be sure.

18. **I prefer to attend a college close to home.** Unless you're planning to live with Mom and Dad, it may not matter whether your college is a two-hour drive or a two-hour plane ride away from home.

19. **I want city life within walking distance of my campus.** Check out the neighborhood(s) surrounding your campus. Urban campuses—even in the same city—can be wildly different.

20. **I want city life within driving distance of my campus.** Unless you're a hardcore urban-dweller, a suburban perch near a city may beat living in the thick of one. Does public transportation or a campus shuttle help students get around?

21. **I want my campus to be surrounded by natural beauty.** A college viewbook will take you only so far. To really know if you'll fall in love with the campus, visiting is a must.

22. **I like to be surrounded by free-thinkers and non-conformists.** Plenty of schools cater specifically to students who buck the mainstream. Talk to your counselor or browse the *Fiske Guide to Colleges* to find some.

23. **I like the idea of joining a fraternity or sorority.** Greek life is strongest at mainstream and conservative-leaning schools. Find out if there is a split between Greeks and non-Greeks.

24. **I like rubbing shoulders with people who are bright and talented.** This is perhaps the best reason to aim for a highly selective institution, especially if you're the type who rises to the level of the competition.

25. **I like being one of the smartest people in my class.** If so, maybe you should skip the highly selective rat race. Star students at less selective colleges get the best that the institution has to offer.

26. **I want to go to a prestigious college.** There is nothing wrong with wanting prestige. Think honestly about how badly you want a big name school and act accordingly.

27. **I want to go to a college where I can get an excellent education.** Throw out the *U.S. News* rankings and think about which colleges will best meet your needs as a student.

28. **I want to try for an academic scholarship.** Students in this category should consider less selective alternatives. Scholarships are more likely if you rank high in the applicant pool.

29. **I want a diverse college.** All colleges pay lip service to diversity. To get the truth, see the campus for yourself and take a hard look at the student body statistics in the *Guide*'s write-ups.

30. **I want a college where students are serious about ideas.** Don't assume that a college necessarily attracts true intellectuals merely because it is highly selective. Some top schools are known for their intellectual climate—and others for their lack of it.

Putting It All Together

We hope the survey will help you get started on a thorough self-assessment that will continue throughout the college search. After thinking about your priorities, the time is right to begin looking at the colleges. Hundreds of them await! It will come as no surprise that we recommend that you begin with the *Fiske Guide to Colleges*. Use the state-by-state index to search geographically if you like or simply browse to find colleges that interest you. When you find a likely candidate, look to the item called "Overlaps" at the end of the article to find additional possibilities. For more ideas in this book, head to Chapter 4, Getting a Jump Start.

3. The College Universe

The most striking fact about American higher education is its diversity. Though our economy might be uncertain, our politics mired in sleaze, and our cultural life at the depths of the latest lurid reality show, the United States still has the richest assortment of colleges and universities in the world. Our twenty-two hundred four-year schools are a smorgasbord unrivaled by any other nation on Earth. American higher ed offers everything from tiny schools where students number in the dozens to massive ones with dorms that have their own zip codes; from colleges so remote that the nearest pavement is miles away to those that are surrounded by the high-rise growth of the urban jungle; from schools where the students wear prints and pastels to those where the preferred uniform is combat boots and chains.

There are virtually as many colleges as stars in the sky and sorting out the college universe is no easy task. To help, this chapter describes the most common varieties. Though not every school fits neatly into every category, an understanding of the trade-offs between the various types can help applicants make intelligent choices.

Size

One of the most important forks in the road to college happiness is the dilemma of big versus small. Do you want to attend a university with ten thousand or twenty thousand students? Or would you prefer a small college with, say, two thousand students?

Before you can answer, we need to define some terms. Though the word *college* is used loosely to refer to a variety of institutions, strictly speaking, it means a program leading to a bachelor's degree. All students enrolled in any college are *undergraduates*—that is, they have not earned a bachelor's degree. Some colleges are devoted to the liberal arts, others focus on business, engineering, architecture, or another pre-professional field. Some are free-standing institutions, others are part of a university. Colleges tend to be small, generally enrolling one thousand to five thousand students.

A *university* is an institution that combines one or more undergraduate colleges (including one for the liberal arts) with graduate schools that give PhDs, MDs, and other degrees. Universities vary widely in size. Most private ones have an enrollment between five thousand and twenty thousand students. Public ones range upward to behemoth Ohio State University, which tips the scales with nearly fifty thousand students, including thirty-five thousand undergraduates.

The Popularity of Universities

In recent years, more top applicants have been choosing universities. Bigger doesn't necessarily mean better, but it often means better known. Leery of going to a "no-name" school, today's students are flocking to universities that have well-established programs in law, medicine, and other prestigious professions.

Aside from name recognition, there are a number of reasons why universities are attractive. Most importantly, they offer more courses to choose from. If you're undecided, that means more potential majors. If you're eyeing a highly specialized major or one that requires expensive facilities, a big university may be the only place to find it. Larger schools often have the strongest departments in less prominent majors, such as anthropology or astronomy, that often get short shrift at a small school.

Outside the classroom, universities generally offer superior opportunities for people who are really good at one thing. If you want to be a newspaper reporter, a high-powered daily at a big university will probably offer much better experience than the sleepy weeklies that inhabit most small colleges. If you want to be the next Michael Jordan, the Big Ten is better than the Little Ivies. Though the competition to get the editorship or make the team is intense, those who have the talent can perform at a higher level. Socially, a large university can be welcome relief from the high school fishbowl. Many students enjoy the anonymity that comes with thousands of classmates and the ability to move in and out of social groups without being stereotyped. The excitement of big-time sports is a strong lure and there is also something special about that "hub of the universe" feeling in the air at great universities.

Though large universities offer unparalleled opportunities, they also put more pressure on students to take initiative. Students should enroll with a particular course of study in mind and be ready to fight the bureaucracy. Go-getters tend to do best. Passive types generally spend too much time falling asleep in the back of huge lecture halls.

The Case for Small Colleges

We now turn to one of higher ed's most underappreciated resources: the small college. Today's applicants seem to have a mental block about them. A large university might be the right choice for many students, but other students would do better at a small school if only they did not fall victim to some persistent myths. Let's dispel a few of these myths:

> **Myth 1.** *I'll never find a job or get into grad school if I go to a small college.* Absolutely wrong. While the names of big universities are more familiar to the general public, people in graduate school admissions and corporate recruiting offices are well aware of the smaller schools. "Hands-on experience" has become one of today's buzzwords and small colleges almost always provide the best opportunities for undergraduates to do their own research, lead an organization, and so

on. In a tight job market, the all-around small college do-er beats the face-in-the-crowd large university type of person every time.

Myth 2. *Small colleges aren't diverse.* If you look at student bodies by their percentage of students from various backgrounds, most small schools are every bit as diverse as the big ones. Small schools also tend to provide the best chance to sample that diversity because they aren't big enough to become segregated by special interest groups.

Myth 3. *A small school would be too confining.* Well, maybe. But remember this: A small college and a small high school are not the same thing. Often, students at a small high school (say, four hundred students) will be determined to attend a "big" university. They forget that a small college might be five or six times as large as their small high school. Do you know anyone who attends a high school of two thousand students? If so, when was the last time they complained about it being "too small"?

The most compelling arguments for small colleges are academic ones. By definition, these schools have few if any graduate students, so you won't find yourself eyeball-to-eyeball with a teaching assistant in introductory math or English. Many large universities like to boast about their distinguished faculty, forgetting to mention that some do not teach undergraduates and many others have only a class or two. For many university faculty, "teaching" means two or three command performances a week in an overflowing lecture hall while graduate students conduct all the discussion sections, do all the grading, and answer all the questions.

Another small college selling point can be summed up

in one word: involvement. Studies show that students who are active in the college community perform best in the classroom. Small colleges generally offer the best chance to sample, explore, and get involved in lots of different things. On paper, the large universities offer more variety, but, in practice, they often have less. Whereas most courses offered at a small college are fair game for anyone, large universities often have strict limitations on cross registration between divisions. If you're a business major at a big university, don't count on getting into that nifty course in the school of journalism without some fast talking, half a dozen signatures, and a lot of luck. On the other hand, small schools give you the freedom to explore varied interests. You can be a jack-of-all-trades—as you were in high school—without being elbowed aside by quasiprofessionals who are on their way to fame and glory.

Do you know anyone who attends a high school of two thousand students? If so, when was the last time they complained about it being "too small"?

Campus housing is more likely to be guaranteed for all four years at a private college. At some large state universities, freshmen become unwilling apartment hunters if they don't send in their housing application on time.

Socially, small colleges usually have a stronger sense of community. If claustrophobia does set in after a year or two, you can always take part of your junior year abroad—a staple of the small-college experience.

Location

Perhaps the biggest difference in college admissions from a generation ago is the mobility of today's applicant. Most don't hesitate to scour all corners of the nation to find the best college. Indeed, many applicants seem to care more about where it is than how good it is.

Different regions evoke different images in the minds of high school students, often depending on where they grew up. In the age of cyberspace, college is still synonymous with a quaint New England town featuring the traditional red brick, white columns, and ivy all around. That enduring mental picture combines with the seemingly inborn cultural snobbery of the East Coast to produce millions of students who think that civilization ends at the western edge of Pennsylvania—if not the Hudson River. For Midwesterners, the situation is just the opposite: a century-old cultural inferiority complex. Many applicants from those states will do anything to get the heck out, even though there are more good colleges per capita in states like Iowa, Minnesota, and Ohio than anywhere else in the nation. The West Coast fades in and out as a trendy place for college, depending on earthquakes, the regional economy, and the overcrowding and tuition increases that plague the University of California system. Among those seeking warmer weather, the South has become a popular place, especially since Southerners themselves are more likely to stay close to home.

Collective perceptions of the various regions have some practical consequences. First, most of the elite schools in the Northeast are more selective than ever. In addition, a lot of mediocre schools in the Northeast, notably Boston, are being deluged with applicants simply because they are lucky enough to be in a hot location. In the Midwest, many equally good or superior schools are much less difficult to get into, especially the fine liberal arts colleges in Ohio. In the South, the booming popularity of some schools is out of proportion to their quality. The weather may be nice and the football top-notch, but students who come from far away should be prepared for culture shock.

We encourage applicants to consider schools in all parts of the nation (especially those applicants looking mainly at private colleges). Students or parents may have the impulse to say, "Nothing east of the Rockies," or "Texas is too far," but barriers like these are mainly psychological. If a student lives in Virginia, the flying time to Texas or California isn't much more than that to Boston or than the drive time to Ohio or upstate New York. Though air fares vary, they will usually add no more than fifteen hundred dollars or so to the annual bill. Many colleges give out larger travel allowances to students from far away in their financial-aid packages, in part because applicants from far afield increase campus diversity. In recent years, the specter of international terrorism has reared its head, and some students have become reluctant to stray too far from home. Psychologically, a car ride seems safer than a plane ride, especially to anxious parents. Memo to Mom and Dad: driving to the local grocery store is more dangerous than a transcontinental flight. In today's hyper-competitive admissions scene, students can significantly enhance their chances for admission if they are willing to apply to a college or university outside their home area.

Applicants must also choose whether to be in or near a city or whether to attend college in a rural area. City sub-urbs are always a favorite because they combine access to the urban area with the safety that parents crave. During the 1970s, rural hideaways were popular among students who wanted to curl up with a book on bucolic hillside. Today, cow colleges are out as students hear the siren song of the city. Boston has always been preeminent among student-friendly big cities, offering an unparalleled combination of safety, cultural activities, and about fifty colleges. Chicago and Washington, D.C., are also immensely popular. On the West Coast, Berkeley, California, is a mecca for the college-aged, though today an overcrowded one. Legendary college towns like Ann Arbor, Michigan; Boulder, Colorado; and Burlington, Vermont, provide wonderfully rich places for a college educa-tion. Perhaps the hottest place of all among today's students is New York City, where private institutions such as Columbia

University, Barnard College, and New York University are enjoying record popularity.

The biggest red herring out there is the idea, "I need to be within an hour or two of a city." That is the sort of issue that, while applicants spend a lot of time thinking about it, has almost no effect on the college experience. Visit any campus and you'll hear things like, "New York is only two hours away, but I can never find the time to get down there," or, "I thought I would visit Boston a lot more than I do." More and more, colleges are becoming self-contained communities. Glitzy new student centers have everything from banks to nightclubs to fast-food joints. One college may look isolated on a map, while another appears closer to major cities, but that does not necessarily mean that the latter has more activity. Rural colleges realize that they are operating at a disadvantage in the eyes of some applicants and they usually do everything in their power to bring arts, culture, and social life to their little corner of the world.

As you think about the role that location will play in your college search, here is another item to reflect on: proximity to cities is often less important than proximity to other colleges. Potential benefits of a nearby school include cross registration, expanded library privileges, and a fresh supply of new faces. Sometimes, students can get the best of both worlds by enrolling in a small college that has a coordinate relationship with a nearby large university. In the East, a shining example is the Massachusetts Five-College Consortium in which four small colleges (Amherst, Hampshire, Smith, and Mount Holyoke) pool resources with the University of Massachusetts at Amherst. In the West, the Claremont Colleges have a similar setup and dozens of other institutions in all corners of the nation have formed similar partnerships.

Finally, try to avoid rigid thinking as you consider location. Don't eliminate whole regions of the country without giving them a chance. If you grew up on the East Side of

Manhattan, avoid the knee-jerk elimination of any school across the George Washington Bridge. Part of being educated is seeing how the other half lives and college provides the perfect opportunity.

Public vs. Private

No matter what their size, American colleges and universities come in two basic types. Some are supported by the state where they are located and hence called *public*. Others are independent or affiliated with a religious group; they are called *private*.

All public universities were originally founded to educate the citizens of their state and all are subsidized by taxpayer money. These universities have traditionally had far lower tuition and less selectivity than their private counterparts, which generally serve a regional or national student body rather than residents of a particular state.

All the country's oldest colleges are private, founded when the United States consisted of the East Coast. To this day, the Northeast is still a stronghold of private colleges and universities, with few prestigious public ones. When the country expanded westward in the 1800s, public education became a reality and thus the state university systems in the Midwest, South, and West are much stronger.

In the past two decades, more and more top students have gotten fed up with private college tuition and begun to look seriously at public alternatives. In response, the public universities have devoted more resources to merit scholarships and various other enticements to encourage the best students to enroll. But such institutions have also jacked up

> **Better Check Those Numbers**
>
> The "sticker price" of a public university is often about half that of a private college. But since public universities offer less need-based aid than private ones, out-of-pocket costs can be higher at public universities for middle and low income families.

their prices, often because of declining or stagnant state support. Today, in-state tuition at public universities is still less than half that of a private college, but out-of-state tuition is soaring. At some popular public universities, including the University of California, the University of Colorado at Boulder, the University of Michigan, and the University of Vermont, out-of-staters pay as much as students who attend expensive private colleges.

Public universities tend to be strong in professional fields like business and engineering, though some also have good programs in the liberal arts. In recent years, they have devoted increasing resources to special programs that give selected students the intimacy of a small college within the context of a major university. Honors programs are nearly universal and more and more public universities have also created programs known as *residential colleges* or *living/learning communities* in which participating students share special housing, community activities, and contact with affiliated faculty. Not all public universities are large, and another growth sector in state-supported education consists of smaller liberal arts institutions that provide private-college opportunities at a fraction of the cost. For some general thoughts on these programs, plus descriptions of some of the best, see Public Universities: The Honors Programs and Residential Colleges and Small-College Bargains in Chapter 6.

With so many high-quality public options available, why pay an extra hundred thousand dollars for a private education? Consciously or not, most private college applicants are buying prestige. Some experts may hold their noses at such a crass reason for choosing a college, but it is interesting to note how many of these same folks themselves attended a prestigious private institution. If prestige is one of your priorities, be honest with yourself and weigh it with your other criteria.

A more substantive benefit of private colleges, especially

the elite ones, is the chance to rub shoulders with some of the best and brightest students from across the nation and around the world. There is a special intensity generated by the convergence of so many extraordinary minds—alike and yet different. Though public institutions attract their share of top students, even the best are limited by the mandate to enroll mainly the residents of their state.

Though the quality of their academic programs may be just as strong, public universities can seldom match the atmosphere of intellectual stimulation at the best private institutions.

The case for private colleges and universities rests mainly on intangibles. Each family must make its own decision.

Personality

Colleges are just like people. They have personalities, too. Some are laid-back and some are intense; some are friendly and some are reserved; some are spirited and some are blasé; some are conservative and some are liberal. These personalities have extraordinary staying power. Benjamin Franklin founded the University of Pennsylvania in 1740 to further the "useful arts" and, today, Penn still reflects his career-oriented approach to education.

It is easy to underestimate just how wide the differences in personality can be. There are some colleges that resemble 1960s communes; there are others where smoking, drinking, and even dancing are banned. You'll find football, fraternities, and homecoming weekends at some colleges; at others, the students scoff at the mere mention of such frivolities. At some colleges, homosexuality is a chic alternative lifestyle that many students try out because it is cool or "politically correct"; at others, gays and lesbians are practically tarred and feathered if they come out of the closet.

To highlight some of the contrasts, we offer descriptions of two colleges that represent the poles of the spectrum. They're both the same size—approximately fourteen hundred students—and both have combined average SAT scores for critical reading and math in the 1300 range. In short, they are both highly selective, small liberal arts colleges.

School No. 1 is the University of the South, a Tennessee liberal arts college with a handful of graduate students, known informally as Sewanee (because that's the name of the town). The first thing you'll notice on visiting Sewanee is that many of the men are wearing jackets and ties, while most of the women are wearing makeup and skirts. Forty years ago, many colleges had a similar dress code. Today, Sewanee is one of a handful. The majority of students pledge fraternities and sororities and social life revolves around a never-ending stream of "big-weekend" beer bashes. The biggest of them all is homecoming weekend, where students get a date and dress up for a huge see-and-be-seen fashion show that includes innumerable cocktail parties before and after. Conservative, well-heeled, and All-American, Sewanee is the perfect place for a carefree 1950s-style college education. In the words of one student, Sewanee has "the happiest college student body I have ever encountered."

No one would ever say such a thing about Bard College, a school of similar size about an hour north of New York City. Though the students may find happiness there, too, it is well hidden beneath a thick veneer of liberal artistic angst. Bard students, it seems, carry the weight of the world on their shoulders. If there is an oppressed group anywhere to be found, Bard students can be counted on to buy T-shirts, sell buttons, and organize protests on its behalf. As for clothes, you would be hard-pressed to find a Bard man who even owns a jacket and tie. Nor would the typical Bard woman be caught dead in a dress—unless it was paired with combat boots. Jewelry and makeup worn in traditional ways are nonexistent, but there is plenty of spiked hair, fluorescent hair, tattoos, and piercings protruding from every conceivable body part. As for football and fraternities? Take a wild guess. The biggest social event of the year at Bard is called Drag Race, where everyone dresses in drag and parties nonstop.

Admittedly, these two examples are near the extremes. But they illustrate some universal tendencies. Where would you feel more comfortable? Do you have a strong antiestablishment streak? Do you feel confined by the conventional norms of our society? Or are you looking for a more traditional college experience? Fortunately for most of us, the majority of American colleges lie somewhere between the Sewanees and Bards of the world. Most colleges include a mix of progressive elements and traditional ones. When you take the time to consider a personality match with a school, you help to ensure a positive college experience for yourself and others you'll meet on campus. Don't forget to think about the emotional wellness resources available when looking at prospective schools—including transition supports like academic tutoring and mental health counseling, which are valuable assets for adjusting to the personality of any school. Once you've figured out the combination you're looking for, the hard part is finding a match (preferably several schools) that fits your criteria. How to find the college that's right for you is one of the topics that we deal with in the next chapter.

4. Getting a Jump Start

You've got a mailbox full of brochures and a slew of unanswered questions. So many colleges out there. So much information to absorb. Fortunately, the college admissions process is not a sprint but a marathon. No one is going to demand that you pick a college today. Or next week. Every time you read a brochure, talk to a friend, or visit a college you add a few more bits of information to your memory bank. The hard part is maintaining your resolve when the whole thing seems hopeless. Disaster comes only when you allow yourself to be paralyzed.

By now, you've thought a little about yourself and your priorities and you've had a general introduction to some of the different types of schools. Below, we offer seven ways to get a start on finding a list of colleges that meet your needs. Notice we said, "get a start." The purpose of these methods is merely to identify possibilities—colleges that fit one or more of your criteria and may be worth further investigation. The real work, that of choosing from among those possibilities, comes later.

Of the seven methods listed here, no one way is the best. We even recommend doing three or four of them simultaneously. Each one you try can provide another piece of the puzzle. Whatever your strategy, the most important thing is merely to get the ball rolling. Now is the time to start naming names—to develop a list of approximately twenty to thirty colleges that you would like to learn more about.

Seven Ways to Jump-Start Your College Search

1. Read Chapter 6: The One-Hour College Finder. This chapter is designed for students applying to selective schools. It provides lists and thumbnail sketches of colleges appropriate for students with various academic and nonacademic interests. Use it as a seedbed for ideas on colleges to investigate further in the next phase.

2. Browse a college guide. Consult Chapter 7: Where to Learn More for some ideas on good guides. For ambitious students, we recommend—surprise!—the *Fiske Guide to Colleges*, which includes in-depth profiles of more than three hundred of the best and most interesting colleges. This is the best place to draw a bead on the personalities of the schools. When you find one that seems like a good match, make a note and then look in the last line of the article for the Overlaps. These are the other colleges to which students most often apply when considering the one profiled in the article. Then read about those colleges and consult *their* overlaps. In short order, you'll have the beginnings of a good list.

3. Run an online search. If your typical day includes any time at all in front of a computer screen, you'll probably want to use your computer to look for colleges. You can easily find a search program on the Web. These programs allow you to make choices among ten to twenty variables (for example: size, location, majors). Once you have entered your specifications in each category, the program identifies all the colleges that meet your criteria. Unfortunately, computer programs are generally not much help when it comes to the personality of the schools, but they can be a big help in sorting with objective criteria. For a more in-depth look at online information, go to Cyber-Sources, later in this chapter.

4. Poll friends, teachers, and relatives. If you're a junior in high school, there is no better place to begin a college search than with members of the senior class whom you respect and who share your interests. Why not benefit from their extra year of experience? Older friends at colleges you are considering can also be a fertile source of information, as long as you keep in mind that the same student who sings his school's praises during spring break may curse it up and down if you happen to catch him during exams. If there are any teachers you respect and who know you well, by all means ask if they have any schools to recommend. Try to keep an open mind to all suggestions at this early stage. As long as no one is trying to cram anything down your throat, welcome the free advice and take it seriously.

5. Talk to some experts. Few people are better positioned to give advice than those who work in a field that interests you. This method is particularly useful for those who have a particular career path in mind. Interested in architecture? See if someone in your circle of friends and relatives knows an architect whom you might be able to call. An even bigger coup would be to talk to someone involved in hiring architects. Another approach is to visit a college—not necessarily to look at that particular school, but as a fact-finding mission on a particular career. Most college admissions offices will happily help you arrange an appointment with professors in just about any field. See also, Private Counselors, later in this chapter.

6. Sample some nearby college campuses. Most applicants think that to go on college visits they must first create a list of likely schools. Not so. One way to begin your list is to sample various kinds of institutions. Say you live in Colorado. To start your search, you might see the University of Denver for a peek at a middle-sized institution in a city. Half an hour to the northwest, the

University of Colorado at Boulder offers a taste of life at a large public university. An hour south of Denver, Colorado College is a small private college with a much more intimate feel. It makes no difference if you are interested in these particular schools. By sampling all three, you can clarify your preferences for large, medium, and small schools and big cities vs. college towns.

7. Read college viewbooks and catalogs. This method comes last—mainly to follow up leads from other sources. That's because anything produced by the colleges—from posters to videos to websites—is little more than glitzy advertising. You probably wouldn't buy a soft drink on the basis of an ad, so why buy a two-hundred-thousand-dollar college education based on one? In the next chapter, we discuss the right way to use college literature. For now, we merely say: buyer beware.

Discerning readers will note that we have yet to mention one of the most important sources of college information: the guidance counselor. Ideally, your counselor will be your most trusted ally throughout the process. Unfortunately, most counselors are overworked, underpaid, and responsible for everything from suicide prevention to watering the principal's plants. If you don't have ready access to a good counselor, this book can act as a substitute.

We save the guidance counselor for last to encourage you to do a little homework before meeting with him or her. Any of the seven strategies above would be a great prelude to your first meeting with a counselor during January of your junior year. (The counselor just might fall out of her chair at the sight of an applicant who has actually done some homework.) The best use of the guidance counselor is as a sounding board and a reality check. At very small high schools, the counselor may be able to give you a personalized list of colleges, but most schools are way too big for that kind of service. Every counselor can respond to a list and provide some idea of whether or not you are being realistic in your plans. Many keep records of how past applicants from your school fared and they may be able to give you an informed opinion of your chances for admission. They can also discuss the pros and cons of the colleges on your list and perhaps suggest others where students with your interests and grades have had success. Finally, they can give you the names of everyone from your school who attends the colleges you're interested in.

> ### Getting to Know You
>
> Some counselors use the college search as a measuring stick for evaluating applicants. Students who are organized and ahead of the game often get a better recommendation.

As the application process moves forward, your counselor should continue to be a vital resource. Make a point of seeing him or her as much as possible without being a pest. In the words of Teresa Lahti, former director of admissions at Kalamazoo College, "Start early in developing a relationship with your counselor by seeking advice on curriculum choices, activities, etc., before you begin to seek help in more pressured situations."

Though most counselors want only what is best for their counselees, watch out for the ones who have other agendas. Some counselors have pet schools that they peddle indiscriminately, while others are under pressure from principals or parents to steer applicants toward (or away from) certain "designer label" schools. Some like to place students at tried-and-true in-state schools, while scoffing at the idea of attending one that may be "too far away." Still others will try to discourage you from applying to certain colleges because they think too many other students from your school are already applying there. Richard Hallin of Eckerd College warns, "Beware of the guidance counselors who attempt to restrict options by giving such advice as: it's too costly or too far away; no one I know goes there; it's not right for you. A good guidance counselor will expand horizons and help find information." In any case, be sure to ask your counselor to explain his or her recommendations.

Remember also that even the best counselors are fallible. All know more about some schools (especially those nearby) than others and, occasionally, their preconceptions will be dated or based on inaccurate information. Whenever possible, double-check what your counselor says with teachers, college guides, and other sources.

As white-knuckle time nears, give the counselor plenty of advance notice before deadlines. Don't just assume that everything is done once you hand in your part of the application. You may have five applications to process; your counselor probably has five hundred. A little double-checking on your part is a wise move. Even the best guidance offices slip up occasionally. Polite but diligent follow-up with your guidance counselor and the colleges can help prevent a snafu that could jeopardize your chances.

The Rankings: Read with a Critical Eye

Be wary of sources that purport to offer numerical rankings of the colleges. Such efforts give an illusion of precision while missing the main point of the college search: different schools are right for different people. Avoid at all costs *The Gourman Report*, a book that uses bogus methodology to generate bizarre rankings. Though now out-of-print, *The Gourman Report* is still kicking around the shelves of many high school guidance offices. The annual *U.S. News & World Report* rankings can be useful as a seedbed of possible choices, as long as you realize that the difference between No. 5 and No. 15 is probably insignificant. Their rankings change yearly with little rhyme or reason—the better to sell each new edition of the magazine.

Cyber-Sources

The Internet is an essential reference tool for the college search. A few keystrokes can lead applicants to information that once required a letter or a trip to the library. Some of the best uses of the computer in college admissions include searching online databases for colleges and scholarships, communicating with colleges and filing applications, and registering for standardized tests and submitting aid forms. But before you log on, know the potential pitfalls. The Web is great for sending messages and sifting through objective information; it is less reliable in offering judgments of quality. The Web will show you where it is and what it offers—but not how good it is.

Literally hundreds of websites are devoted to serving the needs of college applicants. Unfortunately, many of them sell products that are not worth buying, such as scholarship searches or consulting services. The cardinal rule for Internet surfing is to be stingy with the family credit card; limit yourself to convenience purchases of products or services that you would otherwise buy in person or through the mail.

The most useful college-related sites are often—though not always—produced by familiar names in publishing, testing, and test preparation. In addition to selling and excerpting their offline publications, these sites typically offer a range of items including college and scholarship search programs, test preparation, online applications, message boards with discussions of admissions topics, and information about the college and financial aid process. Some of the most prominent options include:

College Board (www.collegeboard.com) The testing giant boasts one of the most comprehensive sites, with college and scholarship searches, registration for the SAT, a financial aid eligibility estimator, online applications, and general information on the college search.

CollegeNET (www.collegenet.com) This site offers more than 1,500 online applications and features enhanced message boards with picture profiles. Also offers its long-standing Mach 25 scholarship search program.

CollegeView (www.collegeview.com) CollegeView combines a college search with interactive presentations about colleges. It also includes content for students with special interests ranging from health professions to Christian colleges.

Peterson's (www.petersons.com) Peterson's is one of the biggest publishers on topics related to the college admissions process and its site includes a full package of application and financial aid tools.

The Princeton Review (www.princetonreview.com) Among the most active on this list, The Princeton Review's site excerpts content from its college guides, while also offering message boards, a financial package comparison calculator, online applications, and advice from experts.

Transition Year (www.transitionyear.org) The source for information on emotional health at college, as well as specific emotional health resource information on over 1,500 schools.

Unigo (www.unigo.com) A relatively new Web enterprise that offers student reviews, student-produced videos, and message boards about hundreds of colleges across the nation.

U.S. News & World Report (www.usnews.com) U.S. News posts its annual college rankings on this site, as well as content from its print guide. It also offers a college search program, message boards, and articles on every aspect of the admissions process.

Though websites like these can be very useful in the preliminary stages of the college search, they don't replace the need for printed college guides. Except for promotional excerpts, you'll find little of the best descriptive information free online. After you've mined the sites above, head to the sources listed in Chapter 7: Where to Learn More.

The websites of the colleges themselves are another obvious source. Some are just billboards with basic information; others include hundreds and even thousands of pages produced by various academic divisions within the institution. Much of their content is a rehash of printed brochures, but *An online version of the campus newspaper is a great way to get the inside scoop on a college.* persistent surfers will uncover layers of detail about particular departments and professors that are unavailable anywhere else. These sites are an excellent source of email addresses for admissions officers, professors, and other university personnel. Some colleges post the entire text of their catalogs online, affording students an opportunity for thorough research on courses and programs.

In addition to the official university site, surfers can usually find links to student publications and homepages. An online version of the campus newspaper is a great way to get the inside scoop on a college. By dropping in on a selection of student blogs, college shoppers can get to know an interesting cross section of students. Readers who feel comfortable doing so can email a student or two who seems to share their interests. Most will welcome the opportunity to tell you about their school.

Private Counselors

Technology aside, some school guidance offices are simply unable to offer good advice on college. Many public school districts have experienced deep budget cuts in recent years, resulting in staggering workloads for overburdened counselors. If you are one of those unfortunate applicants who cannot get adequate advice from your school, you may want to consider hiring a private college counselor. It'll cost you a fair piece of change—from a few hundred dollars up to several thousand dollars for a full admissions-process package—but the bill could be worth it if the counselor you hire is a good one. Services range from helping you draw up an application list to advice on test-taking, filling out applications, writing essays, and managing the waitlist. An experienced independent counselor can be invaluable as a sounding board and as a source of knowledge about the colleges. Just don't sign on under the illusion that he or she will somehow get you in through inside connections or by pulling strings. Used this way, independent counselors are little more than hired lobbyists—a fact not lost on the admissions officers. As a rule, it is best to make sure that your independent counselor's fingerprints don't show up on your applications and raise questions as to whether the work is really yours. If you can't stand on your own qualifications, no amount of high-priced consulting and packaging will make any difference.

A final word of advice as you seek college information: listen to your parents. Improbable as it may seem, Mom and Dad can often be an excellent source of information. Even when they seem hopelessly out of touch with your world, you might be surprised by how much they really know about you and what makes you happy. Furthermore, your parents will never forget (and you shouldn't, either) that they are the ones who are going to pay the bills. Try to settle on some ground rules from the beginning as to how much they are willing to pay, how much input they will have in the final choice, and so on. In general, it is best to avoid the extremes—relying exclusively on their advice or locking them out of the process altogether. Your parents should recognize that the choice of college (within limits) is yours to make, while, at the same time, you can acknowledge that they have an important role to play. A firm understanding early in the process can prevent a lot of heartache and bitterness at the end.

By the spring of your junior year, your college search should be in high gear. You should be able to winnow your list of twenty to thirty "possibles" down to a more manageable list of ten or twelve by about May or June. That's when the serious comparison shopping begins.

5. Cutting through the Hype

If you're wondering why Joe Admissions Officer from Most Desirable University—which you've never heard of—sent you a warm, personal letter and a slick multicolored brochure that reads, "Uncle Joe Wants YOU to go to Most Desirable U.," chalk it up to what one admissions dean calls "the mass-marketing mania." The truth is, Uncle Joe wants you—and the one hundred thousand or so other prospective applicants who also received his letter.

The world of higher ed used to be a dignified place where administrators turned up their noses at anything that smacked of advertising or public relations. But that changed thirty years ago when the baby boom generation graduated and colleges found themselves hard up for students. The competition for students has since become increasingly cutthroat and even elite institutions are hawking their wares with a vengeance. When "sell, sell, sell" is the motto, truth in advertising often takes a beating. We're not accusing the colleges of lying, exactly, but some of them come pretty close. Don't play the role of starry-eyed sucker. Kick the tires, look under the hood, and find out exactly what you'll get for all that money.

College literature is a good place to cut your teeth as a comparison shopper. It can be fun. You'll soon be able to pick out all the hidden ploys and not-so-subtle persuasions built into the viewbooks, brochures, and catalogs that will be bombarding your mailbox. You can also find some valuable information for your college search, but only if you read with a critical eye.

Where It Comes From

How did all those email messages find their way to your computer? And why is the U.S. mail suddenly your personal pipeline for all this advertising? Think back to the last time you took the PSAT, SAT, or ACT. In addition to answering some questions about yourself, those forms asked if you wanted to receive a free service—the Student Search Service for the PSAT and SAT or the Educational Opportunity Service for the ACT. By selecting yes, you authorize them to sell your name, address, test scores, and personal information to any college admissions office that wants to buy them. Items include:

- test scores
- family income
- place of residence
- intended major
- ethnic background
- religious affiliation
- high school grade point average

The list covers almost everything except sexual preference. Every year, the College Board's Student Search Service sells millions of names and addresses to more than twelve hundred colleges and educational organizations. Some schools might want to send viewbooks to all the students who score above 600 on math and plan to major in science or to minority students with strong scores and grades. Others might target wealthy students from certain zip codes who have reasonably good credentials. When you factor in the cost of buying the addresses plus the expense of printing and mailing the brochures, colleges invest a pretty penny to court you through the U.S. Postal Service. (And that's in addition to all the work they put into creating a website with the same panache.) Just because you receive promotional literature doesn't mean you'll get in, but colleges wouldn't waste the money on students who are unrealistic candidates.

Picking through It

Most of your mail will consist of glossy publications with few words and lots of pictures—what the colleges call search pieces. These are the college admissions equivalent of a thirty-second commercial. Just as a soft-drink maker or tire manufacturer does, the college often pays a marketing firm to help hone the message. On TV, the persuaders use catchy jingles, gurgling babies, and celebrities. In higher education, the marketers generally try to sell an image. Among the most popular is the aura of traditional college life: white columns, ivy-covered walls, and majestic trees aflame with the colors of autumn on a crisp afternoon. Another favorite is the "hipper-than-thou" image, which usually includes splashy New Age script, loud pastel colors, and pictures pasted at odd angles. And, of course, every campus is a mosaic of racial and ethnic diversity in the pages of a promotional viewbook.

If you want to play a game, try guessing which photos are staged and which are candid. (Hint: any picture of three or more people in which all are facing the camera is probably staged.)

Perhaps we are too cynical. Though viewbooks usually say more about the skills of the marketing firms than the quality of the colleges, there are a few things you can learn. Pay attention to the message amid the puffery. What are the two or three basic ideas being conveyed? What does the college want you to know about it? Look for a business reply card or an order form in the back. Or give the admissions office a call or an email message telling them you want more information. But beware: any show of interest triggers lots more mail from the computer that controls the whole process.

If you want to play a game, try guessing which photos are staged and which are candid.

Lest there be any doubt, viewbooks are probably the least useful kind of college literature. More helpful is the college's catalog, an official document that lists course offerings, faculty, rules and regulations, the calendar, and so on. Since a catalog doesn't try to sell you anything, it is a welcome refuge of reliable information. But because catalogs are big and expensive to print and mail, colleges usually reserve them for serious customers who request them. Be sure to check the college's website before mailing off for one; more and more colleges are posting the text there.

After your initial browse, set aside the material of each college that seriously interests you. Then read them again—comparatively—when you've whittled your choices down to a manageable list. Look at how the catalogs are divided and how much space is allocated to various departments or majors. This gives you an idea of the colleges' academic structure. For example, is there a separate division of environmental studies or are those students lumped in with the biology majors? Read the short bios of the faculty members. Do they all have PhDs? Did they earn them at creditable institutions? Does each department have a good mix of faculty who specialize in different areas of your intended major? Find the section that discusses freshman requirements and when students must declare their majors. Skim through the history of the college. How long has it been around? Who founded it and why?

Image-Mongering Run Amok

A few years ago, the University of Wisconsin–Madison made the embarrassing admission that the face of a black student was cut-and-pasted into a sea of whites on the cover of its viewbook. The idea was to make the crowd at a football game look more diverse, but the student whose mug was superimposed into the picture said he had never been to a game. Oops.

A Peek Behind the Statistics

Another piece of literature that you should definitely consult is the college's report on its admissions statistics and student body. Most colleges refer to this document as their Profile; others call it Report to Secondary Schools or Admissions Report. This is the place where you'll find the information on a college's acceptance rate, SAT profile, geographical distribution, and a host of other important topics. You'll also find the potential for deception. Since colleges live and die by how selective the public thinks they are, the temptation to fudge the numbers often proves too much. "I have learned over the years not to trust the data that admissions people give to the public," says one financial-aid official who chose to remain nameless. "They gild every lily in sight."

Of the various statistics, applicants inevitably zero in on SAT profiles. The most common mistake is to view median or average freshman SAT scores as cutoffs. If a college says that last year's freshmen had median SAT scores of 600 on the math section and you got a 570, you may be tempted to think that you don't have a shot at that institution.

Think again. Median scores tell you where the middle of the class fell. In the instance above, half of the class had scores above 600, while half scored below that figure. For a more accurate picture of where you stand, find out the college's SAT ranges that encompass the middle half of the class—from the twenty-fifth to the seventy-fifth percentile. In general, this figure will range forty to fifty points on either side of the median score. For example, if the median is 600, then the middle half of the freshman class will probably have scores between 550 and 650. Furthermore, many colleges exclude certain "special admits" from their reports. With one eye on the selectivity rankings, they lop off the scores of foreign students, the economically disadvantaged, children of alumni, minorities, and other groups. The result is an artificially inflated profile. This widespread practice became a national scandal after a *Wall Street Journal* exposé a few years ago. Another widely used deception is to report the SAT ranges of admitted applicants rather than enrolled applicants. The admitted range is always higher because top students will always have more options to enroll elsewhere. The good news for you is that the real SAT profile is often lower than what the colleges advertise to the public.

If your scores fall within the range of the middle half, you can assume that you will be comfortable academically at that institution. If your scores would put you in the upper quartile, you might want to consider a more academically demanding institution. If your scores would put you in the bottom quartile, you probably want to think about whether that school would be too much of a struggle.

The good news for you is that the real SAT profile is often lower than what the colleges advertise to the public.

The listing of the high school class rank also provides fertile ground for creative marketing. Most schools quote the number of their students who ranked in the top tenth, the second tenth, and so on for their most recent freshman class. In fine print at the bottom is a category for "no rank," which generally includes about a third of the students. The secret here is that the unranked group often comes from high-powered private schools. Even students with mediocre grades from these schools are welcomed by many colleges, and the absence of a rank gives the colleges cover to accept less-than-stellar performers without 'fessing up publicly. In recent years, more and more high schools have decided to discontinue class ranking—so don't be concerned if you come from a school that doesn't do so.

Despite all the tinkering around the edges, a college's profile can still give you an excellent idea of your chances for admission. Assume that it is somewhat inflated but still reasonably accurate.

The SAT and class-rank statistics are most meaningful if examined in combination with the school's acceptance rate. If that rate is 30 percent or below, applicants will probably need credentials that compare favorably with the SAT and class rank listings to have a better-than-even chance for admission (unless they fall into a special admit category, such as recruited athletes or underrepresented minorities). When the acceptance rate is low, it means that a college chooses from among qualified applicants and therefore denies admission to many students with scores and grades that match its profile. On the other hand, colleges accepting 70 or 80 percent will generally admit virtually all candidates who match the profile.

Cooking the Numbers

One of the dirty little secrets of college admissions is that selectivity can be easily manipulated. A well-known women's college in New England was once horrified to discover that it was taking four out of five applicants. So the next year it sent out a huge number of brochures and generated a lot more applications. Image problem solved.

A second figure to which you should pay close attention is a college's yield—the percentage of accepted applicants who choose to enroll. The yield is a good index of a college's desirability among applicants. Any college with a yield of 50 percent or higher is a first-choice school. A yield between 30 and 50 percent is average for a selective private college, while a figure lower than 30 indicates a college that is frequently used as a "safety school." The yield is harder for colleges to manipulate than the acceptance rate—but not impossible. Some colleges have taken to denying admission to top-notch students if they don't show sufficient interest in the college via a campus visit, an interview, etc. This practice is most common in the "almost-Ivy" category at schools which routinely watch their best applicants enroll at more selective institutions. More conventional methods of beefing up the yield include rolling out the red carpet for accepted applicants or plying them with scholarships. The best way to win the yield game is to entice applicants to apply via early decision; the yield on ED students is 100 percent, since all must enroll if admitted (see Chapter 12: The Early Decision Dilemma).

More Fudge from the Confectionery

Of all the statistics quoted by admissions offices, the most misused and misrepresented is the student-faculty ratio. If a college claims to have a ratio of 12 to 1, don't think for a minute that your classes will only have twelve students in them. Faculty may include everyone from part-time lab assistants to medical and law professors who do not teach undergraduates. Moreover, even full-time faculty only teach two or three classes, whereas students take four or five. Large universities are especially brazen in overstating the ratio, as they routinely include graduate students in the calculations. Small liberal arts colleges that don't have graduate programs are usually the most trustworthy on the student-faculty ratio. A better question is, "What's the average size of classes taken by freshmen?" (See Chapter 14: Surviving the Interview.)

Another shady area is the percentage of graduates accepted at professional schools. Most colleges quote figures that are suspiciously high. One reason is that many schools prescreen applicants to law and medical schools, recommending only the top ones for admission (and then counting in its percent accepted only those it recommends). The percentage of students

> ### Who Got in Last Year?
>
> To help assess your chances for admission at a particular college, talk to your guidance counselor. Many will have records of how past applicants from your school with similar scores and grade point averages have fared.

on financial aid is also a less-than-meaningful number that is tossed around in many profiles. Financial aid can include everything from a twenty thousand dollar grant to a loan at the market interest rate. And an institution that has a high percentage of students on financial aid may be less likely to give aid to a typical needy student than a college that has a low percentage of students on aid. Reason? Elite institutions attract a higher percentage of students who can pay the full cost of attendance and therefore have more money available to aid the needy. (See Chapter 18: The New Financial Aid Game.)

We hope you've enjoyed our tour through the jungle of college literature. To be fair, the admissions people are less to blame than the university presidents, who have been known to fire admissions deans if the acceptance rate goes up or the SAT profile goes down. With so much uncertainty surrounding statistics, we conclude with the advice of Michael Behnke of the University of Chicago: "Figure out what question you're trying to get answered by looking at the statistics. Then ask the question and forget the statistics."

6. The One-Hour College Finder

By now, you've done the equivalent of sticking your big toe in the water. You can stand there for hours, timidly gazing out over the ripples, or you can breathe deeply and take the plunge. In this chapter, we offer one way to generate a reasonable list of colleges in an hour or two, even if you're starting from scratch.

Consider this your pocket map to the higher education universe. We've divided several hundred of the most prominent schools into categories based on a variety of factors that will be significant in your college search. Where appropriate, we have included the sort of thumbnail assessment that you might get from a good college counselor. Read the whole chapter if you like or simply browse the lists that seem most interesting. As you go, make a note of the colleges that seem right for you. If you already have particular schools in mind, refer to the index at the back of the book for the pages where they are featured. We suggest that you use this section as a shorthand directory to the *Fiske Guide to Colleges*. The majority of the schools mentioned in this book are described there in much greater detail.

Please note that these lists represent subjective judgments. Though based on years of observing higher education and extensive consulting with other experts, the opinions expressed here are just that—opinions. We recommend that you use the lists to help broaden your horizons. Beware of eliminating colleges from consideration merely because they don't show up in one of our categories.

The One-Hour College Finder is divided into two sections. The first, beginning below, is intended primarily for students intending to major in the liberal arts. Later in this chapter we offer lists of colleges strong in selected preprofessional fields.

Some of these schools also offer liberal arts degrees, others focus exclusively on preprofessional training.

The Elite

These are the places that ooze prestige from every crack and crevice of their ivy-covered walls. If you want to scale these lofty heights, you'd better come armed with an impeccable transcript, stratospheric scores, and/or championship-level talent in one or more extracurricular areas.

The main dilemma: do you prefer a liberal arts college offering small classes, close interaction with faculty, and a better chance to be involved in the extracurricular life of the community? Or do you want a comprehensive university with world-class facilities and a world-class name? As we noted in Chapter 3: The College Universe, many educators favor the former. That's one reason why a high percentage of the children of college professors enroll at the elite small colleges and why graduates of such schools have always earned PhDs in large numbers. The prestigious universities have historically been feeders of the business and professional worlds rather than the academic world. (The University of Chicago is a conspicuous exception.)

No matter what your aspirations, you'll find outstanding opportunities at both types of institutions.

The Elite Private Universities

Brown University. To today's stressed out students, the thought of taking *every* course pass/fail is a dream-come-true. Nobody actually does, but the pass/fail option combined with Brown's lack of distribution requirements gives it the freewheeling image that students love. Bashed by conservatives as a hotbed of political correctness.

University of Chicago. Periodically, the news media reports that students at the University of Chicago are finally loosening up and having some fun. Don't believe it. This place is for true intellectuals who don't mind working hard for their degrees. Less selective than the top Ivies, but just as good. Social climbers should apply elsewhere.

Columbia University. Enjoying off-the-charts popularity due to its location in upper Manhattan. Renowned core curriculum gives substance and coherence to freshman and sophomore years. Harlem is only a few blocks away, but safety is no more a concern here than on any other urban campus.

Cornell University. Cornell's reputation as a pressure cooker comes from its preprofessional attitude and "we try harder" mentality. Spans seven colleges—four private and three public. (Tuition varies accordingly.) Strong in engineering and architecture, world-famous in hotel administration. Easiest Ivy to get into.

Dartmouth College. The smallest Ivy and the one with the strongest emphasis on undergraduates. Traditionally the most conservative member of the Ivy League, it has steered toward more student diversity, more serious scholars, and fewer party animals in recent years. If you love the outdoors, you'll be in heaven.

Duke University. What fun to be at Duke—face painted blue, rocking Cameron Indoor Stadium as the Blue Devils score again. Duke is the most selective private university in the South, though not as tough to get in as arch-rival UNC is for out-of-staters. Duke is strong in engineering but offers public policy rather than business for undergraduates.

Georgetown University. For everyone who wants to be a master of the political universe, this is the place. Only a handful of Ivy League schools and Stanford are tougher to get into than Georgetown. In all the excitement over D.C., students tend to forget the Roman-Catholic affiliation, which adds a conservative tinge to the campus.

Harvard University. An acceptance here is the gold standard of American education. Gets periodic slings and arrows for not paying enough attention to undergraduates, some of which is carping from people who didn't get in. It takes moxie to keep your self-image in the midst of all those geniuses, but most Harvard admits can handle it.

Massachusetts Institute of Technology. If you're a science genius, come to MIT to find out how little you really know. No other school makes such a massive assault on the ego (with little in the way of support to help you pick up the pieces). Technology is a given, but MIT also prides itself on leading programs in economics, political science, and management.

University of Pennsylvania. Though an Ivy League institution in name, Penn has more in common with places like Georgetown and Northwestern—places where the liberal arts share center stage with preprofessional programs. At Penn, that means business, engineering, and nursing. Penn has something else other Ivies don't: school spirit. An Ivy where it's okay to have fun.

Princeton University. More conservative than Yale and with total enrollment a third of Harvard's, Princeton is the smallest of the Ivy League's Big Three. That means more attention from faculty and plenty of opportunity for rigorous independent work. Offers engineering but no business. Affluent suburban location contrasts with New Haven and Cambridge.

Stanford University. If you're looking for an Eastern version of Stanford, try Duke (with a touch of MIT mixed in). Stanford's big-time athletics, preprofessional aura, and laid-back atmosphere stand in marked contrast to the Ivy League. In contrast to the hurly-burly of Bay-Area rival Berkeley, Stanford is upscale suburban.

Yale University. Yale is the middle-sized member of the Ivy League's Big Three: bigger than Princeton, smaller than Harvard. Its widely imitated residential college system helps Yale strike a balance between research university and undergraduate college. New Haven is not New York, but the area around the campus is much more livable than it once was.

The Elite Liberal Arts Colleges

Amherst College. Original home to the well-rounded, super-achieving, gentle-person jock. Compare to Williams, Middlebury, and Colby. Not Swarthmore, not Wesleyan. Amherst has always been the king in its category—mainly because there are four other major institutions in easy reach to add diversity and depth.

Bowdoin College. Quietly prestigious Maine school that specializes in Yankee individualism. Rates with Amherst, Middlebury, and Williams for liberal arts excellence, and along with Middlebury, does not require the SAT. Bowdoin has strong science programs and outdoor enthusiasts benefit from proximity to the Atlantic coast.

Bryn Mawr College. The most intellectual of the women's colleges. Politics range from liberal to radical. Do Bryn Mawrters take themselves a bit too seriously? Still benefits from proximity to Haverford, but the latter's decision to go coed in the early eighties cooled that relationship.

Carleton College. Less selective than Amherst and Williams largely because of central Minnesota location. Our choice as the best liberal arts college in the Midwest. Predominantly liberal school, but not to the extremes of its more antiestablishment cousins. Tunnels between buildings help Carls beat the winter blues.

Davidson College. Runs neck-in-neck with Washington and Lee for honors as the best liberal arts college in the South. Liberal by Southern standards, conservative by Northern ones. Small-town location near bustling Charlotte. At seventeen hundred students, it is slightly bigger than Rhodes and Sewanee and slightly smaller than W&L.

Haverford College. Secluded Quaker enclave in Philadelphia's affluent Main Line suburbs. Superb blend of traditional and progressive. Old-fashioned honor code governs all facets of life. With only eleven hundred students, the most intimate of the colleges on this list. An underrated gem.

Pomona College. Long considered the premier liberal arts college in the West. Serious intellectual climate combines with close proximity to an interesting mix of outstanding colleges in the Claremont group. The surrounding area provides access to mountains, ocean, and the lures of L.A., but there is little geared to students in the immediate area.

Swarthmore College. Don't mistake Swarthmore for a miniature version of an Ivy League school. Swat is more intellectual (and liberal) than its counterparts in Cambridge and New Haven. The college's honors program gives hardy souls a taste of graduate school, where most Swatties invariably end up.

Washington and Lee University. The ideal of the gentleman scholar (now gentleperson scholar) is alive and well at W&L. Went coed in the mid '80s, causing selectivity to skyrocket. Noted for geographic diversity, social science programs, and conservative students. One of the South's most prestigious liberal arts colleges since the days of Robert E. Lee.

Wellesley College. There is no better recipe for popularity than a postcard-perfect campus on the outskirts of Boston. That formula keeps Wellesley at the top of the women's college pecking order—along with superb programs in economics and the natural sciences. Nearly a quarter of the students are Asian American, the highest proportion in the East.

Wesleyan University. Often compared to Amherst or Williams, Wesleyan is really more like Swarthmore. The key difference: Wesleyan is twice as big. Wes students are progressive, politically-minded, and fiercely independent. Exotic specialties like ethnomusicology and East Asian Studies add spice to the scene.

Williams College. Running neck-in-neck with Amherst on the selectivity chart, Williams occupies a campus of surpassing beauty in the foothills of the Berkshires. Has shaken the preppy image, but still attracts plenty of well-toned all-around jock-intellectuals. The splendid isolation of Williamstown is either a blessing or a curse.

Rising Stars

Though we call these rising stars, there is nothing new about the superb academic quality and exclusive admissions standards at any of these schools. As a group, they are relative newcomers to the super-elite of American higher education. Most have benefited from recent surges in applications and a number are actually more selective than some of the colleges on the elite list. They tend to be in "hot" locations and are well positioned to continue on an upward trajectory.

Barnard College. With applications running double what they were ten years ago, Barnard has eclipsed Wellesley as the nation's most popular women's college. Barnard women are a little more artsy and a little more City-ish than their female counterparts at Columbia College. Step outside and you're on Broadway.

Bates College. Bowdoin got rid of its frats, Bates never had them, and therein hangs a tale. With its long-held tradition of egalitarianism, Bates is a kindred spirit to Quaker institutions such as Haverford and Swarthmore. Month-long spring term helps make Bates a leader in study abroad.

Claremont McKenna College. Watch out, Pomona—this up-and-comer is giving you a run for your money as the most popular of the five Claremont Colleges. McKenna is small (one thousand) and dedicated to business and politics. More regional than Pomona, but rapidly acquiring a national reputation. Formerly Claremont Men's College.

Emory University. Often compared to Duke and Vanderbilt, Emory may be most similar to Wash U. in St. Louis. Both have suburban locations in major cities and both tout business and premed as major draws. If the campus is uninspiring, the suburban Atlanta location is unbeatable.

Franklin W. Olin College of Engineering. Olin is the most prestigious ten-year-old institution in America. The secret? Scholarships for all of its 200 undergraduates. A campus on the outskirts of Boston adds attractive geography to the mix and a spanking new physical plant is state-of-the-art in everything.

George Washington University. A generation ago, GW was a back-up school with an 80 percent acceptance rate maligned for its lack of unity. A few tens of thousands of applications later, the university accepts less than half who apply and is still not much for school spirit. GW is the nation's leader in internships per capita.

Middlebury College. One of the small liberal arts colleges where applications have surged significantly in the past ten years. Students are drawn to the beauty of Midd's Green Mountain location and strong programs in hot areas like international studies and environmental science. Known world-wide for its summer foreign language programs.

New York University. Don't count on getting into NYU just because Big Sis did. From back-up school to the hottest place in higher education, NYU's rise has been breath-taking. The siren song of Greenwich Village has lured applicants by the thousands. Major draws include the arts, media, and business.

Northwestern University. The most selective university in the Midwest. The Big Ten is not the Ivy League, and NU has more school spirit than its Eastern counterparts. Much more preprofessional than its nearby rival University of Chicago and than all of the Ivies but Penn. World renowned in journalism.

Rice University. One of the few elite private colleges that is also a best buy. Rice is outstanding in engineering, architecture, and music. With less than three thousand undergraduates, Rice is smaller than many applicants realize. In lieu of frats, Rice has a residential college system like Yale and the University of Miami.

University of Southern California. USC's old handle: "The University of Spoiled Children." USC's new handle: highly selective West Coast university with preeminent programs in arts and media. The difference: a deluge in applications of historic proportions as students flock to L.A. and the region's only major private university.

Tufts University. Tufts will always be a second banana to Harvard in the Boston area, but given the Hub's runaway popularity among college students, second is not so bad. Best-known for international relations, Tufts is also strong in engineering and health-related fields. In the Experimental College, students can take off-the-wall courses for credit.

Vanderbilt University. More "southern" than Emory or Duke, Vandy has traditionally been a preferred choice in the deep South suburbs of Atlanta and Birmingham. Secluded Nashville campus is among the prettiest in the South. Becoming more national as the admissions office lures increasing numbers of non-Southerners.

Wake Forest University. Another middle-sized (six thousand) Southern university on the move. Conservative by national standards, although Wake severed its ties to the ultraconservative Southern Baptists in 1986. ACC athletics and Greek parties shape the social scene. The strategic central North Carolina location provides access to mountains, beaches, and the famous research triangle.

Washington University in St. Louis. In the space of little more than a decade, Wash U. has gone from Midwestern back-up school to elite private university close on the heels of Northwestern. Wash U. is strong in everything from art to engineering. The halo effect of the university's medical school attracts a slew of aspiring doctors.

See Also:

Bard College (Top Nonconformist Colleges)
Duke University (The Elite Private Universities)
University of North Carolina (The Budget Ivy League)
Pepperdine University (Top Conservative Colleges)
Spelman College (Historically Black Colleges and Universities)
University of Virginia (The Budget Ivy League)

Top Colleges, Better Odds

This information is for students who plunge into depression every time they look at Ivy League acceptance rates. Instead of beating your head endlessly against that ivy-covered brick wall, why not consider one of the outstanding schools on this list? You'll get an education on a par with the fanciest designer label college, maybe better, and all these places have excellent national reputations. The only difference is that applicants are not clamoring for admission in quite the same numbers.

The reasons vary. Some have such strong reputations for academic rigor that mediocre students would never dare apply. As they say in admissions, the applicant pool is self-selected. Whereas the Ivies always attract stacks of applications from wannabes, hangers-on, and various other prestige hounds, the ratio of serious students tends to be higher at many of these schools (which is, by the way, a good reason why the acceptance rate is not always the best indicator of a school's quality).

In other cases, location plays a role. Many Easterners seem to think they'll fall off the edge of the Earth if they venture past Buffalo or Pittsburgh, but it just so happens that many of the finest colleges in the nation are tucked away in places like Ohio, Iowa, and Minnesota. The schools in trendy locales like Boston or Washington, D.C., tend be deluged with applications, while better ones in the Midwest often attract far fewer.

All of the colleges on this list are well-known in higher-education circles, especially in the admissions offices of top graduate and professional programs.

Case Western Reserve University. CWRU is still trying to catch up with Carnegie Mellon. Students may sing its praises, but Cleveland isn't exactly Boston, or even Pittsburgh. On the plus side, students get an outstanding technical education at Case with solid offerings in other areas.

Grinnell College. Is this heaven? No, it's Grinnell College, tucked away in the Iowa cornfields. Competes with the top liberal arts colleges in the nation, though hamstrung by location. Very liberal, attracts lots of Chicagoans. Savvy financial management has created huge endowment. With nation's highest literacy rate, Iowa gets a bad rap.

The Johns Hopkins University. The Hop makes this list mainly because of its (somewhat misleading) reputation as a premed factory. While future doctors stampede the admissions gate, humanists and social scientists can waltz in with much less difficulty. JHU is the heavyweight champ of federal grants. Located in downtown Baltimore.

Kenyon College. Kenyon is a pure liberals arts college plunked down in the middle of the Ohio countryside. More mainstream than Oberlin, more serious than Denison, and more selective than Wooster, Kenyon is best-known for English and a small but distinguished drama program.

Macalester College. Former U.N. Secretary General Kofi Annan, '61, typifies one of Mac's hallmarks: an internationalist view of the world. Carleton has a slightly bigger national reputation, but Mac has St. Paul, a progressive capital city. Mac is the only leading Midwestern liberal arts college in an urban setting.

Oberlin College. The college that invented non-conformity. From the Underground Railroad to the modern peace movement, Obies have been front and center. As at Reed and Grinnell, Oberlin's curriculum is less radical than its students. Oberlin is especially strong in the sciences, and its music conservatory is among the nation's best.

Reed College. Legendary as a countercultural mecca and also for intense introspection. Combines far-out students with traditional academics, including a senior thesis that would earn a master's degree at many schools. Low graduation rate attests that the Reed experience is overwhelming for some. Student body consists mainly of urbanites from both coasts.

Rensselaer Polytechnic Institute. One of the nation's premier technical institutes. Only top students apply, but over two-thirds are accepted. Rensselaer is a leader in the use of interactive technology for hands-on learning. School of Management and Technology specializes in entrepreneurship.

University of Rochester. The name may conjure up a nondescript public university, but Rochester is a top notch private university in the orbit of Carnegie Mellon, Case Western Reserve, Johns Hopkins and Washington U. (MO). The university has a scientific bent and is known as a haven for premeds.

See Also:
University of Chicago (The Elite Private Universities)

The Best Bargains

Anyone who purports to name the best college bargains begins on shaky ground. Every student has different needs and interests. What looks like a bargain to one person may be too expensive at any price for the next. Furthermore, because high-cost colleges frequently offer extensive financial aid, institutions that charge a higher sticker price can still turn out to be bargains for students who get scholarships based on merit or need.

With those caveats, we offer several lists to cover our picks for the best bargains in American higher education. Most of the institutions in this section are publicly supported. For in-staters, these schools typically cost a third to half as much as their private counterparts. For out-of-state students, the bill usually totals about two thirds the cost of a private institution. Colleges and universities on the Budget Ivy League list enroll more than five thousand students, while the Small-College Bargains list includes those that enroll under five thousand.

The Budget Ivy League

This list includes most of the premier public universities in the nation. (A few of the most expensive ones, such as University of Michigan and University of Vermont, are listed under Other Well-Known Universities.) All combine superb academic programs and low cost.

University of Arizona. Best value for out-of-staters in the desert Southwest. Known for astronomy, engineering, and a top-notch honors program. Sunny Tucson is a haven for sun-worshippers and outdoor enthusiasts. Top-ranked hoops team always a national championship contender.

University of California–Berkeley. Makes this list because it is still cheap for in-staters and retains tremendous prestige. Struggling to cope with budget cuts, tuition increases, and overcrowding. Self-starters will find unparalleled opportunities, more passive types will get lost in the herd.

University of California–Los Angeles. Ditto what we said about Berkeley. Cloistered away in exclusive Beverly Hills, UCLA is the more conservative of the two. The beach, the mountains, and chic Hollywood hangouts are all in easy reach. One of the world's best places to study the arts, film, or television.

University of Florida. It should come as no surprise that UF is a world leader in citrus science. Throw in communications, engineering, and Latin American studies to the list of renowned programs. Among Deep South public universities, only the University of Georgia rivals UF in overall quality.

Florida State University. With an assist from its football program, FSU's popularity has burgeoned in recent years. Not that there weren't some quality programs to begin with. The motion picture school is among the best around, and business and the arts are also strong. So long as the football team beats the hated Gators, all is well.

Georgia Institute of Technology. The nation's top public technical institute. Ma Tech is a leader in every imaginable engineering field. Undergrads often suffer from large classes and the research orientation of the faculty. Atlanta and big-time sports teams offer plenty of excitement.

University of Georgia. What a difference free tuition makes. The Hope Scholarship gives a free ride to in-staters with a 3.0 GPA, and top in-state students now choose UGA over highly selective private universities. Business and journalism head the list of sought-after programs. College town of Athens features the music scene that spawned R.E.M. and the B-52s.

University of Illinois–Urbana-Champaign. Half a step behind Michigan, neck-in-neck with Wisconsin among top Midwestern public universities. Strengths include business, engineering, architecture, and the natural sciences. Only 10 percent of the student body hails from out-of-state.

University of Iowa. A bargain compared to other Big Ten schools such as Michigan, Wisconsin, and Illinois. Iowa is world-famous for its creative writing program and writers' workshop. Other areas of strength include health sciences, business, and the arts. Future scientists should check out the Research Scholars Program.

University of Kansas. Memo to out-of-staters: Lawrence is not flat as a pancake and does not resemble Dorothy's home in *The Wizard of Oz*. University of Kansas has a gorgeous campus and is one of the premier college bargains in the United States. Strong programs in a full slate of professional schools.

Miami University (OH). Rather than disappear into the black hole of Ohio State, top students in the Buckeye state come here to feel as if they are going to an elite private university. MU has a niche like William & Mary's in Virginia—though MU is twice as big. Miami's top draw is business, and its tenor is conservative.

University of Minnesota–Twin Cities. Not quite as highly rated as U. of Wisconsin or U. of Michigan, but not quite as expensive, either. Strong in the standard preprofessional areas, plus forestry and Scandinavian studies. Housing shortage limits campus cohesiveness. The Twin Cities are among the nation's most livable.

College of New Jersey. Once known as Trenton State University, now a perennial in the "best buys" category. A former teachers' college that has remade itself into a selective university stressing the liberal arts, business, and accounting. Beautiful suburban campus with the feel of a private school.

University of North Carolina–Chapel Hill. Close on the heels of UVA as the South's most prestigious state university. With more than 80 percent of the spots in each class reserved for in-staters, admission is next to impossible for out-of-staters who aren't 6'9" with a 43-inch vertical jump. Chapel Hill is a quintessential college town.

University of Oregon. UO may be the best deal in public higher education on the West Coast. Less expensive than the UC system and less selective than the University of Washington, UO is a university of manageable size in a great location. The liberal arts are more than just a slogan, and programs in business and communication are strong.

Rutgers, The State University of New Jersey. Includes over fifty thousand students on six campuses. Rutgers College is the most selective, followed by Douglass (all women) and Livingston. Ninety percent of the students are homegrown Garden Staters.

SUNY–Binghamton University. If one hundred thousand screaming fans on a Saturday afternoon tickles your fancy, head two hundred miles southwest to Penn State. Binghamton has become the premier public university in the northeast because of its outstanding academic programs, such as the Binghamton Scholars and Discovery Initiative, and its commitment to undergraduates.

SUNY–Geneseo. Smallish university (fifty-six hundred) with strong programs in business and the liberal arts. Began as a teacher's college and its female-to-male ratio is still two to one. Much excitement revolves around the men's hockey team. Similar in scale to William & Mary and Mary Washington in Virginia, smaller than Miami of Ohio.

University of Texas–Austin. Though the price tag is going up, UT is still one of the cheapest major universities in the nation. The UT challenge: to avoid getting lost in the sea of fifty thousand faces. Top programs include business, engineering, and Latin American studies. Liberal arts majors should check out the Plan II honors program.

Truman State University. Truman changed its name to emphasize that it has more in common with private institutions than nondescript regional publics. Truman is looking for a public-ivy niche like Miami of Ohio and William & Mary. New residential college program increases co-curricular learning.

University of Virginia. Competition for out-of-state admission now at the Ivy League level. Mr. Jefferson's university remains one of America's most beautiful. Combines an aristocratic flavor with Wahoo support of ACC athletic teams. Strong fraternity system rules campus social life.

University of Washington. The Pacific Northwest's leading research university and the toughest for out-of-state admission. Strong across the board in preprofessional areas. In-staters constitute 90 percent of the student body. Sprawling Seattle campus is an urban oasis.

College of William and Mary. Founded in 1693, William and Mary is the original public Ivy. History, government, and international studies are among the strongest departments. With seventy-five hundred students, W&M is really a medium-sized university that is larger than University of Richmond and Mary Washington.

University of Wisconsin–Madison. UW draws nearly 40 percent of its students from out-of-state, the highest proportion among leading Midwestern public universities. Why brave the cold? Reasons include top programs in an array of professional fields and several innovative living-learning programs.

Small-College Bargains

Here is a list for everyone who thought it was necessary to attend a behemoth state university to get an education at a bargain price. Most of the schools on this list are a different breed of cat: public liberal arts colleges. In many ways, they resemble their private counterparts, offering small classes, a strong sense of community, and undivided attention to the liberal arts. The only difference is the price tag: out-of-state students can count on paying at least a third less than at a private college, while in-staters will pocket enough savings to get a good start on graduate school—or that new BMW they've been wanting. New College of Florida is the consensus leader in this category, but the others are gaining momentum.

In addition to the public liberal arts colleges, we include descriptions of three private institutions that offer an unbeatable deal: free tuition. A fourth freebie, Deep Springs College, is described in The Most Innovative Curriculums list.

For additional small colleges at a reasonable price, browse the southern entries in More Excellent Liberal Arts Colleges. Beginning at South Carolina, Tennessee, and Arkansas, students can expect expenses at least 20 percent lower than at schools in other regions.

Berea College. Absolutely tuition-free for students willing to work ten hours per week on campus. The hitch: only needy students can attend this private institution. Christian orientation fosters a strong sense of community and mission work. Most students come from Kentucky and adjacent states.

Cooper Union. In the heart of Manhattan, a small private school (nine hundred) specializing in art, architecture, and engineering. Founded by a philanthropist as a tuition-free school. Campus consists of East Greenwich Village. At 13 percent, acceptance rate is lower than at most Ivy League schools.

The Evergreen State College. There's no mistaking Evergreen for a typical public college. Never mind the way-out garb favored by its students. Evergreen's inter-disciplinary, team-taught curriculum is truly unique. To find anything remotely like Evergreen, you'll need to travel east to places like Hampshire or Sarah Lawrence.

Keene State College. Middle-sized (forty-six hundred) institution in the hills of southern New Hampshire. Primary offerings include liberal arts, education, and management. A taste of small-town New England.

University of Maine–Farmington. Small public liberal arts college (two thousand) tucked away in central Maine.

Seldom discovered by out-of-staters. Programs in education and health-related fields in addition to the liberal arts. Enrollment approximately two-thirds women.

University of Mary Washington. Mary Washington could easily be mistaken for one of Virginia's elite private colleges. MWC offers just as much history and tradition—but at a much lower price. Once a women's college, still over two-thirds female. On the selectivity chart, MWC ranks behind only UVA and William & Mary among Virginia public universities.

University of Minnesota–Morris. If you've ever taken a wrong turn on the way to Duluth, you might have stumbled upon one of the best public liberal arts colleges in the country. Morris combines superb students, small classes, dedicated faculty, and an isolated prairie location.

New College of Florida. Elite liberal arts education at a bargain price. New College is the South's most liberal institution of higher learning—apologies to Guilford. With an enrollment of eight hundred, New College is about one-third the size of a typical liberal arts college.

University of North Carolina–Asheville. The "other" UNC happens to be one of the best educational bargains in the country. At just over three thousand students, UNCA is about half the size of fellow public liberal arts college William & Mary and one thousand students smaller than Mary Washington. Picturesque mountain location in a resort city.

College of the Ozarks. A Missouri version of Berea. No tuition at this private institution, but family income must be low (approximately thirty thousand dollars) to qualify for admission. Work requirements include fifteen hours a week, plus additional hours during school vacations. Conservative in outlook and requires attendance at religious services.

St. Mary's College of Maryland. Often mistaken for a Catholic-affiliated school. Founded as a seminary for women, now a highly selective public college that is rapidly growing in popularity. Small student body (seventeen hundred) makes for close student-faculty relations. Strategically located one hour from both Washington, D.C., and Baltimore.

See Also:
   Deep Springs College (The Most Innovative Curriculums)
   Morehouse College (Historically Black Colleges and Universities)
   Rice University (Rising Stars)
   State University of New York–Purchase (Top Nonconformist Colleges)
   Spelman College (Historically Black Colleges and Universities)

Public Universities: Honors Programs and Residential Colleges

The last in our triad of ways to beat the high cost of college is to enroll in one of the growing number of "school within a school" programs at state universities. State schools typically have much lower tuition than privates, but, for too many students, economy comes at the cost of biding time at the back of huge lecture halls with scant attention from faculty. In an effort to provide education on a human scale, many large public institutions have invested big bucks to create smaller learning communities designed to give students the best of both worlds. They mimic the intimacy of a small liberal arts college, while giving students access to the full range of university resources, from big-time athletics to research libraries.

The most common learning communities are the traditional honors programs open to students who seek a more rigorous course of study than the usual fare. Virtually every public institution now has one and the best offer an education on par with the most selective private colleges—with admission standards nearly as high. In addition to small classes with top faculty, honors programs can provide perks such as special housing, research grants, priority registration, enhanced library privileges, internships, study abroad, and access to graduate courses and combined degree programs. Small wonder that more and more top students are turning up their noses at Olde Ivy (with its fifty thousand dollar per year price tag) to attend public university honors programs for thousands less.

Residential college programs, sometimes known as living/learning communities, are also gaining in popularity. Their aim is to integrate academic and residential life by seeing to it that students who live and socialize together also have some common intellectual experiences. Some residential colleges allow students to share the same floor or wing of a dorm and cater to students with particular academic interests or offer special seminars; most have affiliated faculty and provide enrichment programs such as speakers, artistic events, and visiting scholars. Some programs are even free-standing colleges. Residential colleges typically emphasize participation and give students a large measure of responsibility in the life of the college. Though admission is selective to some programs, most are open to all students who are interested. A few universities, such as SUNY–Binghamton and UC–Santa Cruz listed below, house all their students in residential colleges.

When considering either an honors program or a residential college, it is important to find out the relationship of the program to the university as a whole. Does it have a critical mass of students? How do they relate to the rest of the student body? Does the academic quality rise above the mediocrity of the university as a whole? Most important: what sort of students does it attract? If the program is perceived as an enclave of nerds who study too much or get too excited about learning, you could be headed for a repeat of high school, something most intelligent students will want to avoid.

The following lists offer a sample of the most prestigious public university honors programs and best-known residential college programs in the nation. Rest assured that there are many other fine ones in both categories. If you are considering any large university, especially one in the Big Ten, ask what they have in the way of learning communities.

Honors Programs

University of Illinois–Urbana-Champaign: Campus Honors Program. Allows students to take honors courses to complete the university's general education requirements. Enrichment opportunities range from a lecture series about faculty research to a lunch program featuring international cuisine. About one hundred and twenty-five freshmen are admitted each year.

University of North Carolina–Chapel Hill: Honors Program. UNC consciously avoids separating its honors students from other undergraduates and offers no special housing. Billed as a "learning laboratory," the program includes seminars on interdisciplinary and nontraditional topics. Other features include an honors semester abroad and a senior thesis.

Pennsylvania State University: Schreyer Honors College.
Penn State's highly selective honors program offers
a variety of enrichment opportunities and requires a
senior thesis. Accepted students have an average GPA
above 4.0. Scholarships of up to three thousand dollars
are earmarked for honors students.

University of Texas–Austin: Plan II. Perhaps the nation's
most famous liberal arts honors program, Plan II features year-long core courses and interdisciplinary
seminars. Given UT's bargain-basement sticker price,
this program may be the single best buy in all of
higher education. Limited to less than two hundred
entering students.

University of Virginia: Echols Scholars Program. About
two hundred of UVA's top first-year students get the
Echols Scholar designation. Students are given complete freedom to design their own academic programs.
All Echols students are housed together during their
first year.

Residential Colleges

University of California–Santa Cruz. The entire UCSC
student body is divided into ten residential colleges. Each college has its own core course ranging
from Cultural Encounters: Rediscovering California
to Global Transformations: Environment and
Community. Entering freshmen choose their college
prior to enrollment.

**University of Maryland–College Park: College Park
Scholars.** CPS offers a two year residential college experience in which students take clusters of interdisciplinary courses to satisfy their core requirements. Funds

are available for one-on-one research with faculty. Top applicants to the university who apply by December 1 are invited to participate.

University of Michigan: Residential College. One thousand students live and learn in Michigan's nationally renowned Residential College. All students admitted to the university's college of literature, science, and the arts are eligible on a first-come, first-served basis when they apply for housing. The RC places special emphasis on the arts and is known for its liberal student body.

State University of New York–Binghamton. Binghamton divides all of its campus housing into five residential colleges which include about one thousand students. Each has its own faculty master and sponsors academic and extracurricular programs. Special interest housing modules within the colleges cater to students interested in everything from the performing arts to computers, robotics, and engineering.

University of Wisconsin–Madison: Chadbourne Residential College. Chadbourne seeks to provide "the community experience of a small liberal arts college at the heart of a great research university." Life in CRC is governed by a Community Forum that all students attend. Participants are chosen from those who designate CRC as their first choice in the university's housing lottery.

More Excellent Small Colleges

This list reflects the reality that there are many more good small colleges for undergraduate study than there are good large universities. For every mega-university with twenty thousand undergraduates, there are ten small colleges with two thousand students that are probably superior in most respects.

The colleges on this list are a diverse lot, but all have a total enrollment of under four thousand. Most have no graduate students at all. The rest have a smattering of them, but are still mainly undergraduate institutions. If you're looking for a college and don't find it here, check out some of the other lists. There are many more excellent small colleges that we have chosen to classify by a particular trait.

Albion College. Next to evangelical Hope and Calvin and out-there Kalamazoo, Albion is Michigan's middle-of-the-road liberal arts college. Think Gerald Ford, the moderate Republican president who is the namesake of Albion's Institute for Public Service. A haven for future doctors, lawyers, and businesspeople.

Allegheny College. An unpretentious cousin to more well-heeled places like Dickinson and Bucknell. Draws heavily from the Buffalo-Cleveland-Pittsburgh area. The college's powerhouse athletic teams clean up on Division III competition. If you've ever wondered what lake-effect snow is, you'll find out here.

Austin College. The second-most famous institution in Texas with Austin in its name. Half the size of Trinity (TX), runs neck-in-neck with Southwestern to be the leading Texas college under two thousand students. Combines the liberal arts with strong programs in business, education, and health fields.

Beloit College. Tiny Midwestern college (twelve hundred) known for freethinking students and international focus. Has steered back toward the mainstream after its heyday as an alternative school in the '60s and '70s.

Wisconsin location makes Beloit easier to get into than similar Northeastern schools.

Brandeis University. Founded in 1948 by Jews who wanted an elite institution to call their own. Now down to just over 50 percent Jewish and seeking top students of all faiths. Academic specialties include the natural sciences, the Middle East, and Jewish Studies. Competes with Tufts in the Boston area.

Bucknell University. A very selective "near Ivy" that attracts conservative and career-oriented students. The Central Pennsylvania campus is isolated, but it is among the most picturesque in the nation. A strong fraternity and sorority system offers traditional college social life. The administration is working to expand diversity.

Clark University. Small university (three thousand) that offers unique opportunities for undergraduate research. Often overshadowed by the Boston schools one hour to the east. World-famous in psychology and geography. Easier in admissions than many other schools of similar quality.

Colby College. The northernmost outpost of higher ed in the East. Colby's picturesque small-town setting is a short hop from the sea coast or the Maine wilderness. No frats since the college abolished them twenty years ago. A well-toned, outdoorsy student body in the mold of Middlebury, Williams, and Amherst.

Colgate University. Frontrunner of the upstate New York liberal arts colleges. Attracts an outdoorsy, athletic student body. Fraternities and sororities still well entrenched despite the university's efforts to neutralize them. The most selective school on this list.

Colorado College. Under its Block Plan, students study one course at a time in month-long segments. Great for science labs, in-depth study, field trips. Less well-suited to assignments that take more than a month. Colorado Springs provides easy access to Rocky Mountain playlands.

Connecticut College. Like Vassar and Skidmore, Connecticut College made a successful transition from women's college to coed. The college is strong in the humanities and renowned for its study abroad programs. It is also an SAT-optional school. New London does not offer much but at least it is on the ocean.

Denison University. Denison shut down its frat row in an effort to shift the spotlight from partying to academics. Not quite as selective as Kenyon, draws more Easterners than competitors such as Wittenberg and Ohio Wesleyan. Denison has a middle-of-the-road to conservative student body and one of the most beautiful campuses anywhere.

Dickinson College. Historic small college in the foothills of central Pennsylvania. Operates numerous study-abroad programs and emphasizes foreign languages. Known for interdisciplinary programs. Competes with the elite schools but is often a second choice.

Drew University. From Drew's wooded perch in suburban Jersey, Manhattan is only a thirty-minute train ride away. That means Wall Street and the U.N., both frequent destinations for Drew interns. Drew is New

Jersey's only prominent liberal arts college and one of the few in the greater New York City area.

Elon University. Once the preserve of first-generation college students from North Carolina, Elon has blossomed as a strong liberal arts college with regional appeal. Emphasizes global perspectives and hands-on learning. Takes ordinary students and turns them on to academics.

Franklin and Marshall College. Eastern Pennsylvania school known for preprofessional students and a pipeline of internships to Capitol Hill. Students aim for careers in law, medicine, and business. A conventional, hardworking school that competes with Bucknell, Colgate, and Lafayette.

Gettysburg College. Another central Pennsylvania liberal arts college often associated with Dickinson and with Franklin and Marshall. Nearby Civil War battlefield helps make the history department one of the best and most popular. Strong Greek system includes about one-half of the students.

Goucher College. This is not your grandmother's Goucher. Once a staid women's college, Goucher has added men and a more progressive ambience, similar to places like Skidmore and Sarah Lawrence. Strategically located near Baltimore and not far from D.C., Goucher offers an excellent internship program.

Gustavus Adolphus College. Named for a seventeenth-century Swedish king who defended Lutheranism against the Catholics. Two-thirds of the students are members of the faith and most are homegrown Minnesotans.

Strong core requirements ensure broad exposure to the liberal arts. Offers unusual opportunities for undergraduate research.

Hamilton College. Once a conservative men's college, Hamilton became coed in 1978 when it swallowed artsy Kirkland College. The marriage has ensured more diversity and strength across the curriculum. Set on an opulent rural upstate New York campus. Fights uphill battle for students in competition with schools in the Elite category.

Hartwick College. Hartwick is known for its cozy atmosphere and ability to take good care of students. Combines arts and sciences with a nursing program. The campus is beautiful but small-town upstate New York has proven to be a hard sell in recent years.

Hendrix College. Tiny Hendrix (fifteen hundred) is one of the most economical private liberal arts college in the nation. Tuition is half that charged by most Northeastern schools. Remote Arkansas location belies strong international emphasis. An unusually open and accepting community.

Hobart and William Smith Colleges. Coordinate single-sex colleges overlooking one of New York's Finger Lakes. Each college has its own administration on formerly separate campuses. Fraternities and men's lacrosse dominate the traditional social scene. Geneva is a rusting industrial town.

Lafayette College. Close kin to Colgate, Hamilton, and Bucknell. Provides highly competitive academic climate and traditional college experience. One of the few small liberal arts colleges that offers engineering. Social life revolves around fraternities and sororities.

Lake Forest College. The only small, selective private college in the Chicago area. The college generally attracts middle-of-the-road and conservative students. In the exclusive town of Lake Forest, students can baby-sit for corporate CEOs at night and get internships at their corporations during the day.

Lawrence University. Underrated Wisconsin college combining the liberal arts with one of the best music conservatories in the nation. Despite the word "university" in its name, Lawrence is really a very small college (twelve hundred). Another top Midwest liberal arts college that would be much more selective if on the East Coast.

Lewis and Clark College. The West Coast's leader in international and study abroad programs. Politically liberal, but not so far out as cross-town neighbor Reed. Portfolio Path to admission allows students to finesse standardized tests. With Mount Hood visible in the distance, a wealth of outdoor possibilities.

Muhlenberg College. There is a definite Muhlenberg type: serious, ambitious and buttoned-down. Muhlenberg is the only eastern Pennsylvania/New Jersey liberal arts college with a meaningful religious affiliation—Lutheran. Strong in premed, prelaw, pre-anything.

Occidental College. Oxy is a diverse, urban, streetwise cousin to the more upscale and suburban Claremont Colleges. Plentiful internships and study abroad give Oxy students real-world perspectives. Oxy's innovative diplomacy and world affairs program features internships in Washington and at the U.N.

Ohio Wesleyan University. Often mentioned in the same breath with Denison, but a bit more Midwestern, a bit less preppy than its nearby counterpart. As at Denison, the administration is doing its best to put the clamps on the Greek system and raise academic standards. Students tend to be mainstream and career-oriented.

Rhodes College. Goes head to head with Sewanee for the top spot in the pecking order of mid-South liberal arts colleges. While Sewanee has a gorgeous rural campus, Rhodes has Memphis. Economics and international studies head the list of strong programs. Like Davidson, Rhodes has historic ties to the Presbyterian Church.

Rollins College. Rollins is the marriage of a liberal arts college and a business school. A haven for Easterners who want to their ticket punched to Florida, Rollins attracts conservative and affluent students and world class water skiers. Rivals include Eckerd in St. Petersburg and the University of Miami.

Ripon College. Everything about Ripon is small—the town, the college, and just about all the classes. More conservative than Beloit and Lawrence, similar to places like Depauw and Knox. With about one thousand students, Ripon is the smallest of the five.

St. Lawrence University. St. Lawrence is perched far back in the north country, closer to Ottawa and Montreal than Syracuse. Isolation breeds camaraderie, and SLU students have a special bond similar to that at places like Dartmouth and Whitman. Environmental studies is the crown jewel.

Skidmore College. Like Vassar, Connecticut College, and Wheaton (MA), Skidmore is a successful convert to coeducation. Strong in the performing arts with an unexpected emphasis on business, Skidmore is top-notch when it comes to internships, study abroad, and student research. Instead of green lawns, Skidmore has the woods.

University of the South (Sewanee). Sewanee is like a little bit of Britain's Oxford plunked down in the highlands of Tennessee. More conservative than Rhodes and Davidson, Sewanee is a guardian of the tried and true. Voluntary dress code includes skirts for women and jacket and tie for men. Especially noted for its English department.

Trinity College (CT). While most small colleges have been treading water, Trinity has had a notable increase in applications and selectivity in recent years. Trinity is among the few small liberal arts colleges in an urban setting and security has always been an issue. Trinity joins Lafayette, Swarthmore, and Smith among small colleges with engineering.

Trinity University (TX). The Southwest's leading liberal arts college is also one of the few in a major city. Trinity is twice as big as nearby rivals Austin and Southwestern and offers a diverse curriculum that includes business, education, and engineering in addition to the liberal arts. Upscale and conservative.

University of Tulsa. Tulsa is a notch smaller than Texas Christian and Washington U. but bigger than most liberal arts colleges. The university has a technical orientation rooted in Oklahoma oil, but Tulsa has a much more diverse curriculum than Colorado School of Mines. Tulsa has an innovative program allowing undergraduates to do research.

Union College. Union is split down the middle between liberal arts and engineering. That means its center of gravity is more toward the technical side than places like Trinity, Lafayette, and Tufts, but less so than Clarkson and Rensselaer. Schenectady is less than exciting but there are outdoor getaways in all directions.

Vassar College. It is hard to imagine that Vassar once considered picking up and moving to Yale in the 1960s rather than become a coed institution. Forty years after admitting men, still on its ancient and picturesque campus, Vassar is a thriving, highly selective, avant garde institution with an accent on the fine arts and humanities.

Warren Wilson College. Set in the picturesque mountains of western North Carolina, Warren Wilson offers a unique mixture of solid academics, community service, and on-campus work. Rooted in the culture of Appalachia, this Presbyterian college emphasizes the importance of global perspectives.

Wheaton College (MA). Wheaton is the most recent convert to coeducation among prominent East Coast institutions, and women still outnumber men by nearly two to one. Though in Massachusetts, Wheaton is actually closer to Providence than Boston. One of the few moderately selective institutions in the area.

Whittier College. Whittier's Quaker heritage brings a touch of the east to this suburban campus on the outskirts of L.A. Less selective than Occidental and the Claremont Colleges, Whittier lures top students with an arsenal of merit scholarships. Beware the sneaky October 15 deadline for the best of them.

Whitman College. Whitman has quietly established itself as one of the West's leading liberal arts colleges. Don't sweat the umbrella: Walla Walla is in arid eastern Washington. Whitman's isolation breeds community spirit and alumni loyalty. True to its liberal arts heritage, Whitman has no business program.

Willamette University. Willamette is strategically located next-door to the Oregon state capitol and forty minutes from Portland. Bigger than Whitman, smaller than U. of Puget Sound, and more conservative than Lewis and Clark, Willamette offers extensive study abroad enhanced by ties to Asia.

Wofford College. Wofford is about one-third as big as Furman and roughly the same size as Presbyterian. With more than a few gentleman jocks, Wofford is one of the smallest institutions to compete in NCAA Division I. Fraternities and sororities dominate the traditional social scene.

College of Wooster. Though not well-known to the general public, Wooster is renowned in academic circles and a number of foreign countries. Admission is not difficult, but graduating takes work. All students complete an independent study project in their last two years. More intellectually serious than competitors such as Denison.

More Well-Known Universities

The universities on this list attract many top students, but are not quite as choosy as those on the Elite list. Each of them has its own specialties, usually in preprofessional areas. Self-starters who have a particular program in mind will be well-served.

Liberal arts students should go in with both eyes open. As with large public universities, an honors program would be a good bet. The main priority is to avoid getting lost in the crowd.

Enrollments at these universities range from four thousand to over fifty thousand, placing them in the medium-to-large category. Most are private universities, though the list includes several premier public universities that no longer qualify for bargain status. Finally, each school on this list is located in or near a major city.

American University. If the odds are against you at Georgetown and you can't see yourself on GW's non-campus, welcome to American University. The allure of AU is simple: Washington, D.C. American has a nice campus in a nice neighborhood and easy access to the Metro. About a third smaller than GW.

Arizona State University. Want to get lost in the crowd? ASU is the biggest university in the Southwest—apologies to UCLA. No matter how appealing the thought of fifty thousand new faces, you'd better find the right program to get a good education. Try the professional schools and the honors college.

Boston University. One of the nation's biggest private universities, but you could easily miss it amid the bustle of the city. Boston's Back Bay neighborhood is the promised land for hordes of students nationwide seeking a funky, artsy, youth-oriented place that is less in-your-face than New York City.

University of British Columbia. Natural beauty is the first thing that draws Americans to Vancouver—and western Canada's premier university. A similar scale to places like University of Washington, but with two major differences—no big-time sports to unite the campus and limited dorm life.

University of California–Davis. The agricultural and engineering branch of the UC system. Premed, prevet, food science—you name it. If the subject is living things, you can study it here. A small-town alternative to the bright lights of UC Berkeley and UCLA. As is often true of science-oriented schools, the work is hard.

University of California–San Diego. Applications doubled in the '90s at this seaside paradise. UCSD now rivals better-known Berkeley and UCLA as the Cal campus of choice for top students. Five undergraduate colleges offer varying educational approaches. Best known in the sciences and engineering.

Carnegie Mellon University. CMU is the only premier technical university that also happens to be just as strong in the arts. Applications have more than doubled in the past ten years so it must be doing something right. One of the few institutions that openly matches better financial aid awards from competitor schools.

University of Colorado–Boulder. Boulder is a legendary place that draws everyone from East-Coast ski bums to California refugees. The scenery is gorgeous and the science programs are first-rate. Check out the residential academic programs. Expensive for out-of-staters.

University of Connecticut. Squeezed in among the likes of Yale, Brown, Amherst, Wesleyan, and UMass—all within a two-hour drive—UConn could be forgiven for having an inferiority complex. But championship basketball teams have ignited Husky pride, and the university's mammoth rebuilding project should work wonders.

University of Delaware. Plenty of students dream of someday becoming Nittany Lions or Cavaliers—even Terrapins—but not many aspire to be Blue Hens. The challenge for U. of D. is how to win its share of students without the name recognition that comes from big-time sports. Less than half the students are in-staters.

University of Denver. Middle-sized university known equally for business and skiing. Laid-back atmosphere prevails. Campus in residential Denver is pleasant but not inspiring. Students tend to be outdoorsy and environmentally conscious.

Ithaca College. Students looking at Ithaca also apply to BU, Syracuse, and NYU. The common thread? Outstanding programs in the arts and media. Cross-town neighbor Cornell adds curricular and social opportunities.

Lehigh University. Lehigh is built on the powerful combination of business and engineering. Lehigh occupies a middle ground between the techie havens, such as Rennselaer and Drexel, and the liberal arts/engineering institutions such as Bucknell and Union. By graduation, students are primed for the job market.

University of Maryland–College Park. The name says Maryland, but the location says Washington, D.C. Students in College Park can jump on the Metro just the same as they do at Georgetown or American. Maryland is nothing if not big, and savvy students will look to programs such as the College Park Scholars for some personal attention.

University of Massachusetts–Amherst. Liberal mecca in cosmopolitan and scenic western Massachusetts. Strong study-abroad programs add international flavor. Ties to Amherst, Hampshire, Mount Holyoke, and Smith via the Five College Consortium.

McGill University. The Canadian university that is best-known south of the border. Though instruction is in English, McGill is located in French-speaking Montreal. Americans will not find the degree of extracurricular life available in the U.S. Only the self-motivated need apply.

University of Miami (FL). Football is the main reason UM is on the map, but it isn't the only reason. Renowned programs in marine science and music are big draws; business is also strong. Housing takes the form of a distinctive residential college system that offers living/learning opportunities.

University of Michigan. The most interesting mass of humanity east of UC/Berkeley. Among the nation's best in most subjects, but undergraduates must elbow their way to the front to get full benefit. Superb honors programs are the best bet for highly motivated students. Intensely competitive in admission for out-of-staters.

University of Missouri–Columbia. Mizzou is renowned for one of the top journalism schools in the nation, but engineering, business, and education are also stand-outs. Enrolls only about half the number of out-of-state students as archrival University of Kansas. Columbia is a quintessential college town.

University of New Hampshire. UNH looks and feels like a private college, and its tuition hits the pocketbook with similar force. Expensive though it may be, UNH draws more than half of its students from out-of-state. Strong in the life sciences, especially marine biology, and in business and engineering.

Northeastern University. Long synonymous with pre-professional education and hands-on experience through cooperative education, Northeastern has shed its blue-collar image and is on the way to becoming a "hot" college. With Boston beckoning, campus life is minimal.

Ohio State University. The biggest school in the Big Ten, Ohio State lacks the prestige of a Michigan or a Wisconsin—partly because three major in-state rivals (Miami, Cincinnati, and Ohio U) siphon off many top students. Operates the mother of all college sports programs. Check out the top-notch honors program.

Ohio University. OU is half the size of Ohio State and plays up its homey feel compared to the cast of thousands in Columbus. The Honors Tutorial College is a sure bet for top students who want close contact with faculty. Communications and journalism top the list of prominent programs.

Pennsylvania State University. There are precious few public universities more selective than Penn State. With a student body the size of a small city, the university is strong in everything from meteorology to film and television. The University Scholars Program is one of the nation's elite honors programs.

Purdue University. Purdue is Indiana's state university for science and technology—with side helpings of business, health professions, and liberal arts. Purdue is nearly twenty times the size of Indiana's other technically-oriented university—Rose Hulman. Compare to Big Ten rivals Michigan State and Kansas State.

University of Richmond. The former capital of the Confederacy is now crawling with Yankees—at least at the University of Richmond. Students come from points north to partake of warmer weather and Richmond's business-oriented curriculum. One of the few institutions with an entire school devoted to leadership.

Rutgers–The State University of New Jersey. Rutgers is a huge institution spread over three regional campuses and twenty-nine colleges or schools. Rutgers College on the New Brunswick campus is the most prominent. Literally everything is available: engineering, business, pharmacy, the arts, and the nation's largest women's college (Douglass College in New Brunswick).

Southern Methodist University. SMU is all-but the official alma mater of the Dallas business and professional elite.

The university is best known for business, performing arts, and upscale conservatism. Though tuition is moderate by national standards, SMU is pricey compared to rivals Texas Christian and Rice.

Syracuse University. Syracuse has recast itself to make undergraduate education a top priority. Offerings such as the Gateway program provide small classes for first-year students. World-famous in communications, Syracuse is also strong in engineering and public affairs. Big East basketball provides solace during long winter nights.

Texas A&M University. Coming to A&M is like joining a fraternity with forty thousand members. In addition to fanatical school spirit, A&M offers leading programs in the national sciences, business, and engineering. To succeed in this mass of humanity, students must find the right academic niche.

Texas Christian University. The personalized alternative to the behemoth state universities of Texas. Tuition is thousands less than that at arch-rival SMU. Though affiliated with the Disciples of Christ, the atmosphere at TCU goes lighter on religion than, say, Baylor. Strengths include the fine arts, business, and communications.

University of Toronto. With more than fifty-six thousand students, U. of T. is one of the largest universities in the world. It is also, for most readers, in a foreign country. If ever there were a place where go-getterism is a necessity, this is it. In the absence of American-style school spirit, U. of T. students cut loose to find their fun in the city of Toronto.

Tulane University. Tulane took a body blow from Hurricane Katrina but has recovered nicely. The engineering program was a victim of the hurricane, and a number of others were downsized. But the new Tulane also has an enhanced appetite for community service. High achievers should shoot for the Tulane Scholars program.

University of Vermont. For an out-of-stater sizing up public universities, there could hardly be a more appealing place than UVM. The size is manageable, Burlington is a fabulous college town, and Lake Champlain and the Green Mountains are on your door-step. UVM feels like a private university, but alas, it is also priced like one.

University of Washington. UDub wows visitors with its sprawling park-like campus in hugely popular Seattle. Washington is tougher than University of Oregon for out-of-state admission but not as hard as UC heavyweights Berkeley or UCLA. Location near the coast and mountains makes for strong marine and environmental studies programs.

See Also:
For other lists that include well-known universities, see Historically Black Colleges and Universities, The Roman Catholic World, and Top Conservative Colleges.

The Best-Kept Secrets
No flashy window decals in this category. Though the colleges listed here are well-known in their respective states, on the national level they are largely anonymous outside of a few devoted alumni and graduate school admissions officers. The latter group, however, is an important one. Rest assured that a degree from any of these colleges will get the respect it

deserves when the time comes to apply to law school, medical school, or any other kind of school. As for the window decal, think of it as a well-kept secret—only a select few will recognize its significance.

Alfred University. Rare hybrid that includes excellent liberal arts and nationally known art and design programs. Includes the country's premier ceramic engineering program. Rural location in the Finger Lakes of upstate New York. Total enrollment is twenty-four hundred.

Centre College. Small Kentucky college (one thousand) known for producing Rhodes Scholars and devoted alumni. Traditional liberal arts curriculum, largely conservative student body. Fraternities and football games are the staples of social life. Old grads still talk about gridiron upset of Harvard in 1921.

Eckerd College. Small Florida college (fifteen hundred) best known for marine biology. Combines strong sense of community with liberal, open-minded atmosphere. No fraternities or sororities. Gorgeous St. Petersburg campus overlooks the Gulf of Mexico.

Guilford College. One of the few Quaker schools in the South. Emphasizes a collaborative approach to all phases of life. One of the most liberal student bodies south of the Mason-Dixon. Offers strong study-abroad programs. Central North Carolina location is within easy reach of the Duke–UNC–NC State research triangle.

Hiram College. Tiny Ohio college (twelve hundred) offering strong community spirit and a top-notch biology program. An ecology research station adjoins the campus. All-American, friendly, middle-of-the-road student body. Offers Midwest tranquillity, with Cleveland about one hour's drive away.

The College of Idaho. Got a map? You'll need sharp eyes to spot COI, the *Fiske Guide*'s only liberal arts college in the interior of the Mountain West. Innovative programs include leadership studies and the Center for Experiential Learning. Formerly Albertson College.

Illinois Wesleyan University. Up-and-coming small university (twenty-one hundred) in Middle America. Eighty percent of the students are Illinois natives. Strong in fine arts and pre-anything. Methodist affiliation is low-key. Recent additions include new gym and state-of-the-art science facility.

Knox College. Target of "School of Hard Knox" jokes. Friendly, progressive Illinois college that was among the first in the nation to admit blacks and women. Offers close interaction with faculty and pure liberal arts. Located amid cornfields midway between Chicago and St. Louis. Very small (twelve hundred).

Millsaps College. The pride of Mississippi higher education. Best liberal arts college in the deep, deep South. Largely preprofessional student body has sights set on business, law, and medicine. In Mississippi, known as a liberal hotbed (translation: middle-of-the-road to conservative).

Presbyterian College. Small South Carolina college (eleven hundred) with a big endowment. Despite the name, only about a third of the students are

Presbyterians. Extensive core curriculum covers the liberal arts. Struggling to attract more minorities.

University of Puget Sound. One of a trio of colleges in the Pacific Northwest (along with Whitman and Willamette) that deserve more national exposure. Tacoma campus features easy access to Puget Sound and Mount Rainier. Best known for Asian studies and study-abroad programs.

University of Redlands. One of the West Coast's most versatile small colleges (eighteen hundred). Offers optional individualized program in which students "contract" with faculty to create their entire program. Also offers preprofessional training in business, education, and even engineering.

Washington & Jefferson College. Premed Central would be as good a name as any for W&J, where the proportion of students who go on to medical school is one of the nation's highest. Law school and business school are also popular destinations. The tenor of life is conservative and the Greek system is strong.

Willamette University. Despite the name, Willamette is a small college (twenty-four hundred) with a few hundred graduate students. Adjacent Oregon state capitol bolsters economics and political science offerings. Unusually strong study-abroad programs.

Wittenberg University. Wittenberg is an outpost of cozy Midwestern friendliness. Less national than Denison or Wooster, Witt has plenty of old-fashioned school spirit and powerhouse Division III athletic teams. Top students should aim for the honors and fellows programs, the latter providing a chance for undergraduate research.

See Also:
Small-College Bargains

Top Women's Colleges

It's been a long, strange trip for the nation's women's colleges since the coeducation movement of the late sixties. First, there was much hand wringing and talk of admitting men or even pulling up stakes to move the entire college to join a counterpart male school hundreds of miles away. By 1980, it looked as if women's colleges might one day go the way of leisure suits and eight-track tapes. Then came the discovery that coed schools might not be such a great place for women after all, with classrooms dominated by male counterparts. Study after study detailing "how coed colleges cheat women" saturated the education journals and suddenly women's colleges were riding high. Today, the long-term future of women's colleges seems secure, regardless of the next twist in the gender wars.

History lesson aside, women's colleges are looking like a good bet for today's talented women. With a higher percentage of women on their faculties than coed schools, these colleges offer abundant role models who are committed to helping women reach their full potential. The case is strongest in the sciences, where the evidence is clear that these schools do a better job of turning out female scientists than their coed counterparts. No matter what they study, students cite a sense of acceptance and sisterly camaraderie. The high point of the week at most coed schools is watching male warriors strut around a stadium and beat each other's brains out while women cheerlead.

One myth about women's colleges desperately needs debunking: they are best for shy, wall-flowerish types too delicate to rub shoulders with men. On the contrary, the students who choose women's colleges tend to be confident, outgoing, and self-reliant. When they want to be with men, they know how to find them.

Lastly, a strategic note: most of these colleges are not quite as competitive in admissions as they were before coeducation. It stands to reason: the coed schools have gobbled up a significant slice of their market. But that creates an opportunity for other young women who might not have had it thirty years ago. After all, these colleges are still among the oldest, richest, and all-around best in the nation.

Below is a selection of what we think are some of the top women's colleges in the nation. We have included only those that have a significant degree of autonomy from parent universities or coordinate all-male institutions.

Agnes Scott College. Combines the tree-lined seclusion of Decatur with the bustle of Atlanta. More money in the bank than most Ivy League schools and enrollment is up 50 percent since 1990. Small classes, sisterhood, and a more exciting location than the Sweet Briars of the world.

Hollins University. Traditional women's college in southwest Virginia. Main strengths lie in the humanities and social sciences. Creative writing is a specialty. Social life revolves around frat parties at nearby coed schools, such as Washington and Lee and Virginia Tech.

Mills College. Remembered for the firestorm of protest that torpedoed a Board of Trustees proposal to go coed. Problems remain, but enrollment has inched upward since the decision to stay all-female. One of the few women's colleges on the West Coast. UC–Berkeley and San Francisco are both within easy reach of Oakland campus.

Mount Holyoke College. One of two women's colleges, with Smith, that are members of the Five College Consortium in western Massachusetts. Less non-conformist than Smith and Bryn Mawr. MHC is strongest in the natural and social sciences, and one among the few colleges that has a program devoted to leadership.

Scripps College. Tiny women's college (eight hundred) that is part of the Claremont consortium (with Harvey Mudd, Claremont McKenna, Pitzer, and Pomona). English and the humanities top the list of strong departments. Near L.A., Scripps offers an ideal climate when not shrouded in smog.

Smith College. Like a slice of Greenwich Village plunked down in western Massachusetts. More liberal than its counterparts Wellesley and Mount Holyoke, Smith is the only women's college to offer engineering. Chic Northampton is a mecca for the gay community. Five-College Consortium offers enormous range of opportunities.

Sweet Briar College. Sweet Briar offers the pure women's college experience—served up with plenty of tradition and gift-wrapped in one of the nation's most beautiful campuses. SBC is the country girl next to in-state rivals Randolph College and Hollins. Academic stand-outs include English and the life sciences.

See Also:
Barnard College (Rising Stars)
Bryn Mawr College (The Elite Liberal Arts Colleges)
Spelman College (Historically Black Colleges and Universities)
Wellesley College (The Elite Liberal Arts Colleges)

Top Historically Black Colleges and Universities

Historically black colleges date from the time when African Americans were denied access to predominantly white institutions. There are approximately one hundred historically black schools in the nation, the majority of which are located in the Southeast. They are generally less selective, less wealthy, and less prestigious (at least in white America) than the colleges we have listed so far. Now that the latter are standing in line to recruit talented minority students, is there any reason to consider a historically black school?

In many cases, the answer is yes. From Jesse Jackson to Spike Lee, a high percentage of the nation's most prominent African Americans attended a black college. Though often strapped for cash, the colleges offer things money can't buy: relief from the constant burden of minority status, a chance to study the black experience as a central focus, and closer relationships with faculty and fellow students. Involvement in the community is an important predictor of success in college, which is one reason for higher graduation rates among students at black colleges than blacks at mainstream schools. Though predominantly white schools often roll out the red carpet for minorities during the admissions process, they seldom maintain the same level of attention after enrollment. No matter how much administrators preach about diversity, the black community at many such schools is confined to the fringes of campus life. Though historically black schools are not household names, they continue to pay dividends after graduation. Most have intensely loyal alumni who will go out of their way to help a fellow graduate.

One of the myths about historically black colleges is that they cater to students who would have difficulty functioning in white America. In fact, such schools are often most valuable for those who grew up as the only black face in a white crowd. For these students, a historically black college may offer the only chance in their lifetime to live and learn in a community of fellow African Americans.

One final virtue these colleges offer: a bargain price. Along with the public liberal arts colleges, historically black schools give the most for the money of any category in this chapter.

Clark Atlanta University. The university at the core of the Atlanta University Center, the national focal point of historically black education. Benefits from coordinate relationship with prestigious Morehouse and Spelman Colleges. Strong in business, communications, health professions, and public policy.

Florida A&M University. Public university best known for business, engineering, and journalism. Shares state capital Tallahassee with Florida State University. With an enrollment of nearly ten thousand, it is one of the largest historically black universities in the nation.

Hampton University. One of the best-endowed historically black colleges and also one of the most selective. Best known for its business school. Located on the Virginia coast near Norfolk. Hampton attracts students from both sides of the Mason-Dixon line.

Howard University. The nation's most famous historically black university. Pioneer of the Afrocentric approach to learning across the curriculum. Has recently weathered financial difficulties that forced cuts in administration and staff. Location in Washington, D.C., is ideal for politics and economics.

Lincoln University (PA). Founded in 1854, this is the nation's oldest historically black university. Alma mater of Supreme Court Justice Thurgood Marshall and poet Langston Hughes. Southeastern Pennsylvania location seems isolated to city dwellers.

Morehouse College. Along with sister school Spelman, the most selective of the historically black schools. All-male alumni list reads like a *Who's Who* of the black community. Best known for business and popular 3-2 engineering program with Georgia Tech. Built on a Civil-War battlefield, a symbol of the new South.

Morgan State University. Next to Howard and Hampton, one of the best-known historically black universities in the Middle Atlantic states. Known for business and strong sports teams. Located in Baltimore.

Spelman College. Sister school to Morehouse. The richest of the historically black colleges, thanks in part to a twenty million dollar gift from the Bill Cosby family. Unusually strong in the natural sciences with particular emphasis on undergraduate research. Wooded Atlanta campus provides easy access to urban attractions.

Tuskegee University. Formerly Tuskegee Institute. Historically committed to preprofessional training, rather than the study of black culture. Strongest in engineering, with premed and business also popular. Isolated central Alabama location.

Xavier University (LA). Small Louisiana school with a big reputation for producing successful scientists. Sustained catastrophic damage from Hurricane Katrina that will take years to repair. The nation's only black Roman Catholic–affiliated institution.

The Roman Catholic World

The Roman Catholic–affiliated schools are a distinctive segment of the higher education scene. The advantages to a Catholic student include a strong sense of community, shared values, and a traditional social life (though often without Greek letter fraternities). On the other hand, some students will feel confined by the relative lack of diversity and the "sheep following the herd" mentality that sometimes creeps into the culture.

Catholic schools tend to be traditional in their approach to academics. In the arts and sciences, most have a core curriculum or similar structured approach that accents the Western tradition. These schools also tend to have a strong preprofessional emphasis.

The schools vary in the extent to which religion sets the tone of campus life. Technically, most are affiliated not with the church itself, but with a particular order, such as the Jesuits or the Franciscans. At some, the Catholic religion is barely noticeable except for the fact that the president wears a Roman collar. At others, clergy hold key administrative positions, religion courses are required, monks live in the dorms, and daily mass is a foregone conclusion. A good index of "how Catholic" is the percentage of students who belong to the faith. The range is from about 50 percent to 90 percent.

Boston College. Enjoys booming national popularity among all faiths because of athletic teams and prime Boston location. Comfortable home for students who want a good name and good partying, but popularity appears out of proportion to quality. Enrollment 80 percent Catholic. Now a close second to Notre Dame in the pecking order among true-blue Catholics.

University of Dallas. Bulwark of academic traditionalism in Big D. Despite being a "university," U. of D. has only twelve hundred undergraduates. Except for the Business Leaders of Tomorrow program, the curriculum is exclusively liberal arts. The only outpost of Catholic education between Loyola of New Orleans and University of San Diego.

University of Dayton. Among a cohort of second-tier Roman Catholic institutions in the Midwest that includes Duquesne, Xavier (OH), U. of St. Louis, Depaul, and Loyola of Chicago. Drawing cards include business, engineering, education, and the sciences. The city of Dayton is not particularly enticing and U. of D.'s appeal is largely regional.

DePaul University. Gets the nod over Loyola as the best Catholic university in Chicago. Lincoln Park location is like New York's Greenwich Village or Upper West Side without all the headaches. Student body largely a feeder to Chicago's business community. Almost half non-Catholic. Robust enrollment increases bode well for the future.

Fairfield University. One of the up-and-coming schools in the Catholic universe. Strategic Connecticut location and ready access to New York City are two major assets. Undergraduate enrollment of fifty-one hundred makes Fairfield smaller than many of its competitors. Little known outside the Northeast. Enrollment 90 percent Catholic.

Fordham University. With the current euphoria for colleges in New York, Fordham has climbed a few notches on the selectivity scale. There is no better location than Lincoln Center, where the performing arts programs are housed. The Bronx is less appealing but better than the horror stories you may hear.

College of the Holy Cross. A tight-knit Catholic community steeped in church and tradition. Many students are the second or third generation to attend. Set high on a hill above gritty Worcester, an hour from Boston. Sports teams compete with (and occasionally beat) schools ten times HC's size.

John Carroll University. Although it is called a "university," JC is really a small college (thirty-four hundred students) that is acquiring a big reputation in the Midwest. It occupies a scenic enclave in Cleveland's exclusive eastern suburbs. Enrollment 70 percent Catholic. Many students have aspirations toward joining the Cleveland-area business community.

Loyola University–New Orleans. There are at least four Loyolas in the nation but only one where you can go to Mardi Gras and still get back in time for class. Suffered with the city in the wake of Hurricane Katrina. Among the most progressive of the nation's Catholic institutions.

Marquette University. Best known as a second choice to Notre Dame. Strong programs include engineering, health professions, and business. Downtown campus in so-so neighborhood blends well with Milwaukee's working-class aura. About 80 percent of the campus is Catholic.

University of Notre Dame. The Holy Grail of higher ed for many Roman Catholics. ND's heartland location and 85 percent Catholic enrollment make it a bastion of traditional values. Offers business and engineering in addition to the liberal arts. ND's personality is much closer to Boston College than Georgetown.

Saint Louis University. This is not your father's SLU. The campus and surrounding neighborhood have been spiffed up in the past two decades, and SLU's campus is a pleasant oasis from the bustle of mid-town St. Louis. In addition to strengths in premed and communication, SLU has an unusual specialty in aviation.

University of San Diego. New kid on the block with a beautiful seaside location and burgeoning popularity. Now accepts less than half who apply. A medium-sized university (seven thousand) that features liberal arts, business, education, nursing, and a small engineering program.

University of San Francisco. Talk about prime real estate: USF is next-door to the legendary Haight-Ashbury district, catty-corner to Golden Gate park, and within five miles of the Pacific Ocean. Though USF is a Jesuit institution, only about half its students are Catholic. Pacific Rim Studies is a stand-out.

Santa Clara University. Probably the best Catholic-affiliated school west of the Rockies. Gorgeous Silicon Valley campus is within easy reach of San Francisco. Large endowment also contributes to air of prosperity. About 60 percent of the student body is Catholic.

Villanova University. Set in upscale suburb, Villanova is Philadelphia's counterpart to Boston College. As at BC, about 80 percent of the students are Roman Catholic (compared to a figure of about 50 percent at Georgetown). The troika of business, engineering, and premed are popular at 'Nova, as is nursing.

See Also:
    Alverno College (The Most Innovative Curriculums)
    Georgetown University (The Elite Private Universities)
    Xavier University (LA) (Historically Black Colleges and Universities)

Top Conservative Colleges

There are many reasons why students and parents would want to consider a conservative college. Let's face it, the political climate at most elite liberal arts colleges is dominated by liberals. Even at schools where conservatives may constitute a "silent majority," they are often reluctant to challenge the prevailing political correctness. Furthermore, university faculties are overwhelmingly liberal, almost without exception in arts-and-sciences schools. In recent years, the gap between the values of college faculties and the more conservative segments of society has grown increasingly wide. Many families may be seeking one or more of the following:

- a place that emphasizes the Western tradition rather than multiculturalism
- a place where conservative opinions can be openly expressed without being branded as racist or sexist
- a place where moral and/or Christian values set the tenor of campus life

Obviously, any attempt at a comprehensive listing of such colleges would be impossible. The term "conservative" is itself a broad generalization that encompasses a wide array of values and beliefs. To paraphrase the *Fiske Guide to Colleges*, we offer this diverse list as a selection of the best and most interesting schools that tend toward a conservative perspective.

One pattern you'll probably notice right away: most of the conservative schools are in the South. With few exceptions, colleges in the South are more conservative in a host of ways than their counterparts in the Northeast and Midwest (the West Coast is a mixed bag). Students who are seeking more of the traditional trappings of college life may want to look at some Southern colleges. Note as well that most of the colleges on the Catholic-affiliated list would also fit here.

Babson College. Boston-area school that is devoted exclusively to business. Offers highly touted Entrepreneurial Studies program. Men outnumber women by almost 2–1. One of the few conservative outposts in liberal Massachusetts.

Baylor University. Come to Baylor and Mom can rest easy. Baylor is Southern Baptist, and that means less of the debauchery that is prevalent at most schools. Dad will like it too: Baylor happens to be one of the least expensive private universities in the country. If only the football team could beat UT.

Birmingham-Southern College. One of the deep South's best liberal arts colleges. The vast majority of students come from Alabama and the surrounding states. Strong fraternity system. A throwback to the way college used to be.

Brigham Young University. The flagship university of Mormonism. Visitors will find an endless sea of clean-cut, all-American students (thirty thousand undergraduates). Most men and some women do a two-year stint as a missionary. The mild-mannered campus goes absolutely bonkers for sports teams.

Calvin College. Evangelical Christian school that ranks high on the private college bargain list. Over half the students are members of the Christian Reformed Church. Particularly strong in the humanities. Archrival of Michigan neighbor Hope College.

DePauw University. Small Indiana college that has helped populate the Indiana business and government elite. Making major strides in attracting more minorities. One of the strongest fraternity systems in the nation. Compare with Ohio Wesleyan, Denison, and Dickinson.

Furman University. Furman's campus is among the most beautiful there is—and the swans are definitely a nice touch. At thirty-two hundred total enrollment, Furman is nearly twice the size of Davidson and half the size of Wake Forest. As befits its Baptist heritage, Furman is a conservative place and still a largely regional institution.

George Mason University. Capitalizing, so to speak, on proximity to Washington, D.C. Leading center of conservative political and economic thought. Once a sleepy commuter school, now challenging UVA and Virginia Tech in many fields for primacy among Virginia state schools.

Grove City College. A rising star among conservative colleges. Known for refusal to accept government funds. Low tuition translates to a top rating among bargain schools. Christian values set the tone. Small-town campus is within striking distance of Pittsburgh.

Hampden–Sydney College. Southern Virginia conservative bastion that is one of two all-male liberal arts colleges (without a coordinate women's college) left in the nation. Feeder school to the Virginia political and economic establishment in Richmond. Picturesque eastern Virginia setting where the Old South still lives.

Hope College. Hope has an in-between size—bigger than most small colleges but smaller than most universities. Evangelical in orientation though less than a fourth of the students are members of the Reformed Church in America. In addition to the liberal arts, Hope offers education, engineering, and nursing.

Houghton College. The mid-Atlantic's premier evangelical Christian college. Women outnumber men by nearly two to one and enjoy perks such as a 386-acre horseback riding facility. All students are required to take a Biblical literature class and most go to chapel three times per week.

Pepperdine University. With apologies to Wellesley and Furman, Pepperdine has the most beautiful campus in America. Small wonder that its acceptance rate hovers at about one in three. Students must come to Pepperdine ready to embrace an evangelical Christian emphasis much stronger than, say, the Roman Catholicism of U. of San Francisco.

St. Olaf College. Lutheran to the core, the well-scrubbed undergraduates at St. Olaf are a stark contrast to the grunge of cross-town rival Carleton. The music program is world-famous, and a whopping 60 percent of the students study abroad. Daily chapel is not mandatory but many students go.

Trinity University (TX). A liberal arts college that has been rolling in dough ever since the 1970s oil boom. Has used its money to lure a high-powered student body heavy on National Merit Scholars. Though middle-of-the-road by Texas standards, it is conservative by those of the rest of the country.

Wabash College. The last outpost of all-male higher education in the Midwest. The school's small enrollment size (nine hundred) and single-sex status make for unique camaraderie. The student body includes plenty of gentleman jocks and clean-cut future professionals. A huge endowment makes college's future secure.

Wheaton College (IL). The premier evangelical Christian school in the country. All students sign a pledge to abstain from vices ranging from alcohol to "occult practices." School motto: "For Christ and His Kingdom." Ranks high on list of bargain schools, with tuition thousands less than most liberal arts colleges.

See Also:
The Roman Catholic World
Dartmouth College (The Elite Private Universities)
University of the South (More Excellent Small Colleges)
University of Southern California (More Well-Known Universities)
Vanderbilt University (Rising Stars)
Washington and Lee University (The Elite Liberal Arts Colleges)

Top Nonconformist Colleges

Let's get one thing straight: these are not merely colleges with a somewhat liberal bent. Nancy Pelosi is liberal. The *New York*

Times is liberal. Many of the most selective colleges in the country have a mainstream liberal tenor.

These are places where students question the very foundations of what might be termed "the establishment" (though that doesn't mean they won't end up as doctors or lawyers someday). Many of the student bodies call to mind images of the 1960s: long hair, protest marches, communal-style living, and lots of kids who look like Grateful Dead groupies. At others, pink hair blends with purple combat boots and black leather to provide a bohemian, Greenwich Village ambience. Alternative lifestyles such as homosexuality are not merely tolerated—they are embraced. In exchange for increased independence, students lose the traditional trappings of college life—no football games, no fraternity pranks, and often, little sense of their collective identity. For most students at these colleges, that's no big loss.

By and large, the academic caliber of these places tends to be high. The act of questioning authority is generally a sign of intelligence and students at these colleges do more than their share. Virtually all of these colleges offer a nontraditional twist to the curriculum and many are among the leaders in innovation across the curriculum. Elements may include self-designed majors, broad thematic courses, hands-on experiences, and de-emphasis of letter grades. Most of these colleges tend to be strongest in the arts and humanities, though science is a specialty at a few.

The downside of these schools is the fact that they are so far out of step with the mainstream of society. A generation ago, a number of them were hot among legions of rebellious youth that numbered among the best and brightest. Today, most of these colleges are less selective than they once were, though interest has rebounded somewhat in recent years. They also suffer, in varying degrees, from the blight of political correctness that stems from their lack of conservative and even moderate voices. Finally, they often have far less endowment than their more mainstream cousins and often run on shoestring budgets.

Antioch College. Part Goth, part granola, and part anarchist—with plenty of none-of-the-above mixed in—Antioch is a haven for square pegs. Yet Antioch offers something very practical: the chance for sixteen-week co-op experiences interspersed with academic study. March and protest, then get a job. Cool.

Bard College. Welcome to Nonconformity-Central-on-Hudson, the only major U.S. institution where cross-dressing en masse on Parents' Weekend is a time-honored tradition. More selective than Hampshire and with a better male-female ratio than Sarah Lawrence, Bard is an up-and-comer among the non-traditional liberal arts colleges.

Bennington College. Known for top-notch performing arts and lavish attention to every student. Arts pro-grams rely heavily on part-time faculty who are practi-tioners in their fields. Less competitive than Bard and Sarah Lawrence, comparable to Hampshire. Enrollment is robust after a dip in the '90s.

University of California–Santa Cruz. From its flower child beginnings, UC–Santa Cruz has come back toward the mainstream. The distinctive flavor is still there, but the students are a lot more conventional than they once were. Santa Cruz's relatively small size and residential college system give it a homey feel.

Earlham College. Small Indiana college (twelve hun-dred) of Quaker origins. Similar in character to Oberlin and Grinnell, though less selective. Strong ties to Japan accentuate international outlook. An alien presence in conservative southern Indiana.

Eugene Lang College. Smack in the middle of Greenwich Village, Lang is the ultimate in bohemian funkiness. Offers little sense of community and virtually no campus life—New York City is Lang's campus. Tiny enrollment of nine hundred, but part of The New School, a major university.

Hampshire College. Child of the 1960s nestled in Massachusetts's prestigious Five-College Consortium. Best known for photography and film. Unique features include substantial individual projects and thematic approach that integrates traditional academic subjects.

Marlboro College. Hilltop home to three hundred and fifty nonconformist souls. Each develops a Plan of Concentration that culminates in a senior project. The college is run in the style of a New England town meeting. Students have veto power over faculty hiring. Unable to lure minorities.

State University of New York–Purchase. Small state university (four thousand) that specializes in the arts. Wooded Westchester campus is a hop and a skip from New York City. Greenwich Village is a frequent destination on the weekends. Large homosexual community.

Pitzer College. Offers a haven for the otherwise-minded without the hard edge of non-conformity at places like Evergreen and Bard. Traditional strengths lie in the social and behavioral sciences. Still more than 60/40 female but much more selective than it was ten years ago.

Sarah Lawrence College. Favored outpost of the New York City–esque avant garde. Located in affluent Bronxville, half an hour from the city. Coed for several decades, but still overwhelmingly female. Students design their own curriculums with the help of a faculty don. Best known for writing and the arts.

See Also:

College of the Atlantic (The Most Innovative Curriculums)
Beloit College (More Excellent Small Colleges)
The Evergreen State College (Small-College Bargains)
Grinnell College (Top Colleges, Better Odds)
Lewis and Clark College (More Excellent Small Colleges)
New College of Florida (Small-College Bargains)
Oberlin College (Top Colleges, Better Odds)
Reed College (Top Colleges, Better Odds)
St. John's College (The Most Innovative Curriculums)

The Most Innovative Curriculums

As a group, the following colleges are much more diverse than those in the previous group. The unorthodox colleges listed above are, first and foremost, magnets for unconventional students who want to be part of an unconventional community. Though many of those colleges also offer innovative curriculums, what defines the tenor of daily life has more to do with the kind of student they attract than what goes on inside the classroom.

The following list, on the other hand, includes colleges that are doing interesting things with curriculum that may appeal to a wide spectrum of students. Some of these colleges attract mainly traditionalists and others attract mainly liberals, but all assemble students united by their willingness to try something a little different. If that includes you, read on.

Alverno College. Small Wisconsin women's college that has pioneered competency-based education. Instead of letter grades, students receive "validations" in practical areas like communication, problem-solving, and citizenship. The student body is overwhelmingly from Wisconsin. The school is Roman Catholic–affiliated.

Champlain College. A cozy New England college that offers practical career training with a personal touch. Champlain's "upside-down" curriculum allows students to take in-depth courses in their majors from day one. Upperclassmen have more time for internships, which are offered in virtually all majors.

College of the Atlantic. Oceanfront college in Bar Harbor, Maine, where everyone graduates with a degree in "human ecology." Dedicated to the study of humankind's relationship to the environment. Still has trappings of its founding in the late 1960s as an alternative school. Tiny enrollment of about two hundred and fifty.

City University of New York–Brooklyn College. Has an innovative core curriculum that occupies students throughout freshman and sophomore years. Includes a comprehensive overview of Western culture and non-Western cultures. The college is a branch of the City University system. Most students are native Brooklynites.

Cornell College (IA). Along with Colorado College, one of two schools in the nation where students study one course at a time. Not to be confused with the "other" Cornell of the Ivy League. Small-town Iowa location makes Cornell the less selective of the two.

With eleven hundred students, Cornell is half the size of other "small" schools. No classes with more than twenty-five students.

Deep Springs College. Picture twenty-five Ivy-caliber men alone in the desert for two years—that's Deep Springs College. Set on fifty-thousand acres at the arid border of Nevada and California. Campus consists of a few ranch-style buildings. Quirky, intellectual students transfer to top colleges after two years to finish undergraduate degrees.

Kalamazoo College. The "K" Plan should appeal to both the non-traditional student and the practical-minded. Those with wanderlust get to travel the world while enjoying hands-on learning experiences. Those looking for a leg up on the job market get it through K-zoo's extensive internship program.

St. John's College. Books, books, and more books is what you'll get at St. John's—from Thucydides to Tolstoy, Euclid to Einstein. St. John's attracts smart, intellectual, and non-conformist students who like to talk (and argue) about books. Easy to get in, not so easy to graduate.

See Also:
Top Nonconformist Colleges
Colorado College (More Excellent Small Colleges)

Environmental Studies and International Studies: The Hottest Interdisciplinary Majors
It is a safe bet that all the colleges on any of our lists are going to have an English or history department. Not all, however, will offer majors in environmental studies or

international studies. Though a student at any university can stitch together a concentration in one area or the other, we thought it would be useful to readers to list some of the best colleges that have particularly strong programs. Keep in mind that both lists include a wide assortment of colleges that may have absolutely nothing else in common. In the liberal arts, the personality match between the institution and the student should remain paramount.

Environmental Studies
Allegheny College
College of the Atlantic
Bowdoin College
University of California–Davis
University of California–Santa Barbara
Clark University
Colby College
University of Colorado–Boulder
Dartmouth College
Deep Springs College
Eckerd College
The Evergreen State College
Hampshire College
Hiram College
Hobart and William Smith Colleges
McGill University
Middlebury College
University of New Hampshire
University of New Mexico
University of North Carolina–Asheville
University of North Carolina–Greensboro
Oberlin College
Prescott College
St. Lawrence University
Tulane University

University of Vermont
University of Washington
Williams College
University of Wisconsin–Madison

International Studies

American University
Austin College
Brandeis University
University of British Columbia
Brown University
Bucknell University
Claremont McKenna College
Clark University
Colby College
Connecticut College
Dartmouth College
Davidson College
Denison University
University of Denver
Dickinson College
Earlham College
Eckerd College
Georgetown University
George Washington University
Goucher College
Hiram College
The Johns Hopkins University
Kalamazoo College
Lewis and Clark College
Mary Washington College
University of Massachusetts–Amherst
Middlebury College
Mount Holyoke College
Occidental College

University of the Pacific
University of Pittsburgh
Pomona College
Princeton University
University of Puget Sound
Randolph College
Reed College
Rhodes College
University of Richmond
St. Olaf College
Scripps College
University of South Carolina
Sweet Briar College
Tufts University
Wesleyan University
College of William and Mary

Study-Abroad Programs

We would also like to offer a word about study abroad. If that is one of your interests, the above international studies list is a good place to look. Virtually all those colleges also have strong study-abroad programs.

In general, the best study-abroad programs are offered by small liberal arts colleges. The Ivy League universities, except for Dartmouth, have always been lukewarm to the concept. (Princeton makes the list above because of its famed Woodrow Wilson School of Public and International Affairs.) A much higher percentage of students at the top liberal arts colleges spend a semester or year abroad.

If someone pulled out a gun and said, "Name the top five colleges in the nation for study abroad," we would probably list: Colby, Connecticut College, Dickinson, Kalamazoo, Lewis and Clark College, Middlebury, Occidental, and St. Olaf. (That's eight, but who's counting?)

Colleges for Students with Learning Disabilities

Accommodation for students with learning disabilities is among the fastest-growing—and most controversial—academic areas in higher education. A generation ago, few colleges paid much attention to LD students. But that changed in the 1990s with the sudden discovery that a significant segment of the population may suffer problems that qualify as learning disabilities. Services have multiplied on virtually all campuses. But so, too, has the concern that some students are trying to use questionable LD classification to get special treatment.

No one denies that many students do suffer from learning disabilities. The diagnosis must be made by a certified professional—usually a physician, psychologist, or learning specialist. Students are judged to be LD if their performance on particular types of tasks shows a pattern of being lower than their intelligence would suggest. These students suffer impaired performance not because of an inability to comprehend, but because of breakdowns in their ability to perceive and process information.

A learning disability should not be confused with low achievement. Every student has strengths and weaknesses. Some work harder than others and do better as a result. But recently, some families have begun to press for LD classification with dubious evidence. Why? With increasing competition for good grades and admission to college, an LD diagnosis is an easy way to explain mediocre grades. More to the point, certified LD status allows students extra time on the PSAT and SAT. In the past ten years, applications to the Educational Testing Service for extra time have doubled, with most of the requests coming from affluent families who know how to use the system to their benefit.

Meanwhile, some colleges have begun to wonder whether the LD movement has gone too far. Boston University, an erstwhile leader in LD services, has made sharp cuts in its program. Many colleges have become more skeptical of LD classification when the initial diagnosis is made on the eve of the college search.

Despite the doubts, students with legitimate disabilities will find high-quality services at many colleges. Virtually all major institutions, from Harvard to the local community college, provide support for the learning disabled. Assistance may include printed notes of lectures, tapes, or extended time on exams. Our first list includes major universities offering particularly strong services; the smaller schools in the second list all devote major emphasis to LD students.

Our advice for LD students? Check out the support services yourself at each college on your list. If possible, pay a visit to the LD support office or have a phone conversation with one of the administrators. Since many such programs depend on the expertise of one or two people, the quality of the services can change abruptly with changes in staff.

Major Universities with Strong Support for Students with Learning Disabilities

Adelphi University
American University
University of Arizona
Clark University
University of Colorado–Boulder
University of Connecticut
University of Denver
DePaul University
Fairleigh Dickinson University
University of Georgia
Hofstra University
Northeastern University
Purdue University
Rochester Institute of Technology
Syracuse University
University of Vermont

Small Colleges with Strong Support Services for Learning Disabled Students

Bard College
Curry College
Landmark College
Lesley University
Loras College
Lynn University
Manhattanville College
Marist College
Mercyhurst College
Mitchell College
Muskingum College
New England College
University of New England
St. Thomas Aquinas College (NY)
Westminster College (MO)
West Virginia Wesleyan College

For Preprofessionals Only: A Subject-by-Subject Guide

Though liberal arts education is the best springboard to most careers, there are a few professions that require specialized training. If medicine is your goal, a standard list of science courses found in most liberal arts colleges will be all you need at the undergraduate level. But if you want to be an engineer, it takes more than just a strong background in science. You need highly technical preparation in a structured sequence, the kind of preparation that you simply can't get outside of a college of engineering. If you like music, you can dabble in performance at a liberal arts college and maybe even do a major. But if your life's dream is to be a headliner at Carnegie Hall, you'll probably need to prepare at a conservatory where people give their heart and soul to music. Likewise, you can do a studio art major at most colleges and universities. But if you're the type who never does a lick of academic homework, yet stays up until 3:00 AM doing art assignments, that's a clue that maybe you should be ticketed for art school.

Below, we offer lists of prominent schools in seven academic areas in which students may choose specialized undergraduate training: engineering, architecture, business, art/design, the performing arts, communications/journalism, and film/television. In compiling the lists, we drew on data from the thousands of surveys used to compile the *Fiske Guide to Colleges*. We examined the strongest majors at each college as reported in student and administrative questionnaires, and then weighed these against the selectivity and overall academic quality of each institution. After compiling tentative lists in each subject, we queried our counselor advisory group, listed at the back of this volume, for additional suggestions and feedback. The final product is necessarily subjective. We intend the lists below as a beginning point. If a particular college isn't under your intended major, don't panic! It may have a fine program. The lists are best used to broaden your options rather than limit them.

If you are planning a career in one of the following subjects, your college search will consist largely of finding the best program for you in that particular area. In contrast to the liberal arts section, we list only names here. It is your job to assess the strengths and weaknesses of each program, according to your needs. You may notice, however, that some of the schools mentioned here for specialized training are also described in one or another of the liberal arts categories. We encourage you to consult the *Fiske Guide* for a full write-up on most institutions listed in this section. If you cannot find them there, consult the recommended reading chapter for other publications that will include descriptions. We also recommend that you shop for a school that will give you an adequate dose of liberal arts. For that matter, you might consider a double major (or minor) in a liberal arts field to complement your area of technical expertise. If you allow yourself to get too specialized too soon, you may end up as tomorrow's equivalent of the typewriter repairman. In a rapidly changing job market, nothing is so practical as the ability to read, write, and think.

Engineering

Were you the kind of kid who always made a beeline for the blocks in nursery school? Or spent years trying to blow up the family garage with your chemistry set? Are you the kind of person who gets a kick out of staring into a computer screen for hours to solve an obscure problem? Is your idea of a good time to curl up with a description of Albert Einstein's theory of relativity?

If some or all of the above apply, you could be ticketed for a career in engineering, a field that combines chemistry, physics, math, and computer science for building and design. Getting the degree, however, is easier said than done. Would-be engineers must persevere through a highly structured curriculum that includes heavy doses of higher math and science (and often takes five years to complete). If that doesn't sound like your cup of tea, it probably isn't. The pathway to an engineering degree is littered with students who went into it for the wrong reasons, such as, "My dad wanted me to be an engineer," or, "I wanted a job." The only good reason to be an engineer is that you enjoy the work. Otherwise, you'll soon find out why they call it "prebusiness" at many universities.

Play the Field

If you think engineering is for you, there are a number of different routes you can take. The purest dose of engineering education is found at technical institutes and universities that specialize in engineering. Nothing in the world of technology can match the intensity of thousands of bright minds living and breathing computers and engineering. The downside of these sorts of places comes from the very thing that makes them great: they tend to be one-dimensional. A technical community without English majors or artists tends to take on a slightly bizarre, ingrown quality. Technical institutes are also overwhelmingly male and the skewed gender ratio doesn't help social life.

If a technical institute seems a bit hardcore, there are other options. Most top students choose to study at a large private university that has a college of engineering. These universities have a critical mass of engineers, but also offer a broad spectrum of courses in the arts and sciences, business, and numerous other fields. Cost-conscious students often opt for a variation on this theme: the large public university. In effect, these students trade a little prestige for an education that is easier on the wallet. The major drawback of both these types of institutions, and many technical institutes as well, is that they are so darn big. As in every other field, the lowly undergrad engineers can get stuck playing second fiddle to the graduate students—or worse, taking their courses from the graduate students.

This leads us to a fourth type of engineering school, the small college or university. As you know by now, small is beautiful in education because students get more attention from faculty and more chance for involvement. At many of these institutions, undergraduates are able to perform the kind of research that only graduate students are allowed to do at big universities. Engineering education also tends to be more firmly rooted in the liberal arts at the smaller schools. Often, though not always, engineering students at these colleges complete much of the same liberal arts core as every other student. The questions to ask at these schools include: Do they have a critical mass of engineers? Do they have facilities that stack up well with the larger universities? Do they have the same access to engineering employers? If the answer to these questions is yes, you may have found the best place to get an engineering degree.

A final way to get an engineering degree is to enroll in a 3–2 program. The numbers refer to the years spent at each of two schools. For the first three, a student enrolls in a small liberal arts college and takes a variety of pre-engineering courses, as well as a full helping of the humanities and social sciences. For the last two years, the student transfers to a university with an engineering program to complete the technical education. The program is a year longer (and a year more expensive), but the student finishes with two degrees—one in engineering and one in the liberal arts. Most of the top liberal arts colleges in the nation offer 3–2 programs and many come with virtually guaranteed admission to the engineering programs at prestigious universities such as Columbia or Washington University in St. Louis.

Top Technical Institutes
California Institute of Technology
California Polytechnic Institute–San Luis Obispo
Colorado School of Mines
Cooper Union
Florida Institute of Technology
Franklin W. Olin College of Engineering
Georgia Institute of Technology
Harvey Mudd College
Illinois Institute of Technology
Massachusetts Institute of Technology
Michigan Technological University
Montana Tech of the University of Montana
New Jersey Institute of Technology
New Mexico Institute of Mining and Technology
Rensselaer Polytechnic Institute
Rochester Institute of Technology
Rose-Hulman Institute of Technology
Stevens Institute of Technology
Worcester Polytechnic Institute

Private Universities Strong in Engineering

Boston University
Bradley University
Brigham Young University
Brown University
Carnegie Mellon University
Case Western Reserve University
Catholic University of America
Columbia University
Cornell University
Drexel University
Duke University
George Washington University
The Johns Hopkins University
Northeastern University
Northwestern University
University of Notre Dame
University of Pennsylvania
Princeton University
University of Rochester
Rochester Institute of Technology
Santa Clara University
University of Southern California
Southern Methodist University
Stanford University
Syracuse University
Tufts University
Tulane University
University of Tulsa
Vanderbilt University
Villanova University
Washington University in St. Louis

Public Universities Strong in Engineering

University of Arizona
University of California–Berkeley
University of California–Davis
University of California–Los Angeles
University of California–San Diego
University of Cincinnati
Clemson University
University of Connecticut
University of Delaware
University of Florida
University of Illinois–Urbana-Champaign
Iowa State University
University of Kansas
McGill University
University of Maryland
University of Massachusetts–Amherst
University of Michigan
Michigan State University
University of Missouri–Rolla
University of New Hampshire
College of New Jersey
North Carolina State University
Ohio State University
Oregon State University
Pennsylvania State University
Purdue University
Queen's University (Canada)
University of Rhode Island
Rutgers, The State University of New Jersey
SUNY–Binghamton University
SUNY–Buffalo
Texas A&M University
Texas Tech University
University of Texas–Austin

University of Toronto
Virginia Tech
University of Virginia
University of Washington
University of Wisconsin–Madison

Small Colleges and Universities Strong in Engineering
Alfred University
Bucknell University
Butler University
Calvin College
Clarkson University
Dartmouth College
Gettysburg College
Lafayette College
Lehigh University
Loyola University (MD)
University of the Pacific
Rice University
Smith College
Spelman College
Swarthmore College
Trinity College (CT)
Trinity University (TX)
University of Tulsa
Tuskegee University
Union College

Architecture

Learning to be an architect consists of two basic elements that don't always go together. A student must master the physics and structural fundamentals of building, as well as the aesthetics of building and how architectural structures meet human needs. A good architect combines the eye for physics of the engineer with the humanistic sensibility of the artist. Unfortunately, engineers and artists mix like oil and water and it is rare to find either a student or an architecture program that offers a perfect combination of the two. Most architecture programs look very much like engineering schools, but some have an artsy streak that gives them more of an alternative flavor (purple hair is always a good tip-off). Before you choose an architecture program, think about what sort of architecture "personality" best fits your needs.

Most aspiring architects get their training in a conventional college or school of architecture. The students at these schools may not design the prettiest buildings, but at least you know the buildings won't fall down. A smaller number of architecture programs exist within a more liberal arts context, sometimes in a department of architecture within a college of arts and sciences. Usually, though not always, these programs place more emphasis on aesthetics. When looking at an architecture program, check out its ties to engineering and/or the art program. That will provide an important clue as to where it stands.

The size of the program is a consideration, as well as the ratio of graduate students to undergrads. See if there will be any opportunities to work with the graduate students, as opposed to merely being taught by them. Similar to engineering, students may opt for a 3–4 program—three years at a liberal arts college doing "prearchitecture" and the liberal arts, followed by four years in an architecture program to complete the professional training. Though 3–4 takes seven years, the end product is a broader education and degrees in both a liberal arts field and architecture.

Private Universities Strong in Architecture
Carnegie Mellon University
Catholic University of America
Columbia University
Cooper Union

Cornell University (NY)
Drexel University
Hobart and William Smith Colleges
Howard University
Lehigh University
Massachusetts Institute of Technology
University of Miami (FL)
New Jersey Institute of Technology
Northeastern University
University of Notre Dame
Princeton University
Rensselaer Polytechnic Institute
Rice University
Temple University
Tuskegee University
Tulane University
Washington University in St. Louis

Public Universities Strong in Architecture

University of Arizona
University of California–Berkeley
University of Cincinnati
Clemson University
University of Florida
Georgia Institute of Technology
University of Illinois–Urbana-Champaign
University of Kansas
Kansas State University
University of Maryland
Miami University (OH)
University of Michigan
University of Nebraska
SUNY–Buffalo
University of Oregon
Pennsylvania State University

Texas A&M University
University of Texas–Austin
Virginia Tech
University of Washington

A Few Arts-Oriented Architecture Programs
Barnard College
Bennington College
Pratt Institute
Rhode Island School of Design
Savannah School of Art and Design
Wellesley College
Yale University

Business
Preparation for a career in business is a much-misunderstood subject. There are approximately one hundred seventy million people between the ages of eighteen and sixty-five in the United States and most of them are in business of some sort. Everything from aardvark farming to zeppelin repair falls under the heading of business. Yet a myth persists that the only path to enter the business world is through an undergraduate business major. In fact, many people major in something else and find that experience is the best teacher when it comes to business skills. Others wait until graduate school to get their business training.

If you want to climb the corporate ladder, you shouldn't necessarily go off to business school right away and hit the library every night with *Principles of Accounting*. Consider the example of Michael Eisner, chairman and CEO of the Walt Disney Corporation. Eisner went to Denison University, a small institution that doesn't even have a business program, and majored in English literature and theater. With no other degrees, he rose to become one of the most powerful executives in the entertainment industry. The biggest titan of the business world, Bill Gates, is a college dropout—albeit from Harvard (which, by the way, does not have an undergraduate business program).

There are advantages and disadvantages to majoring in business at the undergraduate level. In the short run, graduates are probably better positioned for entry level jobs in accounting, marketing, banking, and similar fields. When the job market is tight, that can be a real plus. Unfortunately, an undergraduate business major can also be a limiting factor. Most top graduate programs prefer applicants who have majored in something else, preferably the liberal arts. These schools want applicants who got a broad education and learned to think; they supply the business training. (Most of the top business schools don't even offer undergraduate programs and generally prefer incoming students who have spent time in the working world.) Among mid- and top-level managers, very few will have made it to their positions with only an undergraduate business major. The accounting major who feels so smug about his job prospects now may someday find himself taking orders from a hopelessly impractical art history major who went back five years later for an MBA.

If you do want business training at the undergraduate level, there are two primary choices: a college of business or an economics major in a college of arts and sciences. The college of business will offer a full range of majors in all the primary business areas, including specialties like international business and management information systems. The business training is likely to be specialized and extensive, but it may come at the cost of a firm grounding in the liberal arts.

An economics major can be had at just about any liberal arts college or university. The treatment of business-related topics is likely to be more theoretical than practical, but included in the deal will be a liberal arts degree.

Major Private Universities Strong in Business

American University
Baylor University
Boston College
Boston University
Carnegie Mellon University
Case Western Reserve University
University of Dayton
Emory University
Fordham University
Georgetown University
Howard University
Ithaca College
Lehigh University
Massachusetts Institute of Technology
New York University
University of Notre Dame
University of Pennsylvania
Pepperdine University
Rensselaer Polytechnic Institute
University of San Francisco
Santa Clara University
University of Southern California
Southern Methodist University
Syracuse University
Texas Christian University
Tulane University
Villanova University
Wake Forest University
Washington University in St. Louis

Public Universities Strong in Business

University of Arizona
University of California–Berkeley
University of Cincinnati

University of Connecticut
University of Florida
University of Georgia
University of Illinois–Urbana-Champaign
Indiana University
James Madison University
University of Kansas
University of Maryland
University of Massachusetts–Amherst
Miami University (OH)
University of Michigan
University of Missouri
University of North Carolina–Chapel Hill
Ohio State University
Ohio University
University of Oregon
Pennsylvania State University
University of Pittsburgh
Rutgers, The State University of New Jersey
University of South Carolina
SUNY–Albany
SUNY–Binghamton University
SUNY–Buffalo
SUNY–Geneseo
University of Tennessee
Texas A&M University
University of Texas–Austin
University of Vermont
University of Virginia
University of Washington
College of William and Mary
University of Wisconsin–Madison

Small Colleges and Universities Strong in Business

Agnes Scott College
Babson College
Bucknell University
Calvin College
Claremont McKenna College
Clarkson University
Eckerd College
Fairfield University
Franklin and Marshall College
Furman University
Gettysburg College
Guilford College
Hendrix College
Lafayette College
Lake Forest College
Lehigh University
Lewis and Clark College
Millsaps College
Morehouse College
Muhlenberg College
Oglethorpe College
Ohio Wesleyan University
Presbyterian College
Rhodes College
University of Richmond
Ripon College
Skidmore College
Southwestern University
Stetson College
Susquehanna University
Trinity University (TX)
Washington and Jefferson College
Washington and Lee University
Whittier College

Wofford College
Worcester Polytechnic Institute
Xavier University of Louisiana

Art and Design

These days, an art major sounds like something out of a TV sitcom. Picture yourself having a heart-to-heart with dear old Dad—the person who is financing your education to the tune of two hundred thousand dollars—and gently breaking the news.

"Dad, I've decided to be an art major."

When Dad regains consciousness, he'll probably have visions of you selling apples on a street corner or living out of a 1960s Volkswagen van. In reality, Dad is only half right. Making a living as a painter or a sculptor ranges somewhere between difficult and impossible. But an education in art and design is more than just painting pretty pictures. There are plenty of jobs in advertising, publishing, fashion design, animation, illustration, interior decoration, arts management, and a host of other fields for students who can apply artistic skills to practical careers. Much of today's most interesting work in art and design takes place on that most practical of modern canvases, the computer.

If you are looking to pursue an art-related career, a number of choices await. The most important question may well be whether you want to study in a specialized art school or pursue an art major in a liberal arts college or university. Each has its merits. The specialized schools offer the unmatched intensity of collective soul-searching that only a community of artists can generate. The caliber of work is likely to be extremely high and the pathways to careers in art and design are likely to be well worn. Students will also get the benefit of extensive alumni networks and instant school name recognition from those in the field.

As a side note, the nomenclature in art and design can get

pretty confusing. Some institutions call themselves schools or colleges of art or visual arts, others use design, and still others say art and design. In the art world, the term design has a more preprofessional ring to it, while art signifies a purer form of expression. That distinction doesn't always mean anything when it comes to the names of particular institutions, many of which were acquired decades or even centuries ago. But the difference is significant in your choice of major. At some schools, the art and design departments work closely; at others, the two are worlds apart.

The main drawbacks of an art school are the lack of broad liberal arts training and the inability to major in non-art fields. These schools are probably not the best choice if you have any doubts about your commitment to art or if you would like to combine art or design with another major. Most good colleges and universities have departments of studio art and graphic design and many of them offer superior training as well as chances for cross-disciplinary work in seemingly unrelated fields. The atmosphere is likely to be less single-minded and more relaxed, though a high-powered art department can generate plenty of intensity with a core of committed students.

Top Schools of Art and Design

Art Center College of Design
California College of the Arts
California Institute of the Arts
Cooper Union
Kansas City Art Institute
Maryland Institute, College of Art
Massachusetts College of Art
Moore College of Art and Design
North Carolina School of the Arts
Otis Institute of Art and Design
Parsons School of Design
Pratt Institute

Rhode Island School of Design
Ringling School of Art and Design
San Francisco Art Institute
Savannah College of Art and Design
School of the Art Institute of Chicago
School of the Museum of Fine Arts (MA)
School of Visual Arts (NY)

Major Universities Strong in Art or Design
American University
Boston College
Boston University
Carnegie Mellon University
University of Cincinnati
Cornell University
Drexel University
Harvard University
University of Michigan
New York University
University of Pennsylvania
University of Rochester
Syracuse University
Washington University in St. Louis
University of Washington
Yale University

Small Colleges and Universities Strong in Art or Design
Alfred University
Bard College
Brown University
Centre College
Cornell College
Dartmouth College
Furman University
Hollins University

Kenyon College
Lake Forest College
Lewis and Clark College
Manhattanville College
Mills College
SUNY–Purchase
Randolph College
University of North Carolina–Greensboro
Sarah Lawrence College
Scripps College
Skidmore College
Smith College
Southwestern University
Vassar College
Wheaton College (MA)
Willamette University
Williams College

The Performing Arts

The story on the performing arts is similar to the one for art and design. Earning a living on the stage is even harder than in the studio and performing skills lead to fewer related professions. Aside from teaching and arts management, there is not much a performer can do besides playing or singing. (Even areas such as production and set design are tough to crack.) If music is your passion, you have at least three options: you can study performance in a conservatory dedicated entirely to music; you can get a conservatory education in a program at a full-service university; or you can earn a liberal arts degree in music with an eye toward teaching or some other related career. The conservatory route is legendary for intense pressure to perform—literally—but it probably offers the best shot for a career as a musician. If you're not ready to give heart and soul (and possibly sanity) to music, you're probably better off getting a liberal arts degree, perhaps in combination with music lessons or participation in an extracurricular music group.

The same basic advice applies to future actors and dancers. For "Broadway or Bust" types, a handful of the arts specialty schools offer high-powered training. The legendary Juilliard School in New York maintains world-class programs in all the major performing arts. A few others, notably North Carolina School of the Arts and California Institute of the Arts, cover the entire spectrum of art, design, music, dance, and drama. Performance programs within universities give you more flexibility to take courses outside the arts, and to change direction if you decide that performing is not for you.

When looking at a particular conservatory or arts school, pay close attention to its specialties. Music schools are strong in different instruments; dance schools emphasize different types of performing. Creative philosophies at arts schools vary widely and much hinges on working relationships with program mentors. If you do consider a stand-alone arts school, keep an eye out for ties to nearby colleges. Since most arts schools are located in a city, they often have cross-registration with major universities.

Top Music Conservatories

Berklee College of Music
Boston Conservatory
California Institute of the Arts
Cleveland Institute of Music
Curtis Institute of Music
Eastman School of Music
Juilliard School
Manhattan School of Music
New England Conservatory of Music
North Carolina School of the Arts
Peabody Conservatory of Music
San Francisco Conservatory of Music

Major Universities Strong in Music

Baylor University
Boston College
Boston University
University of California–Los Angeles
Carnegie Mellon University
Case Western Reserve University
University of Cincinnati
University of Colorado–Boulder
University of Denver
DePaul University
Florida State University
Harvard University
Indiana University
Ithaca College
Miami University (OH)
University of Miami (FL)
University of Michigan
University of Nebraska–Lincoln
New York University
Northwestern University
University of Oklahoma
University of Southern California
Southern Methodist University
Vanderbilt University
Yale University

Small Colleges and Universities Strong in Music

Bard College
Bennington College
Bucknell University
Butler University
DePauw University
Furman University
Gordon College

Illinois Wesleyan University
Knox College
Lawrence University*
Loyola University–New Orleans
Manhattanville College
Mills College
Oberlin College*
University of the Pacific
Rice University
St. Mary's College of Maryland
St. Olaf College
Sarah Lawrence College
Skidmore College
Smith College
University of Southern California
Stetson University
SUNY–Geneseo
SUNY–Purchase
Wesleyan University
Wheaton College (IL)

*These two are unusual because they combine a world-class conservatory with a top-notch liberal arts college.

Major Universities Strong in Drama

Boston College
Boston University
University of California–Los Angeles
Carnegie Mellon University
The Catholic University of America
DePaul University
Emerson University
Florida State University
Fordham University
Indiana University

University of Iowa
Ithaca College
University of Minnesota
New York University
Northwestern University
University of North Carolina–Chapel Hill
University of Southern California
Southern Methodist University
Syracuse University
Texas Christian University
University of Washington
Yale University

Small Colleges and Universities Strong in Drama

Beloit College
Bennington College
Centre College
Colorado College
Connecticut College
Drew University
Ithaca College
Juilliard School
Kenyon College
Lawrence University
Macalester College
Middlebury College
Muhlenberg College
Occidental College
Otterbein College
Princeton University
Rollins College
Sarah Lawrence College
Skidmore College
SUNY–Purchase
Vassar College

Whitman College
Wittenberg University

Major Universities Strong in Dance
Arizona State University
University of California–Irvine
University of California–Los Angeles
University of California–Riverside
Case Western Reserve University
Florida State University
George Washington University
Howard University
Indiana University
University of Iowa
University of Minnesota
New York University
Ohio University
Southern Methodist University
Texas Christian University
University of Texas–Austin
University of Utah
Washington University in St. Louis

Small Colleges and Universities Strong in Dance
Amherst College
Barnard College
Bennington College
Butler University
Connecticut College
Dartmouth College
Goucher College
Hollins University
Juilliard School
Kenyon College
Middlebury College

Mills College
Muhlenberg College
North Carolina School of the Arts
Princeton University
Sarah Lawrence College
Smith College
SUNY–Purchase

Communications/Journalism

Though the pundits constantly tell us that we live in the Information Age, they could just as easily call it the Communications Age. Demand for graduates with media and other communications skills has soared in the past several decades and so, too, has the number of programs to train them. For students who want an education in communications, there are two ways to get it: (1) attend an excellent college or university and major in a liberal arts field, or (2) enroll in a college of communications for preprofessional training in a particular field. Among the latter, journalism is usually the most eye-catching for high school students. (Though a few universities offer a full-fledged school of journalism, the subject is usually offered as a department within communications.) Other important communications fields include advertising, public relations, speech, and broadcasting. (Students interested in broadcasting should also read the section on film/television that follows.)

Before enrolling in a college of communications, keep in mind that many of the skills important for success are the same ones you learn in a liberal arts program. Writing is the heart of advertising, journalism, and public relations. Corporations won't mind teaching a good writer about the particulars of advertising; few will waste time with a graduate who knows about advertising but can't write. The same applies to journalism. Many journalism programs offer fine preparation, but so, too, do many liberal arts institutions, where a good campus newspaper often provides enough hands-on experience. For budding journalists, a liberal arts education is virtually a trade school course of study—one that teaches curiosity, research skills, communication skills, and a sense of perspective. The best undergraduate journalism programs understand this and build in heavy doses of liberal arts. Beware of any that do not.

For students interested in broadcasting—especially TV—the case for preprofessional training is stronger, largely because of the expensive facilities required for a top-flight program. Up-to-date equipment is crucial; there's no use learning on stuff that is obsolete. Students considering broadcast journalism should remember that unless you are physically attractive, your chances of getting in front of the camera are virtually nil.

No matter what route they choose, students interested in communications or journalism should seek exposure to many fields. Those who specialize too soon may find that they have nothing interesting to say.

As the following list illustrates, communications/journalism programs are confined mainly to state universities and a smattering of private ones. Most of the nation's elite colleges have a program of their own for budding journalists: the English department.

Major Universities Strong in Communications/Journalism

American University
Arizona State University
Boston University
University of California–Los Angeles
University of California–San Diego
University of Florida
University of Georgia
University of Illinois–Urbana-Champaign
Indiana University
Ithaca College

University of Kansas
University of Maryland
University of Michigan
University of Missouri–Columbia
University of Nebraska
University of North Carolina–Chapel Hill
Northwestern University
Ohio University
University of Oregon
Pepperdine University
St. Lawrence University
University of San Francisco
University of Southern California
Stanford University
Syracuse University
Texas Christian University
University of Utah
University of Wisconsin–Madison

Film/Television

When it comes to glamor, few professions can match the film and television industry. But if you're among the thousands who dream of making it big in Hollywood, be prepared to hustle. Getting a toehold in film or broadcasting is no easy task and making it big is even harder.

There is no primrose path to a career in film or broadcasting. As a seventeen- or eighteen-year-old high school graduate, your best bet is to get a well-rounded education. The liberal arts are especially crucial if you are interested in the creative elements of film production. The technical stuff can be learned anytime, but no film course can teach you imagination, creativity, how to write, or how to tell a story. Many film-industry insiders advise students to wait until the graduate level for specialized film training. A good liberal arts college with a critical mass of people interested in film is often the best preparation.

The main advantage of undergraduate film school is the chance to rub shoulders with other aspiring actors, writers, directors, producers, and cinematographers. If intense competition and single-minded focus bring out your best, film school is definitely worth considering. Some programs are part of a college of communications or journalism; others are linked to theater arts. A school or college of broadcasting or film and TV is often (though not always) more comprehensive than a department of film. Among major university film schools, three stand out: University of Southern California's School of Cinema-Television (George Lucas, Ron Howard); UCLA's School of Theater, Film, and Television (Francis Ford Coppola, Tim Robbins); and New York University's Film and Television Department (Billy Crystal, Spike Lee, Martin Scorsese, Oliver Stone). More unusual is tiny Columbia College in Hollywood, one of the few undergraduate colleges in the nation devoted entirely to media arts.

Making your mark in the film industry takes talent, hard work, and a high tolerance for rejection. Though the dream of being the next Steven Spielberg dies hard, a more realistic approach is to consider the many opportunities outside the world of big-budget feature films. As long as the role of media in our society continues to expand, so, too, will opportunities in broadcast- and film-related professions.

Major Universities Strong in Film/Television

Arizona State University
Boston University
University of California–Los Angeles
University of Cincinnati
Drexel University
University of Florida
Ithaca College
University of Kansas
Memphis State University

University of Michigan
New York University
Northwestern University
Pennsylvania State University
University of Southern California
Syracuse University
University of Texas–Austin
Wayne State University

Small Colleges and Universities Strong in Film/Television

Bard College
Beloit College
Brown University
California Institute of the Arts
Columbia College (CA)
Columbia College (IL)
Emerson College
The Evergreen State College
Hampshire College
Hofstra University
Hollins University
Occidental College
Quinnipiac University
Pitzer College
Pomona College
Sarah Lawrence College
School of Visual Arts
SUNY–Purchase
Wesleyan University

7. Where to Learn More

When your parents were in high school, there was no great mystery about where to find information about colleges. The choice was between a few old stand-bys like *Lovejoy* and *Barron's* that offered a column or two of statistics on each school.

But those were also the days when most people still ate Corn Flakes or Rice Krispies for breakfast and got all their television from the three major networks. Today, breakfast cereals take up a whole aisle in the grocery store and people can watch their favorite shows at any time online. Today's college guide shelf is crowded with entries written from every conceivable angle and the rise of the Internet has created a whole new universe of information. The problem is how to sort through it all. You can either hire your own reference librarian or consult the pages that follow for leads on the best sources.

The key is to understand which materials are appropriate for the various phases of the process. If you're just beginning the search, you may want to check out some of the websites listed in Chapter 4: Getting a Jump Start. The Internet is a handy tool for generating names of colleges based on various criteria (size, location, majors, etc.) and linking to colleges' websites. But smart applicants will soon want more in-depth analysis from sources that are independent of the colleges. For this kind of information, printed college guides are still the best source. The pages that follow describe the ones we think are most useful, including a wide variety of publications for students with particular needs and interests.

General Interest College Guides

Fiske Guide to Colleges by Edward B. Fiske. Sourcebooks. The companion volume to this book. Includes critical essays on more than three hundred of the best and most interesting colleges in the nation. The book we recommend as the next step for applicants to selective colleges. Annual.

U.S.News Ultimate College Guide, *U.S.News & World Report*. Sourcebooks. *U.S. News*'s widely read and controversial rankings are published every August. The book includes reporting on college admissions that is generally more insightful than that found in similar publications by *Time* and *Newsweek*. Much of the material is made available at www.usnews.com. Annual.

The Best 373 Colleges, *The Princeton Review*. Random House. Covers a selection of colleges similar to that of the *Fiske Guide*. Useful for comparisons, though you should watch out for the dubious What's Hot/What's Not section. Much of the text of this book is available at *Princeton Review's* website, www.princetonreview.com. Annual.

Choosing the Right College: The Whole Truth about America's 100 Top Schools by Intercollegiate Studies Institute. William B. Eeerdmans Publishing Company. This book criticizes many highly selective schools for political correctness and failure to maintain standards. Spotlights those that feature the Western tradition and core requirements.

The College Finder by Steven Antonoff. Fawcett Books. Features lists of recommended colleges in hundreds of categories, ranging from colleges with the most National Merit Scholars to colleges that operate kosher kitchens.

Colleges That Change Lives by Loren Pope. Penguin Books. Long profiles of forty small colleges "that you should know about even if you're not a straight-A student." Makes the case that these schools give students a better education than the Ivy League.

Four Year Colleges, Peterson's Guides. This massive tome includes statistical information on more than two thousand schools as well as profiles written by the colleges themselves. Will be useful primarily to students looking at institutions not included in the other guides. Annual.

Harvard Schmarvard: Getting Beyond the Ivy League to the College That Is Best for You. By the *Washington Post*'s Education Columnist, this book offers general insight on the college search and a list of schools that the author believes to be under-appreciated.

The Hidden Ivies by Howard Mathew Greene. Cliff Street Books. Profiles thirty colleges "comparable in quality to the Ivies." Based on interviews and surveys with administrators and students.

The Insider's Guide to the Colleges, *Yale Daily News*. St. Martin's Press. A guide to selective colleges, produced by students at Yale. A counterpoint to the *Fiske Guide*. Annual.

Special-Interest Guides

Barron's Best Buys in College Education by Lucia Solorzano. Barron's Educational Series. Profiles three hundred best buys for the college bargain hunter. Limited because it does not include expensive colleges that offer scholarships and financial aid to discount their sticker prices.

The College Majors Handbook by Neeta P. Fogg, Paul E. Harrington, and Thomas F. Harrington. JIST Publishing. Based on a Census Bureau study, this book includes at detailed look at the job prospects in sixty college majors.

Colleges with Programs for Students with Learning Disabilities and Attention Deficit Disorders by Charles Mangrum and Stephen Strichart. Peterson's Guides. Describes the programs for LD students available at more than eight hundred colleges.

Cool Colleges: For the Hyper-Intelligent, Self-Directed, Late-Blooming, and Just Plain Different by Donald Asher. Ten Speed Press. A smorgasbord of information about various colleges that don't fit the mold.

Film School Confidential by Karin Kelly and Tom Edgar. Perigee Books. Offers in-depth profiles of twenty-six top film schools. Useful for undergraduates, though aimed primarily at those seeking graduate degrees.

More Guides in the Fiske Series

If you're reading this book, you probably know about the *Fiske Guide to Colleges*. (If not, see the description earlier in this chapter.) But did you know there are four other Fiske guides?

Fiske Countdown to College: 41 To-Do Lists and a Plan for Every Year of High School—In addition to the to-do lists, this book offers advice from current students on every aspect of the admission process.

Fiske Real College Essays that Work—Features 109 excellent essays written by real students, with commentary that explains how you can use their techniques to create your own winning essay.

Fiske Nailing the New SAT—Based on a survey of more than 800 SAT takers, this book gives the inside story on how to do your best on the big test.

Fiske Word Power—If you're looking to build your vocabulary, try the Fiske system. This book can help you get beyond rote memorization to a deeper understanding of words and their meanings.

Guide to College Majors, Princeton Review. Provides profiles of two hundred and fifty college majors, including necessary high-school preparation and overview of career options and salary potential.

Guide to Performing Arts Programs by Carole J. Everett and Muriel Topaz. The Princeton Review/Random House. Includes descriptions of more than six hundred programs in dance, drama, and music at both the high school and college level.

Honors Programs by Dr. Joan Digby. Peterson's Guides. Includes descriptions of three hundred and fifty honors programs written by administrators from the colleges. Unfortunately, a number of the most notable schools and programs are not covered.

The K&W Guide to Colleges for the Learning Disabled by Marybeth Kravets and Imy F. Wax. The Princeton Review/Random House. Offers factual profiles of LD programs at more than three hundred colleges, with ratings for the level of support at each.

Making a Difference: College and Graduate Guide by Miriam Weinstein. New Society. Profiles of over one hundred "outstanding colleges to help you make a better world." Particular emphasis on environmental studies and community service.

Professional Degree Programs in the Visual and Performing Arts, Peterson's Guides. Factual and statistical descriptions of arts programs at six hundred and fifty institutions.

Visiting College Campuses by Janet Spencer and Sandra Maleson. The Princeton Review/Random House. Includes information on where to stay and how to get there for about two hundred and fifty selective colleges.

Part Two:

Getting In

8. Inside the Admissions Process

Some signs of the times:

A parent calls the Harvard University admissions office asking for advice about the best nursery schools to prepare his toddler for admission. A student at an elite prep school files twenty-five college applications, including one to every Ivy League school. A parent pays a consultant two thousand dollars to help her child fill out college applications and write essays.

Welcome to the brave new world of college admissions. Though getting into college has always been a preoccupation of high school seniors, the intensity and determination of the struggle have reached new heights. In the chapter that follows, we'll take you on a tour of how the highly selective admissions process works. The rest of the book offers some strategies for success.

But we begin this section with another sign of the times that is not as well publicized. While a few dozen elite schools have been flooded with applications, most of the twenty-two hundred four-year colleges in the nation are still hustling to attract reasonably qualified applicants to fill their classes. Literally hundreds of highly reputable institutions accept virtually any student who has graduated from high school. These colleges may not provide a prestigious bumper-sticker for the family car, but many of them do have superb academic offerings and an excellent record of launching graduates into fulfilling careers.

Most Colleges Accept All Qualified Applicants

As we learned in Chapter 5: Cutting through the Hype, colleges often pose as being more selective than they actually are. Just take a close look at the numbers. A generous definition of selective would be a college that turns away as many applicants as it accepts. Of just over three hundred top schools in the *Fiske Guide to Colleges*, less than a third are that choosy. Apply a more stringent definition to selective— accepting only one in four—and you're only talking about a few dozen institutions.

When a college accepts everyone who is qualified, the admissions process is simple. Meet the minimum standards and you're in. State schools generally operate on this model, with a few variations. At the University of Wyoming, for instance, admission is guaranteed as long as you get passing marks in high school. More competitive state schools generally use a formula based on grades and/or standardized test scores. Essays, recommendations, and other paraphernalia are generally unnecessary except for applicants on the borderline. The message of all this? To paraphrase the old recruiting poster: American colleges and universities want you. No matter who you are, if you meet the minimum standards, there are hundreds of colleges ready to offer you a first-rate education.

Selectivity of Institutions in the *Fiske Guide to Colleges*

The *Fiske Guide* includes three hundred and thirteen of the nation's best and most interesting schools. The selectivity of those colleges is as follows:

Admit 5 to 25% of applicants	29
Admit 26 to 50% of applicants	87
Admit 51 to 75% of applicants	130
Admit 76 to 100% of applicants	68

At a Few, the Competition Intensifies

The dark lining to the silver cloud is the growing selectivity of the colleges at the top of the admissions ziggurat. They're the usual suspects in the growing national obsession with prestigious alma maters, the same few that accept a third or less of their applicants. In the past ten years, applications to these schools have risen significantly, making a once competitive situation border on the absurd. The deluge has been especially heavy at prestigious national universities: the Ivy League, Duke, Emory, Georgetown, Johns Hopkins, Northwestern, Notre Dame, Rice, Stanford, and Tufts, to name a few. For a recent freshman class, the admissions office at Harvard University received over ninety-four hundred applications from students with scores above 1400 on the SAT Critical Reading and Math. It accepted fewer than two thousand of these, including many with lower scores who had other compelling qualifications. A recent report to high schools from Brown University revealed that fewer than half of the valedictorians who applied were accepted.

The most prominent public universities have also seen an increase in applications. Some have been aided by media exposure for big-time sports; others, such as the University of Georgia, have garnered a windfall of applicants due to state-sponsored scholarships. Applications to honors programs have skyrocketed at many top public institutions. A handful of them—notably the University of California–Berkeley and Los Angeles, the University of Michigan, the University of North Carolina–Chapel Hill, and the University of Virginia—have entered the ranks of the highly selective elite for out-of-state students.

Applications at highbrow liberal arts colleges have stayed relatively steady, though notable gainers include Barnard, Middlebury, Trinity, and Wellesley.

If you've set your sights on an elite school, join the club. Most of them will give you an outstanding education and open plenty of doors after graduation. But try to maintain some perspective and avoid becoming another pathetic lamb following the herd. Just because a college attracts lots of applications doesn't mean it's a good match for you. Some such schools are overrated; others have become so crowded that they no longer deliver the quality suggested by their name. Ask yourself if all the pressure is really worth it. Some people thrive on the challenge of the competitive college scramble; others suffer from anxiety, depression, anorexia, and worse. The college search should be about picking the right school for you, not picking the most prestigious one you can get into. Don't end up like the student who described his time on a well-known but (for him) inappropriate campus as "serving a four-year jail term with a one hundred thousand dollar fine."

The Highly Selective Applicant Blues

College	Class of 1997		Class of 2012	
	Number of Applications	% Accepted	Number of Applications	% Accepted
Amherst	5,570	21	7,750	15
Columbia	6,590	29	22,590	10
Harvard	13,030	16	22,990	9
MIT	6,670	33	12,400	12
Northwestern	12,640	43	18,800	30
NYU	10,840	50	15,000	36
Princeton	12,860	16	23,370	10
Rice	7,490	19	8,780	24
Stanford	13,200	22	23,960	10
Swarthmore	3,370	31	5,240	18
Wellesley	2,510	49	4,100	35
Wesleyan	4,800	40	7,750	27
Yale	11,950	22	19,320	9

The Admissions Process at Highly Selective Schools

If your resolve is still firm, hang on for the ride. The highly selective admissions process is complicated and subjective. The problem is that these schools are swamped with applications from many more qualified students than they can accept. Who can say how they should choose? Would you rather admit the tennis player with the 3.50 GPA or the concert violinist with the 3.49? How many math geniuses should be admitted for every artsy dilettante? And how many polite Midwesterners should there be to balance out all the pushy Easterners?

Under these circumstances, it's no surprise that desperate applicants will grasp at any straw to set themselves apart from the crowd. One applicant to Stanford took out a full-page ad in the school paper begging the admissions office to admit him. An audacious University of Virginia applicant actually sent a shoe with the message: "Now that I have one foot in the door, I hope you'll let me have the other one." This little stratagem might have worked, but the other shoe dropped when nearby William and Mary received the exact same treatment—and compared notes with UVA. Though gimmicks like these can be amusing, they seldom work. The jaded eye of the admissions officer has seen most of them a thousand times (well, maybe not the shoes).

Before you throw up your hands in despair, take heart. People who think the admissions process is arbitrary don't understand the logic.

How Duke University Rates Its Applicants

Duke's rating system is more elaborate than most. Applicants are ranked on a scale of 1–5 in each of six categories: grades in academic courses (9–12), strength of curriculum, standardized test scores, letters of recommendation, personal essay, and extracurricular activities. The first three are crucial in determining whether an applicant has a reasonable chance for admission; the latter three are used to make distinctions among top students. A host of additional factors come into play that are not assigned a numerical ranking, including ethnicity, geography, legacy status, and interest from a coach. Reports from interviewers are included in the rating for letters of recommendation.

The purpose is not to assemble the best group of students. If that were the case, the colleges' libraries would be overflowing every night, but the gyms, concert halls, and yearbook offices would be vacant. Nor is the aim to assemble a group of well-rounded students. Though every campus needs some, this kind of person tends to be reasonably good in many things, but not a standout in any one.

The ideal of diversity continues to be one of the guiding principles for assembling a class at virtually all institutions.

The true goal is to create a well-rounded community of individuals who each add a unique talent or characteristic to the mix. In the words of one admissions dean at an elite university:

We want a class of serious, bright, intellectually curious students that represents the many populations of our country in terms of geographical, economic, racial, ethnic, religious, and political characteristics: we seek students who pursue one or more school or non-school activities through to levels of distinction. Special efforts are taken to enroll gifted writers, artists, athletes, and musicians, as well as those with diverse interests or experience in specific areas of study.

Strainin' Sal: A Parable for Stressed-Out Applicants

Just because a college is more selective doesn't mean it is a good fit for you. Consider the case of Straining Sal, a slightly above-average student who applied to thirteen highly selective colleges in the desperate hope that one might accept her. She finally got in off the wait-list of her thirteenth choice—and spent the next four years struggling to keep her head above water competing with some of the smartest students in the country. Between review sessions, tutoring, and nonstop studying, poor Sal had no life. Meanwhile, her self-esteem took a severe beating as she constantly compared herself with students with much more ability than she would ever have. When it came time to look for a job, the prestigious name on the top of the diploma couldn't make up for Sal's low grades and her lack of extracurricular involvement. The last we heard, she was working at a local fast-food establishment.

How different her career might have been had she chosen the less-selective college that was right for her! There, she might have found the help she needed to overcome her academic weaknesses. With peers of similar ability, she might have had the chance to grow in self-confidence. Leadership opportunities would have come her way as she continued to blossom. By graduation, she could easily have compiled the combination of high grades and extracurricular involvement that is impressive to employers no matter what college one attends. Most important, she might actually have enjoyed her college experience and emerged from those years a more focused, mature young woman.

What's My Category?

Picture life on a college campus and the organizations that make it go. Each of these is an interest group that the admissions office must satisfy. The alumni office will lobby for the son of their recent million-dollar donor; the football coach will fight for the three hundred-pound noseguard he covets; the multicultural affairs coalition will be rioting in the streets if the number of minority students goes down. Instead of, "What test scores do I need to get in?" a better question might be, "What's my category?" Few admissions offices would admit to having quotas for the types of students they seek, but practically all have rough guidelines for the number they want of each. The more students in your category, the more competition you'll face to win a spot in the class.

Though the system favors many subgroups that are in short supply, critics have charged reverse discrimination, seizing upon the fact that some minority groups are accepted at a higher rate than other races. Lively debate continues in state legislatures and the legal system and states such as California and Texas have been forced to abandon policies that set aside scholarships or places in the class for certain races. (These institutions continue to seek diversity by targeting economically disadvantaged students or those who have overcome obstacles.) Since private universities don't depend on taxpayer money, their policies are less likely to change. The quest for a diverse student body has less to do with affirmative action than the belief that educational communities are enriched by including students from different backgrounds. The ideal of diversity continues to be one of the guiding principles for assembling a class at virtually all institutions.

With all the clamor over favoritism to minorities, an equal preference for children of alumni and major donors goes largely unnoticed. Many colleges will bend over backward for such applicants; if the admissions office thinks they can muddle through until graduation, they're in. Some colleges help the offspring of wealthy alums sneak in the side door by allowing them to transfer in after a year at another school. This strategy allows the colleges to admit weak students without destroying the SAT profile of the freshman class. It also helps the colleges avoid the embarrassment of accepting alumni children instead of others in the same high school class who are obviously better qualified.

The Category Game: Your Chances

Here are the approximate acceptance rates for different types of applicants. The numbers are for a hypothetical private college that accepts 30 percent, but the logic applies equally to most highly selective schools.

Overall Acceptance Rate	30%
Recruited athletes	75%
Underrepresented minorities	60%
Alumni children	50%
"Typical" applicants	15%

The logic of the categories also holds for students who are not in one of the sought-after subgroups. Though yearbook editor or student council representative is a nice activity to put on your list, it hardly sets you apart from the crowd. But if you edit a publication on Jewish culture or are president of a city-wide teenage chess players' society, that's a little more eye-catching. Similarly, admission is always slightly more difficult if you declare yourself a premed because countless thousands of others do the same thing every year. Though applicants should never try to mold themselves into a phony image, it pays to accentuate elements of your record that set you off from the crowd.

One other category that isn't much talked about is what we dub "the underdog factor." Admissions offices dearly love candidates who come from underprivileged backgrounds or who have overcome great obstacles. After sifting through hordes of well-coached, well-manicured applicants, admissions officers find this type of student refreshing. If you fall into that category, don't let any admissions numbers intimidate you. Your qualifications will get their due.

For those of you quaking in your shoes because you're not a star quarterback or a state symphony tuba player, we repeat: the above applies only to a handful of supercompetitive schools. Most less selective private colleges mimic the same process, but their applicant pools are not strong enough for them to be nearly as choosy. At the vast majority of colleges, you don't need to be a superstar to get in.

A final variable that has become increasingly important in recent years is a family's ability to pay the bill. Many colleges, hungry for tuition dollars, give preference to applicants with low financial need. The impact on admission chances is minor at the most selective (and richest) colleges, but those on the next rungs of the ladder often use ability to pay as a key determinant of who gets admitted when they come to borderline decisions. We offer a fuller discussion of the impact of financial aid on the admissions process in Chapter 18: The New Financial Aid Game.

> ### The Right Time to Schmooze
>
> Be extra nice to the admissions representative from Most Desirable U. who comes to visit your high school. He or she will probably be the first one to read your application.

Admissions Officers: Who Are They?

The typical admissions officer (or AO, as they are known) is not at all like the academic stuffed shirt that most high school students imagine. AOs tend to be young, friendly, outgoing, and idealistic. They genuinely enjoy working with high school students—otherwise they wouldn't be in the profession—and they don't mind (much) the fact that they are always underpaid. Recent college graduates (often alumni) generally make up about half the staff. Many of these people stay in admissions for two or three years before moving on to graduate or professional school. Anyone with more than five years' experience is a veteran in the field; even most directors are young, usually in their thirties or forties.

The life of an AO includes three primary tasks: recruiting, interviewing, and evaluating the applications. Most offices assign their staff to particular regions of the country. From September through November, most AOs are on the road visiting a selection of high schools determined largely by the previous year's applications. A high school visit is often the first time an applicant gets to meet an AO in the flesh. Though not a substitute for campus interviews, a high school visit can be a useful introduction to the college search. (See your guidance counselor in the early fall of your senior year for a list of the representatives visiting your school.)

Crunch time begins in November at the nation's most selective institutions, when the AOs come in from the road to deal with the annual deluge of early applications. After a pause in late December and early January, the regular decision round makes for intense reading from January through mid to late March, when most of the applications flood in. The grueling pace during these months is one of the reasons that the admissions field has such a high rate of burnout. How would you like to wake up every morning with the knowledge that you had to read a hundred applicant files before going to bed?

How They Decide

How do admissions offices evaluate applications? Very carefully. From the moment an applicant makes initial contact, generally in the junior year, a file is created in his or her name. When the applicant comes for an interview, a report is added to the file. Standardized test reports, teacher recommendations, and transcripts all find their way inside, and when the student sends the completed application (with fee), the file is complete.

Though admissions offices are formed in a committee structure, much of their work is done individually. Colleges usually divide up the applications geographically, according to the regional responsibilities of each staff member. At this stage, the admissions officer spends an average of, say, ten minutes reading each application. Many schools use a two-part rating system for (1) academic and (2) nonacademic factors. The science nerd with the 4.0 GPA might be a 1E—great academics, lousy extracurricular/personal. The All-American football player who can barely read might be a 5A. After the initial evaluation, most applications are read a second time by another admissions officer. If the verdict is a clear-cut admit or deny, the application will probably be sent to the dean or director for final action.

Most admissions committees include university faculty— sometimes as full-fledged members, more often as expert evaluators in their fields. The tape submitted by an aspiring French horn player is sent to the music department; the line drawings from the budding designer go to the art department. Coaches also get into the act, generally with a list of applicants they want for their teams. (A hint for athletes: get the coach on your side!) Most university presidents do not involve themselves in the fate of particular applicants, but many have indirect ways of making their interests known.

The borderline cases, which can cause protracted haggling, are put off until the end for consideration by the full committee. If your application is in the last batch, all the rating systems go out the window and there's no telling what will decide your fate. How adamantly will the admissions officer that interviewed you argue your case? What will the art professor think of the slides you submitted? Will you be one of the dean's "wild card" admits that he saves for students denied by the committee as a whole? Talk about a cliff hanger!

9. Shaping Your Record

On your day of reckoning with the admissions committee, one factor is most likely to determine your fate: the high school transcript. Unlike essays or SATs, the transcript is a four-year chronicle of your ability, work ethic, and involvement. No amount of cramming, coaching, or fast talking can make it better. That's why admissions officers will consider it the key ingredient in evaluating your potential for success as a college student. After all, the best predictor of how a person will perform in the future is how he or she performed in similar situations in the past.

There are really two elements to your record in high school. The academic transcript—your courses and grades—is by far the most important. Also significant at highly selective schools is your list of extracurricular involvements, including offices held and time committed. Together, they paint a portrait that gives admissions officers detailed insight into just about every character trait you can think of.

A Tale of Two Students

Though admissions policies vary widely across the many types of colleges and universities, the primacy of the transcript is universal. Admissions officers want the answers to three questions:

1. What are your grades?
2. Have you taken challenging courses?
3. Are your grades improving or declining?

The importance of your grades is hardly front-page news, but too many students are fixated with getting a high grade point average and don't understand how thoroughly admissions officers will scrutinize their course selections and grade trend. To illustrate this, we take a peek inside the lives of two aspiring college applicants, Charlene and Charlie.

Charlene is the kind of student teachers love—always doing the homework, always asking a question when she doesn't understand. Because of her weak background from middle school, ninth and tenth grade were a struggle. But her improvement has been steady and she has been fearless in tackling tough courses even in her worst subjects. She has enrolled in two Advanced Placement courses during both her junior and senior years, including the ones in her favorite subjects (calculus and physics) and her least favorite subjects (English and Spanish). As a senior, her overall GPA has climbed to 3.37, which gives her a rank of seventy-third in her class of two hundred and fifty.

And then there's Charlie. He's a fun-loving kind of guy with a quick wit and loads of intelligence. He also seems to have an internal homing device for the easiest path through high school. His transcript is crowded with less-than-challenging, semi-academic courses such as Physical Education for the Twenty-first Century: Getting a Head Start on the Battle of the Bulge. As a junior and senior, he has opted out of the really tough courses, quitting math after Algebra II and loading up on the one subject he really likes—history. Partly because of his course selection, Charlie's GPA is a spiffy 3.97. With only two *B*s on his whole transcript, Charlie ranks fourth in his class of ninety-eight.

So which of our two applicants wins in the highly selective admissions race? Sorry, Charlie, this one is a no-brainer. Admissions committees can see through your charade; they know nobody twisted your arm to take those three study halls instead of physics and precalculus. And as for that Sociology of Sports course, pleeeeease! In the words of George Stoner of

George Washington University, "So-called gut courses taken to fatten a grade average are as easy to spot as cosmetic transcript decoration and equally easy to discount."

On the other hand, Charlene gets major points for tackling the tough courses. "I'd rather see a *B*, or even an occasional *C*, in an AP course than an *A* in an easy course. This is why we do not make decisions based only upon grade point averages," says Ann Wright of Rice University. Almost as important as Charlene's course selection is her upward grade trend. The more recent the grades, the more important they become. A lot of freshman mistakes can be forgiven if there are high grades in the junior and senior year.

Know Your Goals

As the tale of Charlene and Charlie makes clear, highly challenging courses on your transcript are a big plus (aside from their value as a learning experience).

How many honors and AP courses are enough? If you're eyeing a highly selective college, you should probably take as many Advanced Placement courses as you can manage without harming your grades or extracurricular involvement. At the Ivy League and its cousins, nothing less than top grades in most or all of the advanced courses will get you a foot in the door.

If your school doesn't offer honors or AP courses, don't fret. Designing curriculum is the school's job; your responsibility is to take the most challenging courses available, whatever they might be. If you come from a super-competitive school, your GPA and class rank will be evaluated in light of your school's strength. Even students who rank near the bottom at rigorous college prep schools are highly sought after by some colleges. If you come from a high school that isn't so swift, it is more crucial to rank near the top.

Your academic interests will also affect course selection. If you want to be a premed, taking plenty of upper-level science courses is mandatory. But also pay attention to related disciplines. Prospective business majors are advised to take plenty of math. "You'll definitely need four years, preferably through calculus," says Nanette Clift of Washington University. Ditto for future engineers. If in doubt as to your course selection, consult with your guidance counselor or call the colleges on your preliminary list.

To really stand out in the most selective pools—especially if you attend a so-so high school—it helps to find ways of going beyond the standard curriculum. If you've exhausted your school's physics program, take an advanced course at a nearby college. If you finish integral calculus as a junior, work with a teacher to design your own independent study in multivariable equations. To be a scholar in Harvard or Amherst's applicant pool, you'll need to show self-sustaining intellectual energy that seeks new challenges and propels you beyond merely completing all the right courses.

Preferred High School Curriculum for Applicants to Selective Colleges

English	4 years
Math	3 years (at least through algebra II)
Natural sciences	3 years (including chemistry or physics)
Social studies	3 years
Foreign language	3 years

Different rules apply to students who are aiming for a large state university. These schools attract tens of thousands of applicants each year and, as a result, they often rely on formulas for grades and test scores to make their admissions decisions (see Chapter 8: Inside the Admissions Process). Unfortunately, your GPA is often more important at these schools than the level of the courses on your transcript.

For most students, moderation in honors and AP courses is the wisest counsel. As the hype builds for admission to elite colleges, some students overload themselves with too many advanced courses—and then suffer the consequences of lower grades and major stress. Follow your interests and challenge yourself, but don't feel pressured to take every honors course in the book.

Extracurriculars, Jobs, and Summer Programs

Though not as important as the transcript, an impressive record of extracurricular achievement can be a significant factor in admissions success. The more selective a college, the more likely extracurricular involvements will play a significant role. As we illustrated in Chapter 3: The College Universe, the emphasis should be on quality instead of quantity. Try to pick activities at which you can excel or in which you can acquire leadership positions and then stick with them through your entire high school career. When possible, enter contests or take on extra projects that will hone your skills and win recognition.

Instead of doing the extracurricular scene, some students take a part-time job. Which looks better? The answer varies. The best reason to take a job is to help pay family expenses; any college would look with favor on that. Flipping burgers in a fast-food joint to buy yourself a new Harley is a less compelling use of your time. The more responsibility a job allows you, the more impressive it will look in the eyes of the admissions office.

Since time immemorial, college interviewers have asked, "What did you do last summer?" There is no right answer to the question; the main idea is to avoid having to report that you sat around watching *Gilligan's Island* reruns.

An increasingly popular option is to attend a summer program at a college or university. In addition to sampling college-level work, students get a six-week trial of life as a college student. Since summer programs even at highly selective colleges admit every reasonable applicant, getting in for the summer doesn't mean you'll get a fat envelope when you apply for real. Attendance in summer is most likely to have an impact at moderately selective schools that will value the loyalty factor. The best way to get a foot in the door is to build a relationship with a professor who will write you a letter of recommendation.

The main idea is to avoid having to report that you sat around watching Gilligan's Island reruns.

Other perfectly good ways to spend a summer include a wilderness experience, an athletic camp, a service project (at home or abroad), or some comparable experience. Travel can be valuable, especially if it includes exposure to a foreign language. When possible, use your summer to build on skills or deepen interests that you already possess. Most important of all, have fun!

Athletes and the Admissions Process

If you're a high school athlete who dreams of playing on a bigger stage, join the club. Every year, thousands and thousands of students pursue the Holy Grail of a college scholarship, and the path is at least as difficult as anything Indiana Jones ever had to face. Well, maybe not quite that tough, but the competition is keen. NCAA Division I is where the big money scholarships are; if you're going to play D-I, the chances are good that you already have a shoebox full of letters from college coaches. Division II includes smaller schools that offer some scholarship money. Division III schools offer no money but give major preference in admission to recruited athletes.

The road to being a recruited athlete starts years in advance. Playing high school sports isn't good enough anymore. The best athletes showcase their skills for college coaches in summer leagues, camps, and on traveling teams that play year-round. If you want to be a college athlete, ask your current coach for a realistic assessment of your possibilities. If he or she says you have a chance, discuss which colleges might be realistic and ask for help in navigating the process. By spring of eleventh grade, start cranking out letters to coaches at schools you would like to attend. Tell them a little about yourself and ask if there is a time when you could make contact or visit. Mention any upcoming tournaments that you'll be playing in. You'll probably want to send along a one-page sports resume that includes your vital statistics and major accomplishments. Ask your current coach if he or she would be willing to write or call when you have narrowed down the colleges to a reasonable list. Depending on the sport, you may also want to make a video highlighting your skills.

Unless you are 6′ 8″ and can leap tall buildings in a single bound, be prepared for a lot of rejection. In Divisions I and II, the coaches have a limited number of scholarships. Alas, many of them play a shell game by making promises to various recruits before leaving some out in the cold. The sad truth is that outside of the big money sports, the amount of money available for even blue-chip athletes is limited. A coach's promise of a full scholarship can easily morph into a half scholarship or no scholarship at all. Be encouraged if a coach is enthusiastic, but always hedge your bets. You can be sure that the coach is hedging his.

> ### Calling All Athletes
>
> Any student with a notion of playing college sports should surf over to www.ncaa.org. The site includes the information about the Clearinghouse (www.ncaastudent.org), NCAA rules, and a directory of the colleges that offer each sport.

Though coaches in Division III cannot award scholarships, they can deliver admission and extra goodies such as a sweeter financial aid package. Their games aren't on ESPN, but even the littlest Po-Dunk U. loves to beat its arch-rival in the big game. Consider small but prestigious Amherst College. Though mainly for academics, Amherst reserves 15 percent of each class for recruited athletes—and that doesn't count athletes who get in because of their brains or other qualities. Athletes with their sights set on Division III athletics should not expect a cake walk; competition for slots on D-III teams is far more intense than it once was.

Regardless of the level to which you aspire, never forget that the coach and the admissions office are two separate entities that must be cultivated separately.

For hopefuls in Division I and II, there is one more hurdle: the NCAA's Initial Eligibility Clearinghouse. Students must register with the Clearinghouse during grade twelve and satisfy standardized test and GPA requirements. The minimums for Division I are a 2.5 GPA in academic core courses and an 820 on the Critical Reading and Math sections of the SAT or a combined 68 on all sections of the ACT. Students with a GPA higher than 2.5 can get by with lower scores and those with higher scores can have a lower GPA. The high school guidance office is responsible for submitting your transcript and certifying your courses as approved, so check in during twelfth grade to make sure that process is on track.

Playing sports in college at any level is a huge time commitment—far bigger than high school. Being a recruited athlete can get you in, but the real work starts once you're on campus, juggling sports and school work. Smart student-athletes never forget that student comes before athlete.

A Word to Homeschoolers

If you're among the more than one million students who stay home for school, don't panic. College admissions offices are much more receptive than they once were to students who have been homeschooled. Though the lack of a conventional transcript is a hurdle, most institutions make every effort to give fair consideration.

Homeschooled students should prepare a record of their curriculum that is as detailed as possible, including material covered, books read, and any outside enrichment experiences. Students should strongly consider preparing a portfolio that includes examples of their finest work in each subject. Parents can help by writing a statement that gives their perspective on the curriculum along with a balanced assessment of the student's strengths and weaknesses.

As the time for college draws near, homeschooled students should take advantage of summer programs at colleges or courses offered at nearby institutions. Such work will provide an institutional track record and allow the student a chance to establish relationships with faculty who might be willing to write recommendations. Standardized testing also takes on greater significance for homeschooled students, who should consider taking both the SAT and ACT and/or a selection of SAT Subject Tests. Many colleges will also require the GED high school equivalency exam.

Homeschooled students should request campus interviews whenever possible. A student who can speak convincingly about his or her experiences and aspirations is sure to impress. If an interview is not possible, or even if it is, students should consider writing an essay (whether or not one is required) that addresses their homeschool experiences and how those experiences have prepared them for life.

One bureaucratic note: since many homeschooled students take college courses before enrolling as full-time students, some may have the opportunity to enroll with advanced standing as transfer students. Enrolling as a transfer student may speed graduation, but, in some cases, the best strategy may be to enroll as a first-year student in order to qualify for scholarships that are typically available to such students (but not to transfers). Rules vary, so look before you leap.

10. How Important Are Standardized Tests?

Standardized tests cast a long shadow over the selective college admissions process. To hear some people tell it, test scores are the be-all and end-all of everything: the deciding factor on whether you get into a good school and the litmus test of your worth as an individual. "What did you get on the SAT?" will be the eternal question from test day forward and when you die, your scores will be etched forever on your tombstone.

Or will they? Are standardized tests really as important as people think? The answer—as unsatisfactory as this may sound—is yes and no. At some schools, test scores are merely one of at least a half dozen factors that play a significant role. At others, they are pretty darned important. Perhaps David Erdmann of Rollins College said it best, "At most institutions, standardized test scores count less than the students think and more than the colleges are willing to admit."

The hoopla surrounding standardized tests reached a crescendo in 2005 with the introduction of a retooled SAT. After undergoing its biggest overhaul in decades, the SAT includes three sections in place of the traditional Verbal and Math:

- A Writing section with multiple-choice questions and an essay
- A Critical Reading section with emphasis on reading comprehension
- A revamped Math section that includes topics usually covered in Algebra II

To no one's surprise, the introduction of the revised SAT has sparked a new round of controversy over the role of standardized testing in today's educational system. Some people like the new test, some hate it, and some grudgingly accept it as a necessary evil. Neither the test, nor the debate about its usefulness, is likely to go away any time soon. The SAT is owned by the College Board, which hires another organization, the Educational Testing Service (ETS), to handle the details of designing and administering it. The SAT is the only standardized test that purports to measure overall academic aptitude or what the College Board calls "developed ability."

Along with the SAT itself, the College Board also produces a separate set of Subject Tests, once called Achievement Tests. Most highly selective colleges require the SAT, and many also mandate up to three Subject Tests. As an alternative to the SAT and Subject Tests, a student can generally choose to submit scores from the ACT, a test administered by a different company that includes sections on English, math, reading, and science reasoning, as well as an optional essay that some colleges require of students who choose to submit ACT scores. Less controversial than the SAT, the ACT is most prevalent in the Southeast, Midwest, and Rocky Mountain West.

This chapter takes a closer look at the role of standardized tests—and the SAT in particular—in the college admission process. In Chapter 11: How to Prepare for Standardized Tests, we get into the nitty-gritty of how to do your best.

The Long Strange Trip of the SAT

Though the College Board doesn't like to admit it, the SAT has a sordid past. The forerunner of today's test was developed in the 1920s by a Princeton professor who had actively campaigned to weed out "feebleminded" ethnic groups from the American gene pool. Back then, people believed it was possible to measure intelligence and put a single number on it. The modern discipline of psychology has shown intelligence to be far more complicated, but the SAT, which developed out of the original notion, lives on. Meanwhile, studies have shown that the high school transcript is a better predictor of academic performance than standardized tests. In the words of one selective college admissions officer, "You just cannot equate three years of high school with one three-hour test on a Saturday morning."

In recent years, the College Board and the SAT have been under siege on a variety of fronts. Charges have been leveled that the SAT discriminates on the basis of race, sex, and socioeconomic background. Another problem is the reality that preparation for the test may increase scores. If it is true that students can increase their scores with a few weeks of intense cramming—either on their own or under through a high-priced test prep firm—then SAT scores are in part a measure of skill in taking a particular test rather than a barometer of intelligence or ability. There has also been widespread skepticism about the Writing section, and questions about whether one 25-minute essay can provide a meaningful assessment of writing ability.

The College Board itself has appeared confused about exactly how to describe the test.

What does the SAT really measure? The College Board itself has appeared confused about the answer. Until 1993, the letters "SAT" were an acronym for Scholastic Aptitude Test, but the Board changed the name to Scholastic Assessment Test because the word aptitude suggested abilities that could not be learned in school (therefore might be inborn or cultural). In 1995, the Board dropped Scholastic Assessment, making SAT a three-letter brand name that does not stand for anything. That same year, the Board made a questionable decision to "recenter" the test. In part because of a long term increase in the proportion of low-income students taking the SAT, scores had declined from an original average of 500 on both the verbal and math portions to 430 on the verbal and 480 on math. With some statistical jiggling, the averages were restored to 500 on both parts. The new scale means that historical comparisons are harder. If your cousin Joe scored 600 on the Verbal section twenty years ago, you'll need a 650 (more or less) on the Critical Reading to match him. The difference is particularly pronounced on the high end of the scale, where scores in the 700s are much more common than they were before recentering.

LD Students and Standardized Tests

Students with documented disabilities can be allowed to take the SAT or ACT with accommodations, usually in the form of more time to complete the test. This includes students with ADD, ADHD, and other learning issues, as well as those with physical disabilities. The hard part is getting approval. The number of students seeking accommodations for admission testing has increased dramatically in recent years, raising suspicions that a portion of them are simply trying to get an extra advantage. If you believe you may have a learning disability but have never been diagnosed, see a qualified professional. A note from your doctor won't be good enough; the diagnosis must be backed up by diagnostic testing and a report from the school about how it has accommodated your disability. The school will also need to implement accommodations for your regular school work that will bolster the case to get you similar accommodations on the test. A diagnosis before the end of ninth grade should allow you to take all of your PSATs and SATs untimed. But do it sooner rather than later. An initial diagnosis less than a year before the request for special testing may raise eyebrows and delay your approval.

The latest revision of the SAT came in response to a thunderbolt unleashed in 2001 by the president of the University of California, Richard Atkinson. Out of the blue, he announced that he would recommend that UC drop the SAT as an admissions requirement. Atkinson, a psychologist, lashed out at the SAT as "aligned neither to standards nor school curriculums." Atkinson's ire had been raised, among other things, by a visit to a California private school where he witnessed the spectacle of middle schoolers grappling with analogy questions similar to those then used on the SAT. Atkinson stressed that he is not against standardized testing per se—just tests that are not connected to bona fide school subjects. He reaffirmed UC's use of the SAT Subject Tests, describing them as a better predictor of college performance than the SAT itself, and called for design of new standardized tests geared toward what students learn in school.

Almost before the ink had dried on Atkinson's statement, College Board announced work on a new SAT that would appease its critics. Barely four months later, the College Board unveiled plans for a new SAT, and soon thereafter, UC announced that it would not drop the test after all. We offer a more detailed look at the forces behind the remaking of the SAT in *Fiske Nailing the New SAT*.

Where Test Scores Have Clout

The schools that generally put the most emphasis on standardized tests are large state universities. Many of them must accept all "qualified" in-state applicants and the easiest way to adhere to that mandate is to use test score and grade point cutoffs. Scores typically make up a fourth to a half of the "acceptance formulas" at these schools.

A second category of institution where standardized tests carry weight is technical institutes. "At highly selective institutions of engineering, math and science scores must be within certain ranges in order for a student to be competitive," says one dean.

A third type of school that often puts added weight on scores is the small liberal arts college that is struggling to maintain enrollment—or trying to climb the selectivity ladder. Many of these are reluctant to accept students with low test scores because the college's score profile—and hence its place in the rankings—will suffer. Lastly, for better or worse, highly selective institutions of all stripes are paying more attention to standardized tests than they once did. Rising numbers of applications have forced these institutions to emphasize easy ways of making distinctions, and the rise of the *U.S.News & World Report* rankings has compounded the emphasis on test scores.

SAT–ACT Conversion Chart

Here is how scores on one correlate to the other. If you get a 23 on the ACT, for example, that's roughly the same as getting a combined 1070 on the Critical Reading and Math sections of the SAT.

ACT	SAT	ACT	SAT
36	1600	23	1070
35	1560	22	1030
34	1510	21	990
33	1460	20	950
32	1420	19	910
31	1380	18	870
30	1340	17	830
29	1300	16	790
28	1260	15	740
27	1220	14	690
26	1190	13	640
25	1150	12	590
24	1110	11	530

Source: ACT, Inc.

Where Scores Don't Matter (As Much)

At the opposite end of the spectrum are schools that have stopped requiring standardized tests altogether. The staunchest anti-test institutions tend to be liberal arts colleges with a slightly alternative approach to education. For philosophical reasons, they reject any standardized tests to measure academic potential.

A handful of more mainstream liberal arts colleges have decided to make the SAT optional, though they sometimes require the ACT. "Connecticut College has come to the conclusion that the SAT—and the cottage industry that has grown up around it—no longer serves students well," declared the college in announcing its optional SAT policy. According to William Hiss of Bates College, the nonsubmitters tend to be women, minorities, and "every subgroup you could imagine that is being hammered by standardized tests." In recent years, a number of public institutions have joined the SAT-optional bandwagon, though the policy is often limited to students who meet minimum cut-offs for grade point average.

A policy of SAT-optional has the fringe benefit of allowing colleges to tap into the large number of intelligent students who don't do well on standardized tests—without having to report a lower SAT profile. Many observers continue to believe that the ACT and SAT Subject Tests are a better predictor of academic success than the SAT. SAT-optional is a trend to watch in the years ahead.

> **Better Try That Again**
>
> Students who are not satisfied with their SAT scores should probably take the ACT for another chance to do well on a standardized test. Since the pool of students that take the ACT is less competitive, percentile scores will probably be higher.

The Great Middle

Finally, there is the great middle: schools where standardized test scores are important, but not that important (or something like that).

How Accurate Are SAT Scores?

Not very.

Test makers don't exactly shout about it from the hills, but when pressed, they concede that standardized admissions tests are far from precise. Take your SAT score, for example. There's one chance in three that the 550 that arrived in the little envelope from ETS should really be at least 580 or no more than 520. There's one chance in ten that it should be either in the low 600s or the high 400s.

Here's why. The SAT can't measure everything that you know (like your entire vocabulary) in one Saturday morning. So, by necessity, every test is a sample of your academic knowledge and ability and the nature of this sample varies with every edition of the test. The variation, which exists purely because of the random variation of the test, is known as the *standard error of measurement* (SEM). The SEM on the SAT is 30 points. Since roughly 1.8 million students take the SAT every year, this means that about six hundred thousand reported scores are off by at least 30 points and one hundred eighty thousand are off by at least 60 points. And this doesn't include test-day influences, such as the fact that you may have arrived at the site with a headache.

The margin of error can be illustrated graphically. Suppose sixty students have reported scores of 580. According to the laws of statistics, their "true" scores will break down as follows:

520 or below	520–550	550–580	580–610	610–640	640 or above
3	7	20	20	7	3

College admissions officers—the good ones, at least—understand this. That's why they don't pay much attention to score differences of 30 or 40 points.

Neither should you.

At most colleges, test scores are one of a range of factors used in making admissions decisions. Rarely are they as critical as the transcript. Test scores tend to take on larger importance only when they are out of line with the grade point average. Exceptionally high scores coupled with low grades may signal students who haven't applied themselves very seriously and will probably continue this pattern in college. So don't count on acing the SAT as a way to make up for four years of goofing off in high school. "We will always take a student with strong school performance and weak scores over someone with weak performance and strong scores," says Steven Syverson of Lawrence University.

Though it helps to have high scores, the critical thing is to fall in the general range. Don't be too concerned with median or mean scores (see Chapter 5: Cutting through the Hype). At most colleges, you're in good shape between the twenty-fifth and seventy-fifth percentiles of the school's SAT profile. However, schools that accept only a small percentage of their applicants are an exception. At the elite, you'll need to be at the median or better in the absence of consideration in a special category.

The Bottom Line

Standardized tests, most notably the SAT, will continue to hold sway over the lives of aspiring college applicants in the foreseeable future. Admissions officers understand its flaws and hate the idea of pegging applicants with a single number, but to get rid of the SAT is politically impossible. "You have to sit in the chair of an admissions officer to understand the pressures to keep the numbers up," says Thomas Anthony, former director of admissions at Colgate University. "Presidents and faculty don't give a darn about what class rank looks like, but they light up when your scores increase by five points. This is how the nation measures academic quality." All too many colleges publicly downplay their use of standardized tests in admissions, even though test scores continue to be an important factor in most decisions.

Selective Colleges That Do Not Require SAT or ACT Scores

Bard College	Knox College
Bates College	Lake Forest College
Bennington College	Lawrence University
Bowdoin College	Lewis and Clark College
Connecticut College	Middlebury College
Denison University	Mount Holyoke College
Dickinson College	Muhlenberg College
Drew University	Pitzer College
Franklin and Marshall College	St. John's College
George Mason University	St. Lawrence College
Gettysburg College	Sarah Lawrence College
Goddard College	Smith College
Goucher College	Susquehanna University
Gustavus Adolphus College	Union College
Hampshire College	Ursinus College
Hartwick College	Wake Forest University
College of the Holy Cross	Wheaton College (MA)
Illinois Wesleyan University	Wittenberg University

What it all boils down to: don't take the SAT or any standardized test too seriously or too lightly. As with any other important test, you should do your best, but also realize that it isn't the end of the world if the kid down the street gets a better score. Your worth as a human being—or as a potential freshman—cannot be reduced to a three-digit number. After all, when was the last time you saw a tombstone with SAT scores inscribed on it?

11. How to Prepare for Standardized Tests

An old sales pitch for lottery tickets once proclaimed, "All you need is a dollar and a dream." In the world of standardized test preparation, all you need is a thousand dollars and a dream. That's how much you'll pay—at minimum—for a few weeks of intensive work with a brand name preparation company. Their sales pitch is attractive—"guaranteed" score increases in the triple digits—but the reality is a little more iffy. Some students' scores go up drastically after taking a prep course and these people swear by them. But other students' scores stay about the same or even go down (and these students seldom broadcast that fact).

Instead of blindly following the herd, think seriously about what kind of test prep will best meet your needs. There is no doubt that preparation can boost standardized test scores. Even the College Board, which spent years denying that test prep could have any benefit, now sells products to help you prepare. Our view, based in part on the results of a national survey, is that you can do just as well preparing on your own with books and software as you can with an expensive prep course. Either way, the road to successful standardized testing begins long before you sit down to blacken ovals on a Saturday morning.

Get an Early Start

Everybody agrees that the best way to prepare is to work hard in school. Lots of reading and good conversation with intelligent people (maybe even your parents) round out the long-term recipe for success. Some high schools offer free or discounted prep courses that can help you begin preparation in earnest.

Your first move is to decide which tests to take. For the vast majority of applicants, the Preliminary SAT (PSAT) is the first important standardized test to come down the pike. Unlike the SAT and ACT, the PSAT is administered to students at the high school where they attend. The test is administered annually mid-October. Most students take the PSAT in eleventh grade, though many high schools also administer it to tenth graders. If by chance your high school does not administer the PSAT, talk with your counselor about the possibility of taking it elsewhere. Some schools also administer the PLAN test, a pre-ACT, to students in tenth grade.

The next move is up to the student: SAT or ACT? If you live in the Northeast, SAT is the overwhelming choice, though ACT has been gaining ground there in recent years. We recommend that you take the SAT at least once between January and May of grade eleven, and then take it again in the fall. Some counselors recommend taking it twice as a junior—generally in March and May—on the theory that students do better the second time when the first is still fresh in their minds. Taking the SAT twice in eleventh grade leaves applicants well positioned to explore early decision or early action programs. If you have the time, or are disappointed in your first SAT score, consider scheduling an ACT to see if you might do better on it.

There are literally dozens of books and CDs on how to prepare for, beat, ace, and psych out the various standardized tests.

If you live in the regions where ACT is more prevalent, you have a choice. Most applicants to highly selective colleges take the SAT, but ACT scores are also gladly accepted by these schools. Some students, depending on their strengths, do far better on the ACT than the SAT and may enhance their chances by submitting ACT scores. If you are uncertain, compare your scores on the PSAT with those you got on the PLAN. The ACT is administered on a similar schedule to the SAT; we recommend taking one exam in the spring of eleventh grade and a second one in the fall of twelfth grade.

The next hurdle is the SAT Subject Tests. These are recommended or required by a relative handful of the nation's most selective colleges. The optimal time to take them is June of eleventh grade, though many students continue to take them through December of twelfth grade. Students taking advanced courses early in high school may opt to start Subject Tests in tenth or even ninth grade.

For each new test on the horizon, students should review the prep materials published by the College Board or ACT. Familiarize yourself with the format, so you won't need to waste energy reading directions when test day comes. We also recommend that you spend some time browsing the test prep aisle of a good bookstore. There are literally dozens of books and CDs on how to prepare for, beat, ace, and psych out the various standardized tests. They generally fall into two categories: the no-nonsense models, which include vocabulary lists, formula reviews, and practice tests, and the more provocative variety that promises to teach you how to outthink the test maker. We hope you will consider our entry in the field, the *Fiske Nailing the New SAT*. We expose the tricks of the test makers, but our primary emphasis is on teaching you how the right kind of practice can make a big difference in your scores.

If you're the kind of person who prefers preparing on the computer, help may be only a few clicks away. A number of companies offer samples or scaled-down versions of their SAT prep software that can be used on the Web or downloaded free, including most of the sites mentioned in Chapter 4. As long as you expect a sales pitch, Web surfing is a good way to sample the merchandise.

Savvy Test-Taking: The Basics

Answer the easy questions first. An easy question is worth the same as a hard one. If you're stumped, mark the question and move on. The time invested in solving a single hard one is better used on four or five easy ones.

Mark your answer sheet with care. If you get to question forty in your test booklet and notice that the answer sheet says forty-one, you're in trouble. It pays to double-check the numbers—especially if you skip any questions.

Know your calculator. Virtually any four-function, scientific, or graphing calculator can be used for the PSAT, ACT, SAT, and SAT Math IC and 2C. Nothing fancy here—all you'll need are simple functions. Just be sure you have plenty of practice with it, so as to avoid wasting time.

Guessing is good. If you can eliminate even one wrong answer, you should guess. Since you get one point for every right answer and lose only a quarter of a point for each wrong one, educated guessing raises your score. Random guessing neither helps nor hurts on the SAT. By contrast, the ACT has no penalty for wrong answers and thus even random guessing helps.

Watch for tricks. If you find a question that appears strangely easy—especially after a string of hard ones—it is probably a trap. This is especially true in math, where every question assesses a concept or thought process. If you find yourself saying, "Ahh, that's what they want," you're probably on the right track.

Pace Yourself. Standardized tests reward speedy thinking. Some students read and think faster than others, but everybody can improve their speed if they work at it.

Experiment with skipping hard problems and moving faster on easy ones. Find your comfort zone.

Practice, practice, practice. No matter what any test-taking guru says, taking full-length practice tests is the biggest key to success. Analyze your strengths and weaknesses. Learn by doing.

Taking the Tests

Here is a brief description of what to keep in mind as you approach the tests:

PSAT The PSAT includes Writing, Critical Reading, and Math sections. The Writing section features multiple-choice questions that ask students to correct and improve sentences and paragraphs but does not include an essay. Critical Reading is an update of the old Verbal section—minus the dreaded analogy questions. In their place, students must cope with more reading comprehension, including new short passages of about one hundred words to go with the traditional longer passages. The Math section has been beefed up with more advanced topics from geometry, algebra, and statistics, though the material is not as difficult as that on the SAT. For most applicants, the PSAT is merely for practice. But the test carries added significance as the gateway to the National Merit Scholarship Program. Eleventh graders who score in their state's top 4 percent (more or less) are eligible for recognition and possibly a scholarship. Most of these

> **Some Are Pickier Than Others**
>
> Top colleges will accept the ACT in lieu of the SAT but they vary as to whether the ACT can replace the SAT Subject Tests.

students will receive a letter of commendation congratulating them on their high score. But approximately fifteen thousand of the highest scorers, chosen on a state-by-state basis, are designated as National Merit semifinalists and move on in the competition. After completing an application that includes their grades and an essay, approximately 90 percent of the semi-finalists advance to finalist status. From there, just over half of the finalists will receive scholarships. National Merit itself awards scholarships of two thousand dollars to the highest scorers among the finalists. Major corporations award scholarships to finalists who typically are the sons and daughters of employees. Many colleges also make generous awards to finalists who enroll, though the nation's most selective colleges generally do not make such awards.

The PSAT is also linked to separate recognition programs for African Americans and Hispanics.

SAT The SAT also includes Writing, Critical Reading, and Math. The Writing section features a twenty-five minute essay along with multiple-choice questions that ask students to correct and improve sentences and paragraphs. As with the PSAT, the Critical Reading section no longer has analogy questions, meaning less emphasis on vocabulary, and adds more reading comprehension, including new short passages. Reading comprehension often boils down to a test of concentration, a skill you can improve with focused practice. Applicants who do poorly often suffer from the I-just-read-the-paragraph-and-don't-remember-a-word syndrome. The new Math section includes a variety of topics normally taught in algebra II. Though some of the math will be more advanced, the questions won't necessarily be harder. On the old SAT, many of the toughest questions were rooted in simple math. The new SAT Math places more emphasis on knowing the material than sniffing out tricks.

One of the reasons that many students struggle with the SAT is the prevalence of what test-makers mischievously call "distracters"—wrong answers dressed up to look like the correct ones. In a math problem, for instance, a distracter might be a value obtained by an intermediate step on the way to finding the real answer. For a problem with an answer of .15, a distracter would be 1.5 or .015.

For a complete overview of the SAT, see *Fiske Nailing the New SAT*.

ACT   Since the ACT includes four subject areas, diagnosis of your strengths and weaknesses is key. Relative to the SAT, the ACT emphasizes knowledge more than critical thinking and has fewer distracters to throw students off track. By taking practice tests, you can identify areas where you need to brush up. The English section stresses the mechanics of language with fewer mind-bending riddles and less difficult vocabulary. The math questions require ability to plug into formulas and, unlike the SAT, include a touch of trigonometry in addition to algebra and geometry. The reading section includes four long passages. Of all the sections of the ACT, science is the one that most often throws students for a loop. Hint: do not attempt to read the graphs and other information before answering the questions. Students who do so rarely have time to finish. Instead, go directly to the questions and refer to the accompanying information on an as-needed basis. Finishing on time can be a challenge, so be sure to practice under timed conditions. Answer every question since there is no scoring penalty for a wrong answer. Students are allowed 30 minutes to complete ACT's optional essay.

Most students take the ACT in February, April, or June of the junior year, with a second administration in October or December if necessary.

SAT vs. ACT: What's the Difference?

	SAT	**ACT**
Dominant region:	East Coast, West Coast	interior of the country
Subjects:	Writing 33%, Reading 33%, Math 33%	English 25%, Math 25%, Reading 25%, Science 25%
Math emphasis:	problem-solving	knowing the formula
Verbal emphasis:	reading, logic	reading, grammar, usage
Essay:	required	optional
Test's personality:	tricky	straightforward
Scored with:	guessing penalty	no guessing penalty

SAT Subject Tests Timing is the secret to doing your best on the SAT Subject Tests. Since the tests cover academic subjects, the best time to take them is at the end of the most relevant course. Though you can take up to three Subject Tests at a single administration, the many students like to spread them out to ensure adequate preparation and to avoid fatigue.

The best place to begin preparation is often The College Board's *Official Guide to the SAT Subject Tests*. This book includes sample problems from each test and is especially handy for students who haven't decided which ones to take and want to gauge their preparation in each subject. For more in-depth coverage, books devoted to each Subject Test are available.

SAT: Subject Tests

Literature	French***
U.S. History	German***
World History	Modern Hebrew
Math Level I	Italian
Math Level II	Japanese**
Biology E/M*	Korean**
Chemistry	Latin
Physics	Spanish***
Chinese**	

*Students may choose either an ecological or molecular emphasis.
**These tests include a listening component administered via audio cassette.
***These tests may be taken with or without a listening component.

Registration and Score Reporting

Standardized testing can be an ordeal even before the dreaded day arrives. Both the SAT and the ACT require students to register approximately five weeks in advance, either via a paper form available in high school guidance offices or online at www.collegeboard.com or www.act.org. (For the PSAT and PLAN, see your guidance counselor.) The deadlines are published months in advance, but even conscientious students can find themselves scrambling on deadline day. After students have taken the tests once, it is possible to reregister by phone for an extra ten dollars, though the lines are often busy at the last minute. Students who miss the deadline have an interval of about ten days in which they can register late—for a fee. For those who totally space out, both the SAT and ACT offer a stand-by option (at an additional charge of about thirty dollars) in which students can show up at a test site with a check and a completed registration form and take the test on a space-available basis.

After a student takes the SAT or ACT, score reports go to both the student and the colleges within about four weeks. It is not possible to speed up the initial reporting process, but students can request that scores from previous test dates be rush reported to colleges in as little as two business days. (Fees for various options range from ten to twenty dollars.) We recommend that students verify with the colleges that a rush is necessary before laying the money down.

Those for whom test prep has become a neurotic obsession—or a parental crusade—are advised to chill out.

Big Bucks and Bigger Promises

Now that the basics of testing and test prep are out of the way, we come to the punch line of this chapter: whether to spend between five hundred and one thousand dollars (or more) for a class with a coaching firm. At some private high schools, well over half the students sign up. Only you can decide if a prep course is worth the price. We think the answer is often found in careful reflection about your motives and how you learn best.

There are two gremlins that test-prep agencies count on to deliver most of their customers: fear and guilt. The fear is that the boy next door will get ahead of you because he is prepping and the guilt is what your parents would feel if they didn't do everything possible to help you get in. Even though they may be uncertain of the benefits, many families succumb to the philosophy of "it can't hurt." But an extra thousand dollars seems a lot to pay for peace of mind, especially when you can buy the book that includes all the techniques for about twenty dollars.

We confess that we are not neutral observers in the test prep debate. As part of our research for *Fiske Nailing the New SAT*, we surveyed over eight hundred students from coast to coast and were interested to find that students who prepared on their own actually scored higher than those who got face-to-face coaching for the SAT. Part of the reason, we think, is that students who prepare on their own are more likely to take control of their preparation and develop a strategy that fits their test-taking style. *Fiske Nailing the New SAT* offers a blue-print for preparing without an expensive course, including how to zero in on your strengths and weaknesses, and how to fine-tune the pace at which you take the test.

Our opinions aside, we recognize that prep courses are unlikely to go away any time soon, and that some students may reap significant benefits. Likely candidates for a prep course include:

Students who are enthusiastic about a prep course. Improvement is unlikely when mom and dad are the ones pushing the prep course.

Students with room for improvement. If you are a reasonably good student but score low on standardized tests, a prep course could help you adjust your approach to taking the tests.

Students with mediocre preparation. If you have trouble with the material on the test—especially the math—a one-on-one tutor may be your best bet.

Students who learn best with adult direction. These include step-by-step learners who like to ask questions and students who need help in staying focused.

Before you sign up at a particular agency, find out exactly what you'll be learning. The most effective courses emphasize practice tests and keep teacher talk to a minimum. Be sure to meet your instructor before signing on the dotted line; the national reputation of a test prep company means little if your instructor is a mumbler. Pay no attention to guarantees. These merely mean that if your scores don't improve, you get a free second helping of what didn't work the first time. If you're thinking seriously about a coaching course, try to take it before your first test date. That way, you'll avoid an upward blip in your score between the first and second time you take it.

The students in our survey reported that the main benefit of a prep course was to have an adult on hand to force them to take practice tests. Put your money down if you like, but rest assured that most students can do it on their own. The right preparation has the potential to make a big difference in your scores, but the key is not how much you pay, but how hard—and smart—you work.

How Many Times Should I Take the SAT?

Either two or three times. Because of the standard error of measurement (SEM), once is generally not enough (unless you shoot the moon). Since most colleges consider your highest scores on the Writing, Critical Reading, and Math sections—even if those scores come on different dates—we believe that ambitious students should consider taking it three times. Taking it four times is over the top; the odds of a significant improvement on your fourth time are low, and you risk looking like an obsessed geek with nothing better to do than worry about your SAT scores. Two times is generally enough for the ACT, unless you have reason to believe that you can improve your score on the third try.

12. The Early Decision Dilemma

Early decision is a hot topic among today's college applicants. Faced with increasingly long odds for admission to the nation's elite schools, many students are trying to get a jump on the competition with an early application. At many Eastern prep schools, the majority of students apply early and the trend has taken hold in all corners of the country. Should I apply early? Will it help my chances? What if I get deferred? Inquiring applicants want to know.

The early programs come in two basic varieties: early decision (ED) and early action (EA). Both require students to apply by an early deadline, generally between November 1 and December 15. The college generally renders a decision between December 15 and February 1. (A few colleges offer a second round of Early Decision, with deadlines in January or February.) Borderline applicants in the early pool are generally "deferred" for consideration with the regular applicant pool. The key difference between the two—grab your highlighter—is that early decision entails a binding commitment to enroll if accepted, while early action does not. Early decision is the more common of the two; of the three hundred colleges in the *Fiske Guide to Colleges*, roughly half offer early decision, while about 30 percent provide an early action program.

> **Don't Count on Getting In**
>
> After filing an early application, students should continue investigating other colleges and working on applications. Those who do not, risk finding themselves behind the 8-ball if a deferral or denial comes back in mid-December.

Early programs have come under widespread criticism in recent years from those who believe that such programs make the admission process more pressured. Early decision has drawn particular scrutiny because of the binding commitment to enroll if admitted. A number of high-profile institutions, including Yale and Stanford, have abandoned early decision in favor of early action. "Early decision programs help colleges more than applicants," declared Yale's president in announcing the change. "It is our hope to take pressure off students in the early cycle."

Harvard, Princeton, and the University of Virginia have taken it a step further, eliminating all early admission programs in favor of one deadline for all students. Nevertheless, both ED and EA will remain part of the admissions landscape for the foreseeable future.

From the applicant perspective, early action is generally a no-brainer. If you're interested in a college that offers EA, you might as well do it. You will have until May 1 to make a final decision and can consider other offers in the interval. Most of this chapter is about the pros and cons of applying via early decision. A lot of hype has gone into promoting it. And yes, ED usually gives you a boost in admissions. Though ED is right for some students, it is definitely the wrong move for others. We begin with an examination of the colleges' motives and then outline some of the pros and cons.

Why the Colleges Want You (To Apply ED)

Appearances to the contrary, the colleges do not offer early decision merely to ease the stress in your life as a college applicant. Like glossy brochures and "cooked" SAT profiles, early decision is a way for the colleges to compete for students. At most colleges, less than half of those admitted by regular decision choose to enroll. With students applying to more and more schools, the percentage has been has been on a steady decline. Colleges know that ED applicants are in the bag, helping them to predict and control both the size and quality of their enrollment.

Another trade secret: early decision allows colleges to

make themselves appear more selective. The more students a college accepts ED, the fewer acceptances it needs to mail out to fill the rest of its class. If 100 percent of the ED applicants enroll and only 50 percent of the regular applicants enroll, a college would need to send twice as many acceptances to the regular applicants to get the same enrollment.

An additional motive is the fact that most ED applicants tend to be excellent students from upper-income brackets whose families will have no problem footing the bill. These students are more likely to come from high-powered schools that prime them to apply for early decision. Most colleges jump at the chance to lock in ED students who will not need financial aid.

With all these incentives, it is hardly surprising that colleges have been adding early-decision options left and right. It goes without saying that applicants should be wary of the hard sell. The more desperate the college is for students, the more arm twisting you're likely to get.

Early Decision Balance Sheet
Pitfalls

From the moment you mail the application, there's no turning back. You can apply ED to only one school and, if it accepts you, all other applications must be withdrawn. The only exception is when the college's financial aid award does not, in the family's judgment, make it possible for you to attend. If you try to wriggle out of an early decision commitment for any other reason, you'll excite the wrath of the jilted college, which might try to locate your new suitor school and inform it of your shenanigans. If that happens, both colleges might rescind their offers.

Unfortunately, many students are stampeded into applying early instead of making a well-informed choice. "Along about mid-October, something I call early fever hits," says Wynne Curry, a college counselor at Seven Hills School in

Cincinnati. "The seniors get very nervous and think, 'Oh, I should be applying somewhere early.'" The logic should be reversed. Only after a clear first choice has emerged should students consider ED. Even when applicants do think carefully about ED, it shortens the time they get to weigh their options. The six-month period between November and April is a long time.

Another pitfall regards financial aid. At a time when financial-aid packages are highly negotiable, ED prevents applicants from seeing more than one offer. The colleges use merit scholarships as recruiting tools, so they have little incentive to offer them to ED students.

Applicants should avoid the first round of early decision if there is a good chance that their credentials will improve during the first semester of your senior year. This includes anyone who is expecting (or hoping) to make better grades or improve standardized test scores.

Benefits

If you really do have a foolproof, ironclad, cross-your-heart-and-hope-to-die first choice, early decision is worth considering. ED began as a way to help applicants avoid five months of nail biting between filing an application and receiving a decision. When you have an acceptance from First Choice U. in hand, the second semester can be a joyous time instead of a countdown to Judgment Day.

On a more practical level, ED will give you a slight advantage at highly selective schools and a significant advantage at less selective ones. "Applying early really can make a difference, especially if you're a perfectly qualified applicant, but don't have a hook to single you out," says college consultant Susan Case. Colleges also value what one admissions dean calls "the loyalty factor." They would much prefer to enroll students who really want to be there (as demonstrated by an early commitment) rather than others who come only because they were denied admission at other schools. As a rule, the lower the college's yield on accepted applicants (the percentage of those accepted who actually enroll), the bigger the boost your admission chances will be given when you apply early.

A few candidates will find a financial aid bonus from applying early. Some colleges unable to meet the full need of all their applicants will give first dibs on financial aid money to those admitted ED. From a financial point of view, ED can be helpful if you get one of these deals. If not, it could be a bad move.

To sum up, early decision is probably a good idea for borderline students with low financial need who have a clear first choice. Others should be more cautious.

Early Action

If you're applying to a school that offers early action instead of early decision, you're probably wondering if you'll also be more likely to get in. Usually not. Because early action entails no commitment to enroll, it generally gives little advantage in admissions. But EA students are often first in line for merit scholarships, housing, and other considerations that go to accepted applicants.

The number of schools offering early action has grown in recent years. Along with Yale and Stanford, big name schools include Boston College, the University of Chicago, Georgetown, MIT, and Notre Dame. Interest in early action at these schools has exploded in recent years, but be warned that the competition in early action pools at highly selective institutions is generally tougher than in the regular one. Also, be aware that some early action colleges now ask that students apply early only to their institution, though students can still apply regular-decision to any institution they please.

Early action programs are also becoming more widespread at state universities seeking to get their share of the top applicants. Often, the early deadlines correspond to those for lucrative scholarships. Such is the case at the University of North Carolina–Chapel Hill and the University of Maryland–College Park; among private universities, Boston College has a merit scholarship available only to early action applicants.

Timetable for First-Round Early Decision and Early Action

Junior Year

January–May: Take ACT and/or SAT.

Do college visits during Spring Break if possible.

Work hard! The junior year will be the last included in your transcript before decision time.

May–June: If required, take SAT Subject Tests.

Senior Year

September–October: Work on applications. Give teacher recommendation forms to teachers. File early decision or early action applications according to deadlines. Take SAT or ACT if necessary. October is the last test date that will make scores available in time for first-round programs. If necessary, register to receive the CSS/Financial Aid PROFILE via a form from the high school guidance office or register online at www.collegeboard.com.

November: Continue filing early decision or early action applications. Follow up with teacher recommendations. Continue working on regular decision applications and taking standardized tests. File the PROFILE form, if necessary.

Deferral

Early applicants dread getting deferred and with good reason. After waiting anxiously for word from the early round, they find out that the agony will go on for up to four more months until decision letters come for the regular application pool. Furthermore, deferred applicants often face long odds of ultimately being admitted—lower than one in ten at highly selective institutions. The main priority for deferred students is to focus on other applications, at least for a few weeks until the news sinks in.

The amount of hope that can be salvaged from a deferral depends partly on the college's policy. A few institutions, such as Northwestern University, don't defer anyone from the early round. Other schools defer every early applicant with a ghost of a chance for admission or give let-'em-down-easy deferrals that merely string out the process until the inevitable denial. Still other colleges make an effort to defer only realistic candidates, but uncertainty about the size of the regular applicant pool drives most schools to defer many more students than will have a serious chance in a normal admissions year. When a college gets fewer regular applicants than it is expecting, that's a plus for the deferred group.

The amount of hope that can be salvaged from a deferral depends partly on the college's policy.

Other factors can come into play. Early decision candidates are likely to find themselves competing with a slightly stronger applicant pool in the regular round. And because they've already been considered once, their applications generally go to the back burner until near the end of the process. On the other hand, colleges know that deferred early decision candidates generally enroll if accepted, a significant factor, especially on the waitlist. If an application has won support from a particular admissions officer in the early round, that person may push it over the top in the regular round.

To maintain their chances for admission, deferred students should continue to express interest and submit any favorable new information about grades and extracurriculars.

An additional recommendation also helps if there is a teacher who can shed new light on the applicant.

Start Early

Though it is hard to give definitive advice about early decision and early action, one thing is certain. An early start is crucial! Only students who have thoroughly investigated colleges and completed most standardized testing by the end of eleventh grade will be in a strong position to consider an early application.

13. How to Size Up a Campus

Visiting campuses should be the most exciting stage of the college search. After months of hearing secondhand reports, this is your chance to see real college students in their native habitat and get a taste of the lifestyle that awaits you after high school.

College visiting is more an art than a science. Some people have a revelation the moment they set foot on the "right" campus; others keep a methodical checklist to analyze their impressions carefully. The only ironclad rule is to keep your eyes and ears open—you may not know what you're looking for until it hits you in the face.

Plan Ahead

The first step to a successful visit is to make plans early. Since interview schedules at popular schools fill up fast, you should call as far ahead of time as possible to make an appointment. (A note to the faint of heart: It's your visit, so you should make the call, not your parents.) If the school does not give campus interviews, no sweat. You can still get the tour schedule and most colleges host information sessions with admissions officers at least once a day during peak visit times. If you're visiting during the school year and would like to stay a night in the dorms, ask now. You may also want to find out about nearby hotels, as well as driving times and directions to other schools on your itinerary. If you're an aspiring varsity athlete, see if it is possible to meet with a coach. Those with particular academic interests should ask about attending a class in that area or meeting with a professor. Small colleges will be more likely to accommodate requests such as these, but it never hurts to ask.

We recommend that you begin visits in the winter and spring of your junior year and continue them through the summer and fall. Though it's best to visit when classes are in session, many families find that the summer is the only convenient time to visit faraway colleges. A summer visit is better than no visit at all, but keep in mind that the tanned bodies frolicking on the lawns are probably summer school impostors—maybe even high school students. If you see a campus in the summer that you really like, try to get back to it while classes are in session before making a final decision.

A College Visit Appetizer

During your first few college visits, try to sample different kinds of schools, including a small one, a big one, an urban one, a rural one, and so on. An early smorgasbord of the different types can help you sort out your likes and dislikes.

Friday is generally the best day of the week to visit, since you can sample both weekday and weekend activity. Try to avoid exam periods—everyone you meet will be going nuts—and also steer clear of the first week of school in the fall. Though it is natural to want to fit in as many colleges as possible, limit yourself to no more than two per day. Trying to cram in too many, says William Hiss of Bates College, usually results in a student "screaming at Mother or Father to hurry up and find the college when they are lost and five minutes late for the interview." Since the college visit puts your family relationships on public display, avoid any situation that is likely to create tension between you and your parents.

If you live near the college you are considering, you may have the luxury of visiting more than once. If so, our advice is to go the first time with your parents to get the standard information from the admissions office and then go again on your own to stay overnight in the dorms and sample student life.

As the visit approaches, do some hard thinking about what is most important to you in a college. Is the quality of the History Department really such a big deal to you? Are you dead set on going to a school with a strong Greek system? Do drama facilities still loom as large in your mind as they did six months ago? Once you've settled on some criteria, make a list of the questions you want answered and establish a uniform way of recording your impressions so you can compare different schools on key points.

Cutting through the Hype (Again)

On the appointed day, leave early and allow plenty of time to get there, especially if you have any appointments (see Chapter 14: Surviving the Interview). Once you've gotten those out of the way, take a campus tour. It will probably be led by a student, though by no means a typical one. The smiling, affable, oh-so-polite representatives that most colleges recruit as tour guides can lay it on pretty thick. See if your tour guide admits to anything negative; that should give you a good idea of how much of the positive stuff you can believe. Whether or not your guide is completely candid, the tour is valuable because it offers one student's perspective on the college, which you can compare with that of your interviewer or anyone else you happen to meet.

Though listening to the tour guide's monologue is helpful, even more valuable is the chance to engage him or her in conversation. Unfortunately, most high school students seem to develop a sudden case of laryngitis during a campus tour. But why let the pushy mothers have all the fun? Step to the front of the crowd and ask a question! What are the dorms like? Where do people go to have a good time? What are the biggest issues on campus? Don't be afraid to dig beyond the stock answers. If the tour guide boasts about the university's electron microscope, find out if undergraduates get to use it. If the guide says the new gym is state-of-the-art, ask if intramural athletes get the same access as the varsity teams.

There are dozens of questions that you could ask. The box below gives five we think will be especially revealing.

Five Good Questions to Ask Your Tour Guide

Who will teach me next year? At many universities, senior faculty teach mainly graduate students and upperclassmen. Find out who teaches the general education courses that all students must take during their freshman and sophomore years.

How big are the freshman classes? Forget about student-faculty ratios. Find out how big your classes will be during your first year.

What happens on a typical weekend? This will give you a sense of the overall character of the student body, as well as the range of options that would be open to you as a student.

What issues do students talk about? Casual conversation says a lot about the intellectual atmosphere of a college. Political and social issues play a key role in student life at some and are hardly ever mentioned at others. Find out if students would rather talk about the president's economic policy or the fraternity house's beer bash.

What are this college's biggest drawbacks? Honest or not, the answer should be interesting.

Keep Your Eyes Peeled

In addition to being a good question-and-answer session, the tour will give you a sense of the layout of the campus and the rhythms of a typical day. Pay attention to bulletin boards; they will give you a good idea of what is going on. Be sure to ask the guide about any facilities you expected to see if they are not on the route. At the least, the guide can point them out to you on a campus map.

After finishing the standard tour, leave time to roam the campus on your own. This is no time for bashfulness.

Corner some students and see if their answers match the ones you got from the tour guide. "Honesty will prevail... whether we in admissions like it or not," says Martha Quirk of Principia College.

Obvious places to roam include libraries, classrooms, the dorms, and the student center or central gathering place. See if you can feel the pulse of the campus. Do the students seem friendly? Intellectual? Jocky? Are they radical chic? Or does it feel like you've just stumbled onto the set of *Revenge of the Nerds*?

Things to Notice on Campus

Buildings in disrepair: A signal of financial problems. One good place to check out: the bathrooms.

New construction: A sign of financial health and a statement of the college's plan for the future.

Seating in the cafeteria: Are students sitting at the same tables with faculty members? Blacks with whites? A good indication of social relationships on campus.

Computers: How up-to-date are the computer labs? How is access to them controlled? Are all dorm rooms wired for the Internet?

Size of classrooms: Lots of lecture halls suggest big classes. Lots of seminar rooms means a more personal approach.

Bulletin boards: The single best authority on what students care about.

Sit in on a class, eat a meal in the dining hall, go to a sports event. Are these your kind of people? "I usually tell students to look for the intangibles: friendliness of the students, interaction of faculty and students, excitement in the classroom," says one admissions officer. In the end, your gut feeling is probably more important than all the checklists and departmental rankings put together.

Though sizing up the people should be your main priority, pay attention to the buildings, too. Peeling paint and disrepair are signs of a college with financial problems, while new construction is a sign of health. Are the buildings modern and up-to-date? Because of advances in design, new buildings are likely to be far superior to ones that are decades old. A science facility from the 1950s, for instance, might consist of one long hall with conventional labs on either side and professors' offices in a separate wing. New ones often include faculty offices interspersed with laboratories, adjacent seminar rooms to promote discussion, and various nooks and crannies for student use. Does the student center include a modern food court with twelve different restaurant choices? Or is it a conventional snack bar? Check out the student fitness facilities. Many universities offer the same amenities as a modern health club. The quality of facilities is one area in which the nation's most prestigious colleges can suffer by comparison—shackled as many of them are to decades-old buildings.

Sample the Night Life

If you stay in a dorm, your hosts will be a goldmine of information. Get them to show you around and compare what you see with what you were shown on your official tour. If you're interested in a particular program, ask if they can introduce you to a friend who is enrolled in it.

In the evening, relax and hang out with whoever happens to be in the dorm. Apply what Phil Smith, former dean of admissions at Williams College, calls "the 10:30 test." Says he, "Almost all college students get hungry around 10:30 PM. Between then and midnight tends to be 'people time.'

Find out what students are talking about, how they treat one another, the depth of their concerns." Try to stay up for as much of it as you can. Sometimes the most interesting conversations don't really get started until after midnight.

As the visit draws to a close, be sure to get your thoughts down on paper while they're still fresh in your mind. Note all the particulars about the academic programs and facilities, but also remember the big picture. Above all, trust *If you stay in a dorm, your hosts will be a goldmine of information.* your instincts about the people and the place. Can you see yourself as a student? Are these the kind of people you want for friends? Four years is a long time.

14. Surviving the Interview

It is a scene every college applicant dreads: the awkward quiet of an admissions office waiting room filled with nervous students and parents awaiting the call from within. Mother leans over to straighten your collar as you stare blankly at the pages of a catalog. The wait seems like an eternity, but finally an admissions officer beckons and ushers you into her office. After a brief exchange of pleasantries, she asks what books you have read lately. "None!" you blurt out. "I hate reading!" With that, you leap to your feet, lift your chair high in the air, and smash it to splinters on top of her desk. As she flees the room in terror, you watch her with a fiendish gleam in your eye, and laugh and laugh and laugh...

Fortunately for those with an active imagination, few applicants actually go berserk in the interview. What's more, the interview isn't nearly as important in the admissions process as most people seem to think.

Most of the time, interviewers are more intent on making a good impression themselves than evaluating the applicant. Some schools require or recommend interviews merely to make sure applicants come to the campus—those who do are much more likely to enroll. Even colleges that do use interviews to evaluate applicants realize that twenty minutes of chitchat may not reveal much about the real you, especially if you're nervous. When it does count, the interview almost always works in your favor by putting a human face on your application. As James Holmes of Washington College notes, "It's rare that someone shoots himself in the foot with some horrendous blunder." Merely showing up is a point in your favor because it demonstrates interest.

Before you hit the panic button about the interview, check with the admissions office to find out their policy. Are the interviews strictly informational or are they used in making decisions? A growing number of schools, including most large universities and some small institutions, don't even offer campus interviews. With the recent deluge in applications, they simply do not have the time. Bear in mind that the interview isn't so much a judgment of you as it is one more step in a matchmaking process. "Treat it as an opportunity to discover whether or not the institution is right for you, not as an obstacle to be overcome," counsels Steven Syverson of Lawrence University.

If you're still suffering from those pre-interview jitters, here are some tips for putting your best foot forward.

Try to Relax

On the day of the interview, your first dilemma will be picking what to wear. Be comfortable, but dress nicely. You won't need Dad's oversized three-piece suit, but neither should you show up looking like a beach bum. Proper interview attire balances respect for the occasion with the fact that you are a seventeen-year-old.

The first secret to a successful interview is getting there on time. If this is your first visit to the admissions office, leave an extra half hour to get lost on the way. If you do happen to be late, get a grip. Most admissions officers have flexibility in their schedules and won't mind.

The interviewer knows you are going to be nervous and he or she will almost never hold it against you. Indeed, a little nervousness can actually work in your favor. The fact that you care enough to be nervous will endear you to most interviewers. If you feel the need, say so out loud: "I'm a little nervous because I really want to come here." Nervousness is bad only when it causes you to clam up—or worse, to adopt a posture of cool indifference. When in doubt, be open.

Ninety-nine times out of a hundred, the admissions officer will do his or her best to put you at ease.

After the initial pleasantries, there is one major rule to good interviewing: have a conversation. Get to know the interviewer, maintain eye contact, and be responsive. Most students come into interviews like robots programmed to talk nonstop for forty-five minutes and then self-destruct. Better to muster the presence of mind to listen and react spontaneously.

Interviewers come in two basic varieties: talkers and listeners. The talkers are generally more intent on selling their college than on listening to anything you have to say. Don't be frustrated if you have trouble getting a word in edgewise. Affirm what the interviewer says and use openings in the conversation to get your questions answered. If you play the role of interested customer, this sort of interviewer will respond favorably.

The majority of college interviewers are listeners—that is, they view their primary task as getting you to open up about yourself, your ideas, your hopes and dreams. They generally probe for topics that seem to excite passion or interest, while giving you the openings to take the conversation wherever you choose.

We recommend that you go to every interview prepared to discuss at least two or three topics at length. Examples might include your school, your favorite academic subject, important extracurricular activities, current events, or your favorite book. Think carefully about your opinions, how you got them, and what the subject means to you. Many interviewers will use an extended conversation on one subject to measure the depth of your thinking. Be careful not to misrepresent yourself. If you say current events are one of your biggest interests, don't come up blank when the conversation turns to the latest Arab–Israeli peace talks.

> **Practice Makes Perfect**
>
> Never schedule your first interview at one of your top-choice schools. Instead, practice your technique at one or two less-desired options before making a date with First Choice U.

No matter who your interviewer is, don't forget to do your homework on the college ahead of time. Well-prepared interviewees should come armed with at least three questions. Good questions, mind you. While an admissions officer is likely to be impressed by a insightful question, he is just as likely to be turned off by a stupid one ("Do you have a business department?") that is answered on the first page of the viewbook. By asking intelligent questions, you let the admissions officer know that you are serious about the matchmaking process. That alone is a big point in your favor.

Expect Probing Questions

Though most interviewers will let you take the initiative, don't be surprised if you find yourself on the receiving end of one of these time-honored zingers:

What books have you read lately? Try to avoid the usual high school staples like *Lord of the Flies* or *The Scarlet Letter*. Since part of the purpose is to gauge your initiative and creativity, it is generally best to pick a book you found on your own, rather than one that has been assigned. (On the other hand, *The Scarlet Letter* is probably better than *The Michael Jordan Story* or *Paris Hilton: The Untold Story*.) Choose a book that really excites you and that you wouldn't mind discussing at length. An in-depth talk about a book you know well will almost always impress an interviewer. By the same token, if you try to wing it, you'll look like a liar and an idiot at the same time.

Why do you want to enroll here? The trick is to cite at least two or three reasons. Read the college's literature and mention what you've found there—diversity, academic excellence, and so on. Mix that with some reasons of your own, like the fact that it is strong in the

Good Questions to Ask Your Interviewer

What is distinctive about your school? Try to get beyond the usual platitudes about academic excellence. Each school has a different idea of its mission, which tells you a lot about its character.

What sets students here apart from those at similar schools? If this is Yale, ask about the differences from Harvard or Princeton. You'll probably be considering those competing schools (and the interviewer will know it). Try to zero in on where each one stands in relation to the others.

What percentage of entering students graduate within five years? Anything above 85 percent is high; below 60 percent is low. (The rate tends to be somewhat lower at public institutions.) As a follow-up, ask about the main reasons why students leave without graduating.

What are the most common career paths for graduates? Find out whether the aspirations of past graduates match yours. Is this school a feeder for Wall Street or does everyone want to join the Peace Corps after graduation?

Would I have been accepted last year? Whether or not you get into a selective college depends mainly on whom you're competing against. Since admissions officers can't predict the exact mix of applicants in any given year, asking about last year makes it easier for them to assess your chances.

natural sciences or has good performing arts facilities. Strike a balance between the things you are interested in and the things the college is trying to sell you on.

What are your most important activities and why are they valuable? Think this out before the interview and resist the temptation to be too grandiose. Standard answers that cite benefits such as increased self-discipline and experience working with others are fine. If you can think of something more extraordinary—an experience that has transformed your life—so much the better.

What would you add to life at this college? This one is a favorite at highly selective colleges. Hint: List some of the ways that you would affect the lives of others in the community. The purpose of the question is to find out how much you would give of yourself to those around you. Colleges want givers.

What other colleges are you considering? This one is loaded. On the one hand, your list will tell the college something about you and your interests. Your interviewer will know all about the other schools and will be impressed if you can explain your choices cogently. If the list includes colleges that are radically different from one another, explain. Otherwise, it will appear that you haven't done a very good job researching.

On the other hand, the list will give the interviewer an idea of whether his or her college is your first choice—something uppermost in the minds of admissions officers at schools that are usually safeties. If the college is your first choice, stress that fact. If it's your safety, be a little vague. It is always best to give the impression that the college is under serious consideration.

Keep Your Cool and Be Yourself

If—God forbid—something does happen, have a sense of humor. This worked for at least one stressed-out applicant to Franklin and Marshall College, who, sitting with her legs crossed, was so nervous that she kept swinging her foot back and forth. It just so happened that she was wearing wooden clogs. On a particularly long swing, the clog flew off, hit the admissions officer in the head, *"She looked at him in terror, but when their glances met, they both dissolved in laughter."* and then ricocheted off his desk lamp, breaking it. "She looked at him in terror, but when their glances met, they both dissolved in laughter," recalls Ronald Potier. No big deal.

The interview is also a good time to introduce ticklish subjects head on. Too many applicants try to paper over problems because they think colleges are looking for perfect applicants. In reality, college interviewers tend to be impressed by students who are mature enough to be candid about the obstacles they have overcome.

The worst thing you can do is to leave a dip in performance unexplained. If, for instance, you had a poor sophomore year because of switching to a new school, the interview is an excellent time to tell your story. If you have a learning disability that has meant lower grades in certain subjects, say so, and then explain the steps you have taken to compensate and how you plan to cope in college.

In cases like these, applicants should consider bringing a transcript to show what they are talking about. A transcript can also be useful if you are particularly interested in an assessment of your admission chances. In most other situations, a transcript is not necessary. The whole purpose of the interview is to reveal things not included in all the paper that will accompany your application.

Post-Interview Stress Syndrome

One applicant to Haverford College was particularly stressed out at the conclusion of his interview. On his way back to the waiting room, he opened a series of doors. Upon reaching the waiting room, he was too nervous to notice and instead opened one more door—and walked into a closet. He was so embarrassed that he simply stayed there. "It was some minutes before he came out to face the room full of people staring at him," recalls the admissions officer.

Though parents can be very helpful on a college visit, make sure they do not venture into the interview room. Though they mean well, parents can do nothing to help the situation—and plenty to mess it up. They're generally more nervous than you are and they tend to babble. Suggest that they take a tour or get lunch while you're in the interview. If they want to come back at the end for a question or two in the waiting room, that's perfectly okay (but only after you've had your thirty minutes alone with the admissions officer). Above all, don't have a family squabble in the presence of your interviewer. If you roll your eyes at something your mom says, you are broadcasting your immaturity for everyone to see. Even if she says the stupidest thing you've ever heard (a strong possibility), just keep your cool.

When D day arrives, resist the temptation to try too hard. This is no time to create an artificial personality or market yourself as something you're not. "Sometimes applicants are obviously coached," cautions one admissions director. "Their 'image' is overplayed and it looks and feels uncomfortable." Nothing is more irritating than a seventeen-year-old who acts as if he or she has all the answers. Though preparation is important, the golden rule for good interviewing is really quite simple: Be yourself.

15. Getting Good Recommendations

There is a rule of thumb among admissions officers: "The thicker the file, the thicker the applicant." What that means, in practical terms, is that if you're thinking of padding your application with a few recommendations from well-placed friends of the family, think again. "Each year we run an informal contest to determine the candidate with the most superfluous recommendations," reports one admissions dean. "This year's winner had twenty-three and he was denied."

Don't misunderstand. Recommendations can be useful, but only if they come from people who know you well. "Letters of recommendation matter because of substance, not because of who is writing them," says Christoph Guttentag of Duke University. A good letter will tell the admissions committee something about you as a person that comes out nowhere else in the application—your willingness to work hard, perhaps, or your ability to listen to good advice and then use it. Recommendations that begin with phrases like, "I don't know Susie personally, but if she is anything like her parents..." are a cinch to start eyes rolling.

Accent on Academics

To get good recommendations, find people who are familiar with your goals and aspirations and can write about you in vivid detail. You usually won't be able to look at the recommendations before they're sent, so choose carefully. Most selective colleges require at least one recommendation from a teacher. Since colleges want to know what you have done lately, try to pick teachers who have taught you in your junior or senior year.

English teachers tend to write well, so they are usually a good bet. To round out the picture, consider a second recommender in math, science, or a foreign language. An academic teacher who has also known you outside the classroom is generally the best choice, but try to avoid coaches or teachers of fluffy electives. Even if you are pals with the yearbook sponsor, your math teacher is likely to have more clout with an admissions office.

Your Rights under the Buckley Amendment

You might not know it, but, because of an act of Congress, you have the right to look at your recommendations after they are filed at the colleges. The issue is complex, dealing with the limits of your right to privacy, but the upshot is this: most recommendation forms have a place to check off if you want to sign away your rights under the Buckley Amendment. Though a lawyer might tell you never to sign away your rights, we think you should in this instance. Signing the waiver is an expression of confidence in your recommenders, who may feel freer to be candid. Most important, the colleges will be reassured that you are not worried about what your recommenders might say.

In general, it is best to pick a teacher who respects you as a person and who can testify to some of your deeper and less obvious qualities. It is not always best to pick the teacher who gave you the highest grade. Says Tim Fuller of Houghton College, "If a student has cruised through a class and gotten an *A*, a recommendation from that teacher concerning his or her natural abilities may not be as helpful to the student's admission chances as one where the student has had to struggle and work hard to get a *B*."

If you're completely at a loss over whom to ask for a recommendation, talk to your guidance counselor. They often know which teachers write the best letters and can steer you (subtly) in the right direction.

Guidance: Handle with Care

Many colleges require a recommendation from the guidance office. The usefulness of this recommendation will hinge on the extent of the counselor's firsthand information about you.

At a small high school, the counselor often knows everyone and can provide a good overview of your academic career based on his or her knowledge and on input from teachers. At larger ones, there's little chance of that happening unless you're an academic superstar. The only way the counselor will know firsthand of your work is if you keep him or her up to date.

In either case, it is a good idea to establish a personal relationship with the counselor to avoid a recommendation confined to meaningless generalities (see Chapter 4: Getting a Jump Start). Otherwise, you run the risk of suffering a fate similar to that of the luckless applicant to St. John's College in New Mexico who had a recommendation that stated simply, "Joe is really amazing. He does things that are just not normal."

Having chosen your recommenders, don't be bashful. Responsible teachers will rarely say no, but if they hint that someone else might be better, heed their advice.

Popular teachers tend to be snowed under with requests by December, so try to get to them in early fall to make the process as painless as possible. (Waiting until, say, early November is okay if you are thinking about a twelfth grade teacher.) Don't wait to ask until you have figured out all the colleges to which you will apply; you can always add more schools later. In the days before the Internet, students used to show up at each teacher's room with a stack of forms. But with each passing year, more teachers (and guidance counselors) are submitting recommendations online, meaning that you'll need to follow up with an email rather than a physical form. Check with your teacher or counselor to find out your school's procedure.

If a teacher expresses uncertainty about how to write a recommendation, photocopy this chapter and give it to him or her. Try to make the process easy for your teacher—assume that you're the twentieth student who has asked for a recommendation. Complete the top portion of the form and provide a stamped envelope addressed to the admissions office (or email them a digital copy of your personal contact info if they're submitting online). Just as important, give the teacher a brief synopsis of your goals, interests, and the experiences you have shared with him or her on a separate piece of paper. That will help jog the teacher's memory and increase the likelihood that the teacher's comments will reinforce the other points you are trying to make in your application. A list of the colleges to which you will apply, along with the deadlines, would also be much appreciated.

How Thick Is Too Thick?

Occasionally, students may want to send along an extra recommendation beyond those requested in the application. Though the first impulse should always be to send the one or two best recommendations, an extra one from someone who knows you well may not hurt, especially if the extra recommender can highlight a different facet of your record or personality than the others. As a

Scattershot attempts at influence peddling will only succeed in making you look silly.

rule, you should not exceed the number of recommendations requested by more than one. (The waitlist is an exception to this rule. See Chapter 20: Fat Letters and Thin.)

Notwithstanding what we said about friends in high places, some applicants will want to see if their family connections can come through in a pinch. If you are a relative or close family friend of someone who gave millions to the college, that may help. If your best friend's dad is an alumnus, have him write a letter, but don't get your hopes up. A recommendation from someone who knows you a little or not at all—from your local congressman to the president of the United States—is probably worthless. Scattershot attempts at influence peddling will only succeed in making you look silly.

Consider the examples brought to us by former Virginia Military Institute Admissions Dean William J. Buchanan:

> We had an alumnus solicit letters of recommendation for his son from his 2001 VMI classmates. No dice.... One applicant (over 1400 SAT) sent letters of recommendation from an archbishop, an illiterate scoutmaster, and a man identifying himself as a former captain in the czar's Imperial Guard. No sale again. (This lad got As in courses he liked and Fs in those he didn't.)

The reason these examples were no good? No personal insights.

On the other hand, sometimes it pays to consider a slightly offbeat approach. One possibility is a peer reference from one of your classmates who knows you well and is a good writer. Michael Behnke of the University of Chicago was much impressed by a letter from a school custodian about how hard an applicant worked with the custodial staff on school projects: "In broken English, the custodian communicated very effectively that this applicant was the only student in the school who paid attention to those who worked in support positions." That sort of recommendation is generally a lot more valuable than one from even the biggest bigwig.

When It Pays to Be a Packrat

Savvy students save their graded papers from teachers whom they plan to ask for a letter of recommendation. Such papers can help teachers recall specifics that they would otherwise forget.

16. Filing Your Applications

Today's college applicants don't know how good they've got it. Just a few short years ago, applicants spent long hours toiling over paper forms with a typewriter and a bottle of correction fluid. Nowadays, they need only a few keystrokes to access electronic applications that can be transmitted with the push of a button.

Though computers have revolutionized the application process, the top priority is still the same: don't make careless mistakes. Students would be amazed to see how many applications are positively riddled with typos, spelling errors, and other assorted bloopers. After agonizing over the standardized tests, forking over hundreds of dollars for application fees, and traveling far and wide to visit colleges, you owe it to yourself to take the time to do your application right.

Double-Checking Your List

The most crucial act of the college search is choosing the final selection of colleges where you will apply. For most applicants, we recommend a list of about seven schools (more or less). Often, students aim for one or more "reach" colleges that are highly desired, but also highly selective. In this case, it is also wise to include others where the odds are closer to fifty/fifty. Most importantly, we recommend that students include at least one college where admission is highly likely. "The easy part of the college selection process is finding your reach schools," says Christoph Guttentag of Duke University. "The hard part is finding a safety school that is a really good match." Much of the task involves keeping an open mind about the many fine colleges that are not intensely competitive in admission. Out of the many dozens, all you need is one or two. (Two is preferable to guarantee a choice between two offers.) The potential for heartache in April can be drastically reduced by a few good decisions in October and November.

Applications Online

We recommend that every applicant use online applications. Transmission is instantaneous, and you'll have immediate confirmation that each college and university has received your application. More and more colleges now read applications on the computer, so if you send them paper, they'll simply make an electronic copy before reading.

A huge time-saver that has grown by leaps and bounds is the Common Application, available online at www.commonapp.org. Approximately four hundred schools, including the vast majority of highly selective private institutions, accept the Common Application in lieu of their own. (Some have gone so far as to adopt it as their only application form.)

By endorsing the Common Application, colleges vouch for the fact that it carries the same weight as their own application. The CommonApp allows you to input key information only once and then import it to multiple applications. Instead of rewriting your essays ten times for ten colleges, you do them once. The only hitch is that many schools require supplemental forms, which you can link to from the CommonApp site, that ask things such as why you want to attend their particular institution. Note to procrastinators: if you wait until 10:00 p.m. on the due date to look at a CommonApp Supplement, you do so at your peril.

> **Lead Us Not into Procrastination**
>
> Be sure to notify your counselor of where you want to apply long before the deadlines. Straggling in on December 20 for a January 1 deadline will get you an icy reception.

The Internet makes it easy for applicants to create a crisp application no matter what their typing skills, but the convenience itself can create new problems. Students must resist the temptation to impulsively hit the "send" button until they have proofread thoroughly. We recommend that students compose essays and short answer questions offline and then cut-and-paste. Review a printed copy of your work whenever possible before sending and keep it for your records. Don't forget that on occasion, you may need to print and mail a signature page with a check for the application fee. There is also the matter of the school's portion of the application, including the Secondary School Report and letters of recommendation. Check with your guidance office. Many schools are now sending electronic transcripts and recommendations, and if you attend one of those, you'll need to communicate electronically with school staff to bring them into the picture. If your school still sends this material through the mail, you may need to print forms and distribute them to the relevant people.

Cultivating the Colleges

In the age of the Internet and the Common Application— where applying to twenty colleges is almost as easy as applying to two—the premium on showing extra interest in the colleges has never been greater. Once, it was enough to simply apply. Today, as colleges anxiously eye the percentage of their accepted applicants who enroll, many institutions are reluctant to accept an applicant unless they have reason to believe that he or she is seriously interested. Many colleges track every contact that the applicant initiates and are more likely to accept students who have made multiple contacts. A few ways to communicate interest:

- Visit the college. If you don't have a personal interview, be sure to stop by the admissions office to let them know you came.
- If the college sends a representative to visit your high school, come to the session and communicate your interest.

- Attend a college fair in your local area and speak to the representative.
- Get a business card from any college representative you meet and write or email that person to thank them and emphasize your interest.
- Note in your application that a particular college is your first choice school or one of your top choices.
- Write a convincing essay about why you want to attend (usually in response to a question on the school's CommonApp Supplement).

One last tip about cultivating the colleges: make sure your email address stays the same throughout the college search process. If it changes, tell the colleges.

How Many Colleges Should I Apply To?

A good ballpark figure is seven, including at least two from each of the following three categories: (1) reach schools, (2) fifty/fifty schools, and (3) safe schools. The purpose is to apply to colleges of varying degrees of selectivity in order to maximize chances for success.

Most students have no trouble finding the reaches. These are the dream schools, where the odds of admission are long. There is nothing wrong with dreaming, but it also pays to include one or two where the odds are closer to fifty/fifty. Last but not least, applicants should find at least one or two colleges where they would be happy to attend and are reasonably certain of admission.

Though applicants tend to focus more on the reaches, careful selection of the safe ones is probably more important. Getting caught without a school is the ultimate nightmare, almost as bad as attending a poorly chosen safety that doesn't meet your needs.

Some applicants react to runaway college anxiety by applying to a dozen or more schools. We counsel against such a scattershot approach. The overload of completing so many applications often takes its toll and students who put off narrowing their choices in the application process are likely to face a frantic April. Even if you are admitted to ten schools, you can still only attend one.

Use Your Head

When the application asks for a visa number, don't fill in the one from Dad's credit card. The question is for foreign students, a fact that will be clear if you read it carefully. Also, don't answer with strained attempts at humor. One admissions director cited with disgust the applicant who listed one of his favorite activities as, "beating my grand-mother with a tire iron." Ugh! The short answer questions are not the place to be funny.

If Mom and Dad's fingerprints show up on the application anywhere—for example, if it ever uses the words *my child*—you've got a credibility problem. Get them to proofread and make suggestions if you like, but do the final draft yourself.

Choosing a Major

At highly selective schools, even little things like your expected major can have strategic significance. Many universities have different admissions standards across their various colleges and schools. At Carnegie Mellon University, the acceptance rate is about 20 percent in computer science, 30 percent in the fine arts, and more than 50 percent in the liberal arts. At virtually any college, the more people who want to major in your chosen field, the harder it is to get in.

> ### Got Copies?
>
> Never send an application without keeping a photocopy or print-out. The number that gets lost is small, but you never know.

Premed and engineering are notoriously difficult across the board. Other fields vary, depending on the strength of the college's reputation in that particular area (for example, Bard College, a magnet for artists, is much easier to get into for aspiring physicists).

Applicants should be careful not to misrepresent themselves on the application, but they should also think twice before listing a popular major as their first choice. If you are merely considering premed, you should probably list "undecided" for your major, a perfectly respectable choice for any high school senior.

Listing Activities

Always list activities from most important to least important. The ones that are significant, as evidenced by leadership and time commitment, will be obvious. Marginal stuff like membership in SADD or Monogram Club for varsity athletes should be de-emphasized. Don't make a big production out of "honors" from companies that put your picture in a book and then ask you to buy it; such things carry little weight.

Follow the college's preferred format for listing activities. Since the space on the application is often absurdly small, attach extra sheets where necessary. Some applicants prepare their own résumés or activity sheets. Those are often useful as supplemental material, especially when activities of in-depth involvement need further elaboration. But submit one of these only in addition to filling out the college's activity form. When slogging through a pile of a hundred applications, admissions officers prefer to find information in the familiar place and in the standard format rather than finding the words, "see attached."

Marginal stuff like membership in SADD or Monogram Club for varsity athletes should be de-emphasized.

Explain Everything

Most applications have a place for you to address topics that do not fit in the standard boxes. If one of your important activities was chairing the Founder's Day Committee, it won't mean anything to the Admissions Office unless you explain what you did and why the committee was important. If it was an honor bestowed on only one senior, say so. If it involved presentations to alumni and coordination of twenty volunteers for six months, spell that out. Or have the principal write a letter outlining the significance.

The same applies to less pleasant subjects. If there is a black mark on your record—like a suspension or a failing grade—don't just hope that the admissions office won't notice. Any reasonable explanation you can give without sounding whiny or bitter would be helpful. (Even more impressive would be an account of how the experience has helped you to mature.)

Application Extras

Some students may be tempted to send along extra material through the mail to supplement the application. If you are an athlete or a musician, you may want to consider making a tape of a performance. For artists, a portfolio of work can be useful, even if you are not applying to an art program. Don't be shy about sending extra exhibits, but do so only if they show genuine distinction. Just because your mother was enthralled by your recent chorus solo doesn't mean you should send the tape. The music expert on the admissions committee—who has probably received a thousand such tapes—may approach it with a different attitude than your mother.

Before sending extra material, we recommend that you call the admissions office to ask for advice. Some prefer that you forward it directly to a particular person; others request that supplements fit in an 8"x 11" file folder. If you are an athlete, such material should generally go to the coach.

Gimmicks

As "getting-in mania" sweeps the nation each spring, eager applicants shower admissions offices with everything from cookies and flowers to letters with various creative ways of saying, "Please accept me!" We really must recommend that you refrain from acts of desperation like these. In the words of William Hiss of Bates College:

> I don't need a chocolate layer cake, your kindergarten report card, or all the poems you wrote in the ninth grade. I am very interested in seeing the results of whatever it was you consider your finest accomplishment, whether that be photographs of your set designs or genetics research or Scottish dancing.

While we are on the topic of gimmicks, we should point out that the colleges have recently invented one of their own: the so-called "fast track application." These usually appear in your email inbox, with a note saying how wonderful you are and asking would you please consider applying to Most Amazing U? Upon reading further, you may find that MAU has completed part of the application for you (with personal information you supplied while taking a standardized test) and is promising to waive its application fee for you (and a few thousand of your closest friends). Sadly, it is also possible that MAU may not accept you when all is said and done. The university may simply want your application to pad its numbers and make itself look more selective when it says, "Thanks, but no thanks." So handle with care.

Get It in Early

Keep on top of those deadlines. Most come between January and April, but a handful of state universities make priority deadlines as early as October. Find out if your colleges offer rolling admissions (many state schools do) or if they evaluate applications in one big pool. Under rolling admissions, colleges admit the first good applicants who come down the pike, adding to the urgency of prompt filing. At most other colleges, filing by the deadline ensures full consideration, but doing so early shows that you are interested and on the ball. Stronger applicants tend to file early—a fact not lost on admissions officers. A tidal wave of applications pours in as the deadline approaches and the ones caught in that last-minute surge sometimes get less attention.

Most applicants heave a sigh of relief when they submit the application, but the job is still not finished. As the deadline approaches, be sure to pay a friendly follow-up call on your recommenders. If one of your recommendations is late, don't fret. Calmly inquire with the teacher and rest assured that the colleges will not hold it against you.

Making Double Sure

Most colleges also allow students to track the progress of their applications via the college's website. Don't phone the admissions office unless you have checked your status online and still have questions.

When the last application is safely tucked away in the admissions office folder, your part of the job is done. Take time to kick back. You deserve it!

17. Scoring Points with the Essay

Pity the poor admissions officer, sitting alone in his cramped little office, swamped by a stack of essays six inches thick. Talk about an endurance test!

"How My Trip to Europe Changed My Life"
"How I Would Solve World Hunger"
"Why I Want to Be an Investment Banker"

The problem with these essays? No personality. They're written by applicants who don't have a clue how to choose a topic that will reveal something meaningful about themselves. The result is a generic, contrived, fake essay that will bore the socks off even the most conscientious admissions officer.

Your essay will eventually find its way into the same pile as these, so why not try to shake the admissions officer out of his stupor? Let him have a peek inside your world and at the same time show him how well you can write and think. He is interested in learning about you or he would not be in admissions.

Before we launch into our analysis of the essay, we should note that the *Fiske Guide* series includes an entire book on the subject, *Fiske Real College Essays that Work*.

The Write Stuff

What do admissions officers want in an essay? "Spark, vitality, wit, sensitivity, originality, and signs of a lively mind" are some of the qualities, according to Richard Steele of Bowdoin. First and foremost, they want to know how well you express yourself in writing. The sad fact is, many high school students can't write well and, unfortunately, this book can't teach you how. If you doubt your skills, talk it over with your English teacher or get help from your parents or a tutor. (Two good books on the subject are *The Elements of Style* by William Strunk and E. B. White and *On Writing Well* by William Zinsser.)

In the meantime, try to be as concise and specific as possible. Carefully organize your essay around a key theme. Don't waste words that aren't essential to your point and reread the essay several times for word choice and typos. Above all, use your spell checker.

If you have the time, put your essay aside for a week or two and then read it again to see if it still makes sense. You'll be amazed at how many mistakes jump out that were invisible the first time. By choosing your words carefully and proofreading, you show the admissions office not only that you are a good writer, but also that you care about the essay and are willing to take the time to do it right.

Straight from the Heart

Though skillful writing is important, you don't have to be another Joyce Carol Oates to write a good essay. Most admissions offices won't penalize you if there are a few rough edges to it—unless you happen to be applying to places like Princeton or Swarthmore.

Aside from writing skills, the most important thing admissions officers look for in the essay is a sense of who you are as a person. "We look for the applicant's voice," says one. It is generally easier to reveal something about yourself if you pick a topic drawn from your own experiences.

One University of Tulsa applicant scored major points with an essay about looking in the mirror and reflecting on his homely face.

Don't make the mistake of thinking that a good essay must be about something big, like winning the championship game or losing a friend to childhood cancer. The best essays are often about mundane topics. Why? Because an essay about a life-changing experience is dominated by the facts of what happened, rather than by the personality of the author.

Five Fundamentals of a Successful Essay

Show, don't tell. If you want to convince the reader that you never give up, don't tell the reader, "I never give up." Instead, describe how you were cut from the basketball team in ninth grade, sat on the bench in tenth grade, and finally made the team as a junior. A skillful writer lets evidence show that a proposition is true; a clumsy one tells because his writing is not powerful enough to show.

Use your own experiences. The most interesting essay puts you in the starring role and features real life thoughts and feelings. Anecdotes from your world are always more interesting than abstractions. Give the reader a piece of your mind.

Use the first person. Nine out of ten essays should be in the first person, the best vehicle for revealing your thoughts and beliefs. Says Christoph Guttentag of Duke University, "The better we get to know the students as people, the more likely they'll be admitted."

Begin with a flourish. The most important sentence in any essay is the first one. Polish it like a precious stone. Good writers often try to hook the reader with a first sentence that surprises or piques. Often, it is an autobiographical anecdote.

Proofread. Applicants are told over and over again and still they don't proofread! Arrggh! Nothing is more damaging than an essay sull of typoes, speling misteaks, and grammar that ain't no good.

Remember Seinfeld, the television show about nothing? The reason it was (and is) so great is precisely because it is about nothing. With no established story line to hog the spotlight, the writers were free to unleash their creativity. Some of the same logic applies to college essays.

Too many applicants feel they must make a single experience bear the burden of transforming their lives. Nine times out of ten, the "How _____ Changed My Life" essay falls flat. Few teenagers have actually had such experiences, a fact admissions people know all too well. A more believable approach is to write thoughtfully about incremental change, with a particular incident used to illustrate your evolution.

The best topics are often close to the heart. If you have the guts to openly discuss a personal problem or obstacle you have overcome, any admissions officer will be impressed—maybe even touched. A good essay always shares something real, even though baring your soul to complete strangers may feel uncomfortable. One University of Tulsa applicant scored major points with an essay about looking in the mirror and reflecting on his homely face. An applicant to Lewis and Clark College turned the tables by writing as if she were an admissions officer considering her own application. A Rollins College hopeful enhanced his chances with an essay on his guilt over injuring another player in a football game, while a Duke applicant wowed the admissions office with a spoof on the anxiety related to taking the SAT.

One applicant to Hampden-Sydney College wrote about a pair of old but treasured shoes he had worn to his interview despite his mother's protests, ending with, "Tell the truth, Dean Jones, did you notice my shoes?" "My response was yes, but it didn't matter," says Robert Jones, the former dean of admissions, who sent him an acceptance letter.

How to Borrow Without Stealing

Only the dumbest applicants would consider plagiarizing an essay from a book or website. It's wrong, and risky, and completely unnecessary. The hard part of writing is to find appropriate rhetorical devices, and these can be legitimately borrowed from other good writing. For an example, flip back to the opening of Chapter 14. The dream device was purloined from the opening of former Senator Bill Bradley's 1976 memoir, *Life on the Run*.

Don't Try to Save the World

While personal topics work well, stay away from political issues or what one admissions officer calls the "social-problem-of-the-year" bandwagon.

The bandwagon works like this. Consider the huge oil spill in the Gulf of Mexico. Like clockwork, college applicants across the nation will write essays on the environment and why we need to keep it clean. Most of them will say the same thing, more or less, and even the well-written ones will reveal little about the writer and his or her outlook on life.

Essays that are overly self-centered also bomb. "I hated it when an applicant wrote that he had learned from a trip to the ghetto how fortunate he is to live in a nice house," remembers one admissions dean. A societal problem can occasionally be an interesting topic for an essay, but only if you give it a personal slant. Lots of people write about the homeless—usually a mistake. But one applicant to the University of Miami actually went out and interviewed a homeless man—and was accepted.

In addition to open-ended personal statements, many applications ask students to answer a more specific essay question. Most of these are a variation on the theme of "Why do you want to attend our fine institution?" Handle these with extreme care. When you're writing about yourself, the topic is one that you know better than anyone. When you're writing about the college you want to attend, you're writing about a subject that the admissions office knows a lot more about than you do. Do your research. When you visit, remember that in six months you'll need to explain why you want to apply. The best "why us?" essays use concrete details and personal experiences to show why the college is a good match for you.

Essay Turnoffs

Trite phrases. Most admissions officers are near nausea with applicants who "want to help people." Think of something unique about you.

Slickness. An essay that reads as if it has been churned out by Dad's public relations firm will not impress. Let the real you shine through.

Cynicism. Colleges want bright, active people—not wet blankets. A positive approach to life, and to the essay, will score points.

Life histories. Make sure your essay has a point. An endless stream of phrases like "then I did this and then I did this" is sleep-inducing and does not say anything meaningful.

Essay that goes on forever. More is not better. The colleges want a concise, well-reasoned essay—not the sequel to *War and Peace*. Try not to exceed the amount of space allotted for each essay.

The thesaurus syndrome. Don't overutilize ostentatiously pretentious language to delineate the thematic observations you are endeavoring to articulate. Big words aren't impressive; a clear, direct style is.

The most important rule of thumb in cases like these is simple: answer the question. Never substitute the answer to one college's question for that of another unless the two are exactly the same.

Another morsel: if you're doing all your essays on a word processor, remember to change the name of the college before you print. Likewise, heed the advice of Roger Campbell, former dean of admissions at the University of Denver, "Don't send a Xerox copy of your most recent major school paper. We may not agree with your teacher."

The Finishing Touches

An obvious way to make yourself memorable is to use a little humor. Many admissions officers enjoy essays written with a twinkle in the eye. An applicant to Ursinus College made a lasting impression when he wrote his essay on, ahem, sexual fantasies. (He was accepted.)

Be on guard, though, because humor is in the eye of the beholder and it's hard to be sure the admissions staff will laugh when you want them to. Also, "It usually makes the student seem too casual, too uninterested, and/or flippant," says Richard Hallin of Eckerd College. Only excellent writers should try to be funny and then only if they can reveal something important about themselves in the process.

There's a fine line between legitimate consultation and illegitimate misrepresentation.

As for length, we wholeheartedly recommend the KISS formula of Tim Fuller of Houghton (Keep It Short and Simple). Admissions officers reading "their seven hundredth application in two weeks," he says, "are not impressed by long essays."

A final ticklish issue is getting help. There's a fine line between legitimate consultation and illegitimate misrepresentation. The application has your name on it, so most of it should be your work. It's fine to get a parent or teacher to look it over for spelling and make some comments on style and content, but if that person begins writing sentences or paragraphs, it isn't your essay anymore. Many admissions officers have finely honed radar to detect ghost-written essays. If you got straight Bs in English and your essay reads like E. B. White, the admissions office is going to be skeptical.

"Essays are windows into the real you," says David Erdmann of Rollins College. After completing a rough draft, ask yourself: could anybody else have written this essay? If so, you need to think again about the fine art of letting the reader see inside your soul.

Part Three:

Paying the Bill

18. The New Financial Aid Game

Learning about financial aid is the college admissions equivalent of a trip to the dentist's office. Nobody, least of all a stressed-out applicant, wants to spend his or her time contemplating Expected Family Contributions (EFCs), Student Aid Reports (SARs), and the Free Application for Federal Student Aid (FAFSA). But unless your last name happens to be Rockefeller or Gates, you had better sit up and listen closely. Financial aid is a make-or-break proposition in today's world and the path to First Choice U. is littered with unfortunate applicants who realized too late that getting financial aid can be just as important as getting in.

For anyone planning to let dear old Mom and Dad foot the bill, here are some sobering facts:

- The cost of attending the most prestigious private colleges for four years is more than two hundred thousand dollars, double the price of 20 years ago.
- Tuition at public universities has risen more than 50 percent in inflation-adjusted dollars in the past ten years.
- As college costs have gone through the roof, government aid has failed to keep pace. Grant programs have withered, while student debt has ballooned.

For families that don't have an extra one hundred thousand dollars stashed under the mattress, money will influence the college search at every step. The schools don't like to say so in public, but most are forced to admit and deny students according to financial criteria. We'll tell you when it happens and to whom. Colleges are also less and less likely to provide all the financial aid that applicants need to enroll. We'll show you the causes of the money shortage and its impact on applicants like you.

Though the reality of paying for college can be grim, the news is not all bad. While some private colleges charge a sticker price of over fifty thousand dollars for a single year, they also give a growing number of discounts based on need and merit. A few of the most expensive schools have recently changed the way they measure financial need to sweeten aid packages and reduce or eliminate loans. We'll tell you about the new opportunities in financial aid and who will benefit.

We begin with an overview of the aid system in its pure form—how it was designed to work and *did* work once upon a time. We then move on to the wrenching changes of the past two decades and the nitty-gritty of today's aid scene.

Financial Aid 101

The first rule of financial aid is simple: the colleges are the place to find it. About 95 percent of the available dollars are administered through them, including virtually all of the federal money and most state grants. We'll suggest other places to look later on, but this chapter focuses solely on money that comes by virtue of applying for financial aid at a college.

As we have noted, college-administered financial aid comes in two basic varieties: awards based on academic merit or special talents and awards based on need. Your first major decision in the financial aid search is whether or not to apply for need-based aid. In most cases, the answer should be yes. Even if your family income is over one hundred thousand dollars, there is still a chance that you may qualify for something, and some non-need awards require an aid application. (At the richest universities, families with income of one hundred and fifty thousand dollars can still qualify for substantial need-based aid.) We recommend that you sit down with your parents at the outset of the college search and ask a simple question: how much can the family afford to pay each year for college? A ballpark figure will do. Next, compare that number with the total of tuition, room and board, and fees (plus at least three thousand dollars for travel, books, and living expenses) at the college(s) you are interested in attending. If the total of those is larger than what your parents feel they can afford, you should definitely apply for financial aid.

The talk with your parents should inject a dose of reality into your college search. If the figure they can pay is below the cost of your schools, you need to investigate some cheaper options. But don't eliminate the expensive ones just yet. Apply for aid and see what you can get. The time to judge whether a college is too expensive comes at the end of the process, after the financial aid awards have been made. Only then will you know the actual out-of-pocket costs of each school.

To illustrate this point, we offer the following example. Let's assume that a close personal friend of yours named Todd Tight-Wad is applying to two schools: an expensive private college charging forty thousand dollars per year and a state university with a more modest sticker price of ten thousand dollars. Which one do you think will end up costing Todd's family more? The one that costs forty thousand dollars, right? Maybe—but maybe not.

When Todd applies for financial aid, the system reviews his family's assets and calculates something called the Expected Family Contribution (EFC)—the amount Todd's family can afford for college. Let's say his family's EFC is seven thousand dollars. If the colleges are willing and able, they'll give Todd financial aid to *In a few cases, the expensive college might actually turn out to be cheaper.* cover what they consider to be his "demonstrated need"— the difference between the EFC calculated by the aid formula and their sticker price. At the expensive private college, he would qualify for thirty-three thousand dollars in aid, while at the public university he would be eligible for only three thousand dollars. Even though the sticker prices of the two are vastly different, they both end up costing him seven thousand dollars. Even if his EFC were much higher—fifteen thousand dollars or so—he would still qualify for twenty-five thousand dollars from the private college to help soften the blow. In a few cases, the expensive college might actually turn out to be cheaper. Public universities are typically much less generous with need-based aid than private ones. If the private one meets Todd's full demonstrated need while the public one meets none of it, the pricey forty thousand dollar private school turns out to be three thousand dollars cheaper when all is said and done.

> **A Destination for Mom and Dad**
>
> A campus visit is an excellent time to get financial aid information. If a family has special circumstances—medical bills, fluctuating income, and the like—the parents may want to make a date with the financial-aid office to see how their situation might be addressed.

For an early indication of how the system might work for your family, we recommend that you complete one of the financial aid estimators that are available via the Web. (Some financial aid offices make them available on their websites.) These programs replicate the aid formulas used to calculate need. Simply plug in your family's financial data and *voilà*—out comes the EFC. For thoroughness and reliability, we recommend the College Board's aid estimator on its website at www.collegeboard.com.

If you and your parents are careful with your data, the estimator should give a rough idea of how much aid you can expect. The results will help dictate your financial aid strategy. If your EFC is over forty thousand dollars, your best hope of significant aid probably lies in merit scholarships. If your EFC is less than ten thousand dollars, you'll want to look at schools with a firm commitment to need-based aid.

We emphasize that an aid estimator will give only a ballpark figure and its predictive ability is less for those who have complicated finances. With college purse strings pulled tighter every year, the financial-aid system is less reliable than ever before. Families can no longer sit back and trust that they'll get all the money they need. One essential strategy is to apply to one or more schools where you are sure your family can pay the sticker price. Second, you and your parents should do a thorough job of financial aid comparison shopping before you apply.

The Budget Squeeze Hits Higher Ed

To understand the plight of the financial aid system, you need a brief history lesson. The roots of today's crisis go back to the 1960s. The federal government had declared a war on poverty and the colleges were determined to take the lead in breaking down the walls of oppression. College admissions offices made a commitment to admit students without regard for their ability to pay and to then cover the full financial need of any who chose to enroll. Though the most generous support was offered to low-income applicants, affluent families also reaped handsome rewards; even millionaires could qualify for interest-free loans subsidized and guaranteed by the government. No matter what your background or financial circumstances, aid was available for the asking.

Somewhere on the road to utopia, financial reality intruded and the high-minded ideal of need-based aid was compromised. The country took a turn toward conservatism in the 1980s and government spending suddenly went from being considered a noble social cause to being viewed as an excuse to raise taxes. In the new political climate, it was only a matter of time before college financial aid went on the chopping block. The states were the first to go for the jugular, slashing millions in aid to public universities. The changes in federal money were slower, but relentless. Although the total amount of federal assistance is now at an all-time high, the proportion coming in the form of outright grants has declined, while the number and dollar volume of repayable loans has increased. Among loans, there has been a major shift away from subsidized loans, under which the government pays the interest while the student is in college, to ones carrying no subsidies.

As government support waned, expenses were rising steeply at the nation's colleges and universities. The cost of physical plants, maintenance, technology, libraries, faculty salaries, and benefits have all been rising faster than inflation for decades. Yet many colleges put off the day of reckoning, preferring to raise tuition rather than deal with the underlying problems. Oddly, the public played along with the game for many years. In part because the Ivy League led the way with huge tuition increases, high price seemed to equal high quality.

As the new century dawned, the colleges suddenly awoke to the fact that many families could no longer afford their product. As the money squeeze intensified, the old financial aid system quickly became unworkable. The last straw came with the recession of the late 2000s. University endowments plummeted, and even the Harvards of the world were forced to dramatically tighten their belts. Though most institutions have struggled mightily to maintain their affordability, many have been forced to adopt the let's-make-a-deal syndrome. Though the "sticker price" of college may be outrageously high, there is also an endless variety of incentive deals and give-backs to lighten the load. (At one selective university in the northeast, not a single freshman paid full tuition and fees in a recent year.) With millions of dollars at stake, few colleges can afford to give aid without carefully spreading it around to maximize tuition revenue. "The admissions process we knew twenty years ago is radically different," says Thomas Anthony, former dean of admissions at Colgate University. "Today is much more sales oriented and financial aid is now a tool to help colleges in a competitive marketplace."

Merit Scholarships

The typical private college hands out tens of millions of dollars in financial aid each year. Ask a college administrator why colleges spend so much and you may hear the familiar 1960s-style platitudes about helping the needy, access for all, the value of diversity, and so on. In fact, financial aid has become weapon No. 1 in the dog-eat-dog competition for academic prestige and financial stability. Strange as it may seem, colleges have figured out a way that they can make money by giving it away.

The trick is to give non-need (merit) scholarships to students who can pay most of the bill. Once upon a time, selective colleges looked down their noses at the very idea of "buying" students with merit scholarships. Not only were such awards viewed as

> **Good Grades Pay**
> The growth of merit scholarships carries a clear message: work hard in school. A few extra points on your GPA could mean thousands of extra dollars in aid.

undignified, they put a serious crimp in the system of need-based aid for all. The more heavily a college invests in merit scholarships, the less money it has for packages based on need. Since the students who win merit awards (particularly those based on standardized test scores) tend to come from well-heeled families, merit scholarships represent a huge money transfer away from high-need applicants toward low-need ones.

From the colleges' point of view, merit money has become a case of keeping up with the Joneses. As their competitors entice top applicants with lucrative awards, few colleges can afford to sit out the bidding war. Only a handful of the most prestigious schools—with their massive resources and sterling reputations—continue to offer financial aid solely on *The higher you rank in a particular college's applicant pool, the more likely it is that you will qualify for a merit scholarship.* the basis of need. These richer colleges have a secret weapon: because they are so prominent, they tend to attract richer applicants. Thus, at ultra-elite Amherst College, less than 50 percent of the students receive aid from the college, well below the 75 percent that is typical at less selective private colleges. With all the tuition money flowing in from the full payers, Amherst can afford to give aid only on the basis of need.

Colleges that are lower on the prestige totem pole have no such luxury. They resort to merit scholarships to raise their status in the rankings and protect their turf against competitors. Much of the loot goes to top scholars and athletes, with lesser amounts set aside for those with other special talents. Though many schools combine a handful of merit scholarships with abundant need-based aid, those that trumpet dozens of merit scholarships are sending two messages: (1) if you are a well-qualified applicant without much need, a scholarship could be yours, and (2) if you are a middle- to high-need student, you might want to look at schools with a firmer commitment to need-based aid.

For applicants who are in earnest about finding a merit scholarship, we offer an ironclad rule: the higher you rank in a particular college's applicant pool, the more likely it is that you will qualify for a merit scholarship. For example, picture applicant Sarah Superstar with SAT scores in the mid-700s and a 3.9 grade point average. Sarah is applying to only two schools: Top-of-the-Heap University and Up-and-Coming College. At Top-of-the-Heap, Sarah is well-qualified for admission, but doesn't stand out from hundreds of other superstars with similar records. But at Up-and-Coming, Sarah is one of the best applicants of the year and considered a hot prospect for the honors program.

Let's assume that Sarah gets in at both schools. Where do you think she will enroll? Nine times out of ten, Sarah and the other superstars will want to go to Top-of-the-Heap. So how does Up-and-Coming compete? By offering Sarah a full-tuition scholarship and thereby putting her in a dilemma. Does she pay through the nose to attend the college she really wants? Or does she take the money and attend the less selective school? Only Sarah and her parents can make that decision.

No-Need Scholarships from the Government

With so much public concern about the cost of college, it is hardly surprising that the politicians have stepped forward with a variety of relief measures at both the federal and state level. Students in Georgia get a full-tuition scholarship to any in-state public institution (or an equivalent amount at an in-state private one) if they earn a minimum grade point average of 3.0. Florida students receive a similar deal with a 3.5 and other states have enacted or are considering similar programs.

Help is also available at the federal level in the form of the Hope Scholarship tuition tax credit and Lifetime Learning Credit. The Hope takes fifteen hundred dollars off the tax bill of any middle-class family that pays at least two thousand dollars in tuition for a student in the first two years of college. The Lifetime Learning Credit covers 20 percent of the first ten thousand dollars in tuition bills for a student in the last two years of an undergraduate degree. Both phase out for single parents (or independent students) who earn forty thousand to fifty thousand dollars per year and married couples who earn eighty thousand to one hundred thousand dollars.

The most recent addition to the paying-for-college arsenal is the so-called "529 Plan," named for a section of the tax code that allows parents to save tens of thousands tax-free without having to establish a custodial account.

In addition to the full-tuition scholarship that Sarah won, a second variety of merit awards—known to insiders as "discounts"—is now in vogue at many financial aid offices. Discounts come in the form of small cash awards, usually in the five thousand dollar range. Though colleges dress them up like big merit awards—same flattering letter, same fancy stationery—the real purpose is to attract good and even average students who can pay most of the tuition bill. (People are more likely to respond if they believe they have won something—just ask the folks at Publisher's Clearing House.) In the same way that auto makers give factory rebates when they have trouble selling cars at the full price, colleges offer discounts when they have trouble attracting enough full-paying customers. The list of schools offering discounts includes many of the nation's private colleges and a growing number of public institutions.

The financial rewards of discounting can be substantial. Consider the situation of Wannabe Ivy U., a Midwestern liberal arts school with a sticker price of forty-five thousand dollars. Though Wannabe is a selective school, it has been struggling with a tight budget and a declining applicant pool. Let's assume that Wannabe Ivy is trying to decide what to do with a forty thousand dollar piece of its financial aid budget. In past years, it might have lavished the whole amount on an applicant like Monica, who is the daughter of a single parent who can't afford a dime for college expenses. Monica's 3.0 GPA and SAT scores in the mid-500s put her just above the admit-deny borderline at a level where most—though not all—students are offered admission. The fact that Monica comes from a humble background is likely to make her a sentimental favorite of the admissions committee, but with the university's financial security at stake, Wannabe simply can't afford her. Instead, the university has earmarked the forty thousand dollars to try to lure a few more students who can pay most or all of the freight. The beneficiaries are Susan, Joe, Michael, and Jim, four students who all come from affluent backgrounds and don't qualify for aid. All four are average to slightly better than average applicants, with SAT scores around 600 and grades in the *B+* range. Each will get a ten thousand dollar merit award as the equivalent of a cash incentive to enroll.

The obvious winners of the discounting game are the good and average students who don't qualify for much need-based aid.

The rationale behind Wannabe Ivy's decision will be clear from a glance at the impact on its budget. Were Monica to receive the money, her EFC of zero dollars would leave the university with nothing to offset its four-year annual expenditure of forty thousand dollars except the warm fuzzies that come from helping a student in need. (For simplicity, we assume that the five thousand dollar gap between Wannabe's grant and its sticker price will be covered by federal aid.) If the money goes to the other four and all choose to enroll, the college will more than cover its forty thousand dollar outlay by raking in a total of one hundred and forty thousand dollars from Susan, Joe, Michael, and Jim, all of whom pay the balance of the bill after receiving the scholarship. Multiplied over four years, the difference to the college's financial bottom line between giving the money to Monica versus giving it the other four comes to over four hundred thousand dollars. Of course, several of them might enroll even without the ten thousand dollar grant. But if even one or two of them is swayed by it, the college makes money on the deal.

The obvious winners of the discounting game are the good and average students who don't qualify for much need-based aid. They can take comfort in the fact that as tuition costs escalate, fewer and fewer families are actually paying the full price. Less than a third do at most private colleges and the figure is as low as 10 percent at schools that are heavy discounters.

And as for Monica? Every college enrolls a few like her, but most cannot afford very many. With her family's modest finances, she is likely to get a thin letter on April 1—or a hollow acceptance not accompanied by the aid she needs to enroll.

Some final caveats on merit awards: be sure to find out if they are renewable for four years and, if so, what the requirements are. Some colleges lure students with hefty cash awards for the freshman year and then snatch some of the money away once the student is hooked. Other colleges build in sticky requirements for renewal, such as maintaining a 3.5 grade point average on a 4.0 scale.

A merit scholarship is nice recognition for hard work in high school, but never forget that it is also an enticement to buy an expensive product (albeit at a discounted price). Applicants should think hard before changing a college choice over a few thousand dollars. A discount is a good deal only if you like the merchandise.

Where to Learn More about Financial Aid

www.finaid.org Endorsed by the National Association of Student Financial Aid Administrators, the FinAid page offers in-depth coverage of every facet of financial aid.

www.fastweb.com The busiest free scholarship search site online. Students complete an informational questionnaire and receive a list of scholarship opportunities that match their criteria.

Don't Miss Out: The Ambitious Student's Guide to Financial Aid by Anna and Robert Leider, Octameron Associates. Since its initial publication more than twenty-five years ago, this book has offered an excellent one-stop summary of the aid process.

Financing College by Kristin Davis, Kiplinger Books. In addition to covering the aid scene, Davis offers an excellent overview of saving for college that may be of interest to younger parents.

Paying for College without Going Broke by Kalman Chany, The Princeton Review/Random House. The strength of Chany's book is in coaching parents on how to position their income and assets to qualify for the most aid. It also gives detailed guidance on completing the aid forms.

Need-Based Aid

It is time to lift the veil on the most complicated part of our story: the convoluted process by which colleges parcel out need-based aid. Need-based aid used to be the wholesome branch of financial aid in which every deserving student got all that he or she needed. But only the richest colleges can still afford the process we outlined in Financial Aid 101. Today, a growing number of colleges make admissions decisions based on who can pay and the amount of your need-based aid package may depend less on your financial situation than how badly the college wants you to enroll.

One of the big problems is that few colleges are completely forthright about how the system works. Like presidential candidates, they tend to speak in sound bites that mask the complexity of what they do. Applicants who want real answers must dig into the details of each college's policies.

The pages that follow examine the three most important questions facing aid applicants.

1. How does financial need affect admissions decisions?
2. How is financial need calculated?
3. How are aid packages assembled to meet the need?

Each of these questions is complicated. Many colleges, including the majority of the most selective ones, assert that financial need has no impact on admissions decisions. But even at the handful of colleges that adhere faithfully to the policy, the phrase "need-blind admissions" is a misnomer. Communication between the admissions and financial-aid offices is ongoing throughout the process. The financial-aid office will know exactly which applicants are at the top of the list for admission (most colleges have a numerical rating system) and aid packages are constructed accordingly. The more the college wants you, the more aid you are likely to get,

> ### Bagging a Sure Thing
>
> Students with high need should apply to at least one low-cost school where they can pay the "sticker" price.

and the higher the proportion that will come in the form of grants rather than loans.

As colleges ponder the fate of borderline candidates, several incentives work against admitting the high-need students. No college wants to lavish a huge aid award on a marginal admit. Yet if these students are admitted without adequate aid, they are unlikely to enroll (thereby hurting the college's yield and selectivity rankings). Either way, the college loses.

No matter what an institution's policy is, the students who squeak through in the final cut are often the ones who can pay the freight. When considering students on the waitlist, so-called need blind colleges have no qualms about accepting only those with no need (rationalizing that the waitlist is a special case).

One group that almost never has the benefit of need-blind admissions is international students. Even colleges that say they are need blind for everyone else typically admit only foreign students with some ability to pay. (Rare exceptions are limited to the richest of the Ivy League.) Since only U.S. citizens and permanent residents can qualify for federal need-based aid, sources of funding are limited. Many schools say flat out that they have no money available to foreign students; others have merit or need-based money set aside.

Demonstrated Need and Your Aid Package

The impact of financial need on admissions decisions is a crucial issue, but the second half of the equation is just as important. How much of the need will be met? Many colleges offer aid packages that leave a gap between the aid award and the amount a student needs to enroll. This outcome, called gapping, has become more widespread as college costs escalate.

Another fly in the ointment lies in the way demonstrated need is calculated. Twenty years ago, the process was fairly straightforward. All colleges used a government formula for

Selective Colleges that Award Aid Only to Students with Need

One indication of a college's commitment to need-based aid is whether it offers academic merit scholarships. The colleges below devote all of their resources to need-based aid.

Amherst College
Barnard College
Bates College
Bowdoin College
Brown University
Bryn Mawr College
Bucknell University
Colby College
Colgate University
Columbia University
Connecticut College
Cornell University
Dartmouth College
Eugene Lang College
Georgetown University*
Harvard University
Haverford College
Massachusetts Institute of
    Technology

Middlebury College
University of Notre Dame*
Parsons School of Design
University of Pennsylvania
Princeton University
Reed College
St. John's College (MD and NM)
Sarah Lawrence College
Stanford University*
Trinity College (CT)
Tufts University
Vassar College
Wellesley College
Wesleyan University
Williams College
Yale University

*These institutions offer athletic scholarships, but no academic merit awards.

---

determining the Expected Family Contribution (EFC), the amount each family was required to pay for higher education. The difference between the EFC and the total expenses of attending each college yielded the demonstrated need. Though some schools occasionally tinkered with the EFC, there was general consensus on the major ground rules.

Everything changed in the 1990s when the Federal government decided to rewrite the financial aid rules. It replaced the old form for calculating need with a new one, the Free Application for Federal Student Aid (FAFSA), which all students must file to receive aid from any college. The FAFSA examines household income and assets. After factoring in a hefty allowance for your parents' retirement nest egg (the older they are, the bigger the allowance) and performing sundry other calculations, the formula spits out an EFC.

Though the stated goal of the FAFSA was to simplify the aid process, the behind-the-scenes explanation isn't so simple. The legislation was crafted with an eye toward middle-class voters and it gave them a major plum: the value of the family home was no longer to be included in the formula for determining expected family contribution. That may not sound earthshaking, but the effect was substantial. A family earning $50,000 per year and living in a $400,000 home was now considered to have the same ability to pay as a family with the same income that rented an apartment. For many colleges—especially some expensive private ones committed to meeting 100 percent of "need"—the new rules foreshadowed a severe financial hit.

While the private colleges were crying foul, the College Board entered the fray with a new supplementary financial aid form known as the CSS/Financial Aid PROFILE. (CSS stands for College Scholarship Service, an arm of the College Board.) The primary purpose of the PROFILE is to provide a way for expensive private colleges to modify the federal aid formula of the FAFSA. While asking many of the same questions, the PROFILE goes into more detail concerning the nature of family assets and a variety of special circumstances. Among the variables ignored by the FAFSA, but included in the PROFILE are:
- home equity
- trust funds held by siblings
- noncustodial parent income and assets
- medical and dental expenses
- private school tuition
- student's summer earnings

In addition to the standard battery of questions, the PROFILE also includes a number of "institutional questions," which are added only at the request of each college. When students register to fill out the PROFILE, they must list the colleges to which they will apply. From that list, the College Board creates an individualized PROFILE for each family that includes the institutional questions required by the colleges they choose. These questions delve even deeper into topics such as untaxed income, assets in foreign countries, business and consumer loans, and financial issues relevant to divorce. As if all that weren't enough, many colleges also require submission of their own supplemental financial aid form that asks for additional information. Despite the government's talk of simplifying the system, families now find themselves filing as many as three separate aid applications for a single college.

> **Less Income, More Aid**
>
> Since the aid formulas tax income more heavily than assets, parents should minimize sales of stock or property beginning in the calendar year before the student enrolls in college.

The uniform method of calculating demonstrated need is now long gone. Colleges are still bound by the federal rules when distributing federal funds, but they are now free to define demonstrated need any way they like depending on the data in the CSS PROFILE or their own supplemental form that they choose to include in the calculations. Differences in methodology can mean wide variations in a family's demonstrated need from one college to the next.

With such a confusing welter of forms, the task of zeroing in on how your colleges calculate need won't be easy. A good opening question might be, "Do you use the federal methodology (FM)?" A yes to this question will probably spare you the need to file the CSS PROFILE. Most state universities use the FM, as do many moderately selective and nonselective private institutions. On the downside, most FM schools do not presume to meet full need, but instead extend an offer of admission with a gapped aid package. A good question for schools in this category: is there a standard amount of need that goes unmet?

At colleges that use their own institutional methodology (IM) to calculate demonstrated need, information may be harder to get. If the college requires the PROFILE, you can assume that many of the variables discussed above are included.

One of the biggest differences between schools that use FM and those that use IM is their handling of divorce. At FM schools, only the adults in the student's primary household are included in the need assessment formula. But IM schools use the PROFILE and their own aid forms to seek information about the noncustodial parent. Typical of these is Dartmouth College, which stated in a recent publication that "both natural parents have a moral obligation to cover their children's educational costs, despite any legal documents to the contrary." Despite the hard line taken by some colleges, dealing with a divorce can be a judgment call. Schools are much more likely to require a contribution from the noncustodial parent when a divorce is recent, than to go after an absentee father who disappeared fifteen years ago. If your parents are divorced and financial aid will play a major role in your college choice, we recommend that you check out each college's divorce policy before you apply. If there have been unusual circumstances in the family that prevent seeking a contribution from the noncustodial parent, the family can appeal directly to the colleges.

> *The primary purpose of the PROFILE is to provide a way for expensive private colleges to modify the federal aid formula of the FAFSA.*

Applying for Aid: Which Forms?

FORM	REQUIRED BY	WEB ADDRESS
FAFSA	all colleges	www.fafsa.ed.gov
CSS PROFILE	some highly selective colleges	www.collegeboard.com
college form	varies—inquire at financial aid office	

A second item that bears scrutiny is the allowance for travel and living expenses built into demonstrated need. If a college is looking to cut corners, this is an obvious place. For schools more than a few hundred miles away, two round-trip air fares should be factored into the deal.

Though it pays to be well-informed before you apply, many differences in aid policies only become apparent after the aid offers are in hand. We now turn to the various elements that make up those much-anticipated awards.

Building an Aid Package

After a college has arrived at its calculation of demonstrated need, the final piece in the puzzle is how it chooses to respond. The college will either offer a package that will meet the full need or leave the family a gap to pay (somehow) on its own. In both cases, the package will probably include aid in three varieties: grants, loans, and a work-study job. But how much of each? That is a question that bears close scrutiny.

Mix and match is the operative metaphor for financial aid packages. Some of the money will come from the college's own funds and some will be contributed by the federal government and the states. Loans and work study provide the foundation of most packages. The loans might be administered by an outside lender or through the college itself, but the source of the money is much less important than how much the college chooses to give you. The loan plans come under a dizzying array of acronyms corresponding to a variety of federal and institutional programs.

Five Good Questions for the Financial Aid Office

1. **What percentage of the last freshman class paid full tuition?** A rough indication of your odds for getting aid via merit or need.

2. **What percentage of accepted aid applicants were offered aid to meet their full need?** Even if *full* need is subjective, a good index of a college's aid resources and commitment to need-based aid.

3. **Is there a standard expectation for self-help?** Some colleges have uniform levels for the amount of loans, work study, and earnings in the summer that are built into most aid packages.

4. **How will my aid package change after freshman year?** Many colleges will increase loans for upperclassmen. Find out if there are standard increments for such changes.

5. **What happens if my need increases later?** Some schools are reluctant to raise aid amounts for students already enrolled. You'll be at their mercy then, so ask the question now.

Work study is a federal program that subsidizes jobs for students while they attend college. Typically, the college gives the student a job in the cafeteria or an academic office and then the wages are counted as part of his or her EFC. Most colleges generally expect students to work no more than twelve hours per week during the school year and studies show that such a workload rarely affects student performance. One hitch: the money doesn't come in until after it is earned.

The combination of loans and work-study jobs is known in financial aid offices as self-help. Virtually every need-based financial aid package includes self-help, but the amount can vary widely. In the world of financial aid accounting, a five thousand dollar loan meets the same need as a five thousand dollar grant—even though the grant is for keeps and the loan must be paid back with interest. Some colleges maintain an unreasonably high self-help component in their aid packages to preserve the fiction of meeting full need. Savvy financial aid consumers will want to ask the colleges that meet full need if there is a ceiling on self-help as an aid component. A reasonable total for freshmen is approximately six thousand dollars per year (roughly four thousand dollars in loans and two thousand dollars for work-study earnings). There may be an additional expectation for summer earnings of up to two thousand dollars. At colleges that gap, students may be loaded up with loans of thousands more, including supplemental parent loans.

Another important issue is how much the self-help expectation may change in the sophomore through senior years. A hike in loans for upperclass students is standard according to federal guidelines; see if the colleges can give you specific information on how much, if any, your loans can be expected to increase. A few colleges will lure freshmen with generous grant aid and then put the squeeze on them with massive loans as upperclassmen.

Escalating debt is a particular concern at expensive private colleges. Some of the nation's most selective schools have decided to do something about it. The richest Ivy

League universities have replaced loans with grants for students whose families make less than $40,000 per year. A group of twenty-eight other well-heeled institutions, including Stanford, Amherst, and Swarthmore, has significantly changed the way it measures financial need. All have agreed to:

- give more aid to families who live in high cost-of-living areas;
- limit the amount that the value of a family's home affects its financial aid eligibility;
- expect parents to contribute less from tax-advantaged college-savings accounts; and
- be more lenient in expecting contributions from both custodial and noncustodial households in cases where divorced parents have remarried.

Among public universities, institutions such as University of North Carolina—Chapel Hill and University of Virginia have pledged to limit the amount of debt that low income students are forced to take on. Though there have been many hopeful developments in recent years, the state of the economy is always a wildcard. Even when the colleges have the best of intentions, a string of lean years can force deep cuts in any institution's aid budget.

Savvy financial aid consumers will want to ask if there is a ceiling on self-help as an aid component.

Preferential Packaging

Though loans and work study are nice, grants are what financial aid applicants want to get their hands on. That's the real money—the kind you don't have to pay back. When comparing aid offers, families should generally focus less on the total value of the package than the size of the grants. As a simple example, if College A offers a ten thousand dollar grant and four thousand dollars in loans, while College B offers an eight thousand dollar grant and six thousand dollars in loans, both packages meet fourteen thousand dollars worth of need. But College A's offer is better because it includes more grants and less loans.

In today's financial climate, the ratio of grants and loans included in an aid package often depends on how badly the college wants you to enroll. Even at those that meet the full need of all admitted students, some students make out like bandits with large grants and no or few loans, while others get smaller grants and go thousands into debt.

> **Getting Them to Fight over You**
>
> Aid-conscious applicants should consider applying to schools that compete directly with one another. Colleges are more likely to match aid offers from their closest competitors.

This practice, known as "preferential packaging" or "sweetening the pot," is nearly universal at selective private colleges. How likely are you to get your pot sweetened? It depends mostly on your qualifications. The admissions office will rate you against other admitted applicants, then the aid office will build a package that is more generous the higher your standing. Your intended major may also come into play. If you're an outstanding humanities student at a college that attracts mainly science students—or is trying to build up its humanities programs—you may get a sweetened offer. Ditto if you are a recruited athlete or a member of an underrepresented minority group. Increasingly, the bottom line of need-based aid is the same as with merit scholarships: the top students are the winners.

Negotiating for More Aid

After the colleges have loaded all their stocking stuffers, the aid offers are unveiled along with the letters of acceptance (or shortly thereafter). Be prepared for wide variation in the size of your awards. Financial aid is far from an exact science and one of the reasons applicants should apply to more than one school is the chance to compare offers.

The Aid Officer's Toolbox

Your financial aid officer is the point person in helping you pay for your education—like the folks at car dealerships who help finance all those cars. Your aid officer decides on what loans, grants, or scholarships the college is willing to offer from its own funds and serves as the coordinator of outside assistance, including virtually all federal aid.

The Federal dollars come through six major programs: Pell Grants, Supplemental Educational Opportunity Grants, Perkins Loans, Stafford Loans, PLUS Loans, and work-study jobs. Federal loans are administered through lending institutions or through the colleges via the Direct Lending program. The colleges also offer grants and loans of their own and often have preferred arrangements with lenders. A number of state-sponsored grant and loan programs round out the list. In approximately half the states, students who file the FAFSA are automatically considered for most of these funds. In the rest, students should file a separate state aid application.

Students and parents should be less concerned with the source of their money than with the bottom line: grants are free and loans must be paid back. If your aid offers include loans, check to see whether they are subsidized or unsubsidized. The former includes deferred payment and a favorable interest rate; the latter is just a regular loan that requires immediate payback. In the past decade, unsubsidized loans have been the fastest growing form of government assistance for students.

Even families that do not qualify for aid may be eligible for financing options. Some universities will guarantee four years at the freshman year rate if you pay the combined tuition bills at enrollment. (And in case you don't have fifty thousand dollars sitting around in your checking account, they will lend you the money.) Most institutions allow payment by a monthly installment program. The Golden Rule of financial aid: seek and ye shall find.

If your awards seem too low or your dream school offers thousands less than your safety, you and your parents should consider an appeal. With competition for students at an all-time high, it is sometimes possible to wheedle additional dollars from the college of your choice. Rule No. 1: be tactful. Begin the inquiry as an effort to understand the offer and how it was put together.

Outside Scholarships: Can I Keep Them?

It depends. When applicants are awarded need-based aid and receive an outside scholarship from, say, the Rotary Club, federal rules prohibit the college from giving a package that exceeds need as determined by FM. For a student whose need has been met fully, an outside scholarship often necessitates a reduction in the aid package.

Many colleges are willing to deduct the amount of the scholarship from loans rather than grants. But policies vary and outside scholarships are sometimes a topic for negotiation—especially for applicants accepted by colleges that have differing policies.

The most promising appeals are generally based on new information or special circumstances. If Grandma is in a nursing home and your parents pay part of the bill, that's a special circumstance. The same is true if your mom is laid off from her job. If Dad doesn't think the financial aid office understood the magnitude of his business debts, he should definitely call to plead his case. On the other hand, sob stories about lifestyle choices are not likely to carry much weight. If the family is strapped for cash after buying a second Mercedes, don't bother telling the financial aid office.

Colleges are favorably disposed to special circumstance

appeals because those provide an obvious reason for changing the award. Appeals made merely to cut a better deal will encounter more resistance. Few colleges publicly admit to revising offers. "We're not going to bend over backwards and award more aid to a family just because they scream louder," says Elaine Solinga of Connecticut College. The reality behind such public pronouncements will depend on the college. Some truly won't negotiate, but others are willing to up the ante—when pressed—to get a student they want.

Unless a recent development has changed the family's financial situation, the best ammunition in such negotiations will be a superior offer from a comparable school. If the differential will be the determining factor in your enrollment decision, make that fact clear and be ready to fax or mail a copy of the other offer. Your bargaining power is likely to correspond to how high you rank in the pool of admitted applicants and how badly the college wants students like you. Some schools, notably Carnegie Mellon and Williams College, openly encourage accepted applications to come forward if they get a superior offer from another college. No less than Harvard has quietly indicated a willingness to be flexible in such cases. Financial aid appeals don't always work, but there is no better way to find out if you really got the college's best offer. As long as you maintain proper courtesy, you have nothing to lose.

How Much Debt Can I Afford?

Some people will pay anything to attend Dream U., but we recommend that students think twice about borrowing more than about five thousand dollars per year. After four years at this rate, you'll pile up a debt of over twenty thousand dollars that will continue to accrue interest until you pay it back.

If you try to work off twenty thousand dollars of debt in five years, you'll owe roughly four hundred and fifty dollars per month—more than a fourth of the take-home pay of a person who earns twenty-five thousand dollars a year. That's no problem if you're drafted by the NFL or the NBA, but many students will want to attend graduate school and may need—you guessed it—more loans. Spreading the payments over ten years will cut your monthly bill in half, but the total you owe will also be greater because of the additional interest charges. Paying off college debt at age thirty is not an ideal situation, especially if you are trying to start a family.

After all appeals have been exhausted, some unlucky souls will still find themselves gapped. If your aid offers don't meet the family's full need, you have a decision to make. You can either attend a cheaper school or ask the family to help pay your way with additional loans above and beyond what the college has given you. A home-equity loan is the favored choice for many because the interest payments are generally tax deductible. Also available is the unsubsidized PLUS loan program, in which parents can borrow up to the full costs of attendance (minus the aid offer) without regard to need. But those who choose this option risk creating a mountain of family debt. A better strategy for those who are gapped might be to work for a year between high school and college to save the much-needed funds. Most colleges will allow you to defer enrollment for a year if you want to build up your assets.

It is sometimes possible to wheedle additional dollars from the college of your choice.

Though paying for college is still a daunting prospect—especially at private institutions—the future appears much brighter than the immediate past. College costs are still outpacing inflation, but new sources of aid are rising to soften the blow. With that thought in mind, we turn in the next chapter to an applicant's eye view of how to conquer the aid process.

19. Dave's World:
A Financial Aid Timeline

To everyone who persevered through Chapter 18, we offer a hearty round of congratulations. The only thing left is to master the nuts and bolts—forms, deadlines, and all the other details. To reward your persistence, we've created an applicant's helper to guide you through the maze. His name is Dave and he's probably the most conscientious financial aid applicant who has ever lived. (You may be tempted to strangle him after a while, but remember, he's here to help you.) It will come as no surprise that Dave is one of the top students in his class. His grade point average is a sparkling 3.89 and he scored above 700 on each section of the SAT. Follow along with Dave's financial aid search and you won't miss a trick when it comes to your own.

Winter, Junior Year
With college looming on the horizon, Dave calls his parents together for a chat about his prospects. They're committed to paying for his college expenses, but the concern in their voices is apparent from the moment he enters the room. Their incomes total ninety-eight thousand dollars per year— too much, they fear, to qualify for the substantial financial aid they think they might need. Dave's father was recently diagnosed with Parkinson's disease, and though he still holds his job as a sales manager at a pharmaceutical company, the family is already preparing for when he will be unable to work. (He is also contemplating some experimental treatments not covered by his company's health plan.) Will the colleges make an allowance for medical expenses in their calculations? After some preliminary figuring, Dave's

parents conclude that they can afford about fifteen to eighteen thousand dollars per year for his college expenses. Both are somber as they come to the realization that some colleges may be too expensive for them to afford. "That's okay," replies Dave cheerfully. "I'll handle the rest."

Armed with the financial parameters he needs, Dave makes an appointment with his guidance counselor to officially begin the college search. Together, they settle on a two-pronged strategy that will include some schools above the fifteen thousand dollar threshold and some below it. Ever since Dave read F. Scott Fitzgerald's *This Side of Paradise* as an eighth-grader, his dream has been to attend Princeton University, a school in the forty thousand dollar-plus category. Several other Ivy League schools have caught his eye, as well as some elite small colleges that are highly selective and highly expensive. Dave is disappointed to learn that most of these schools do not offer merit scholarships, but his counselor suggests some other slightly less lofty selections that do. Dave knows that neither type will be possible without some form of aid, but he is determined to scrape together the money. Just in case the aid doesn't work out, Dave and his counselor also discuss a range of schools with sticker prices at or near fifteen thousand dollars. He is particularly intrigued by his counselor's list of public liberal arts colleges. Most of them don't have the big reputation of a private school, but she assures him that they provide a comparable education— often at less than half the price. Alas, none of them are in state, but Dave notes that their out-of-state expenses are generally within his price range.

At his counselor's suggestion, Dave asks his parents to complete the financial aid estimator program on the College Board's website. She cautions that it will produce only a ball-park approximation of the EFCs that might be computed by particular colleges. The program is quick and easy, but yields distressing news—an expected family contribution of twenty-four thousand dollars. Without special consideration for his father's medical condition, Dave's family is unlikely to qualify for substantial need-based aid.

Spring, Junior Year

With his prospects for need-based aid looking bleaker, Dave decides to get busy on his search for scholarship money. Though he knows that colleges are the primary source for aid, they're far from the only source. His uncle suggests that he look into Army ROTC, a program that will pay up to twenty thousand dollars toward his education at a number of the schools on his list in exchange for service in the reserves after college. Dave is jolted to learn that his friend Josh is already knee-deep in the application process for ROTC and the service academies. Though he soon decides that the army isn't for him, Dave hastily makes an appointment with his counselor to find out what other deadlines might be sneaking up on him.

> **Aid Tip for Parents**
>
> To maximize your prospects for financial aid, it is best to save in your name(s) rather than in your child's name. The aid formula taxes student assets at a far higher rate than parental ones.

Dave's counselor chuckles to find him in such a tizzy over scholarship deadlines in the spring of his junior year. She commends Dave on his conscientiousness and points him to a shelf of scholarship books and a computer workstation in the corner of the guidance office. During his free periods, he'll devote several hours to picking over those. In the meantime, Dave has a list of questions that are on his mind.

"I've heard that millions of dollars in financial aid money goes unclaimed every year. Is that true?"

"That's just talk," his counselor replies. "I'm sure some scholarships do go unclaimed, but mainly ones targeted to specific populations. Some are for members of a particular church or for inhabitants of a particular county who belong to the Elks Club or the DAR. Sometimes private companies create scholarships for the children of their employees. The state has money set aside for war orphans. How many war orphans do you know?"

"A friend of mine got a letter from a company that guaranteed it could find ten scholarships for him for a fifty-dollar fee. It sounded like a good deal to me. What do you think?"

"I think he had better read the fine print. Most of those outfits say they'll find scholarships 'for which you qualify.' That's not to say you'll actually get them. Give me ten minutes and I'll find ten scholarships for which you qualify, too. There are plenty of free scholarship databases on the Web and here in the guidance office that are at least as good as the one they're using. Never, ever, pay anybody to find you scholarships."

"So how do I find them on my own?"

"My rule of thumb is simple: look locally first. That's where you have the best shot at getting money. I have a file of local scholarships that you should definitely look at. Several of them even guarantee that one person from our school will win. Also check out scholarships relevant to your background and interests—your race, your religion, your parents' employers, your intended major, and so on. You can use our books and database."

"Can you tell me more about the sources on the Web?"

"There are plenty, but I don't recommend random surfing. There are too many hucksters selling information that is either useless or available free elsewhere. As a place to begin, your best bet is the SmartStudent Guide to Financial Aid at www.finaid.org. It includes everything you could ever want to know about financial aid, as well as links to other key financial aid sites. The biggest scholarship search site is at www.fastweb.com, a database of several hundred thousand scholarships and loans."

"Any other places to look?"

"The state has a number of scholarships, including one that is awarded on the basis of your class rank and SAT scores—I'll set it aside for you when I get the announcement. If you're really ambitious, you can try for some of the national scholarships. I receive notices for them all the time. Just remember: most scholarship programs get hundreds or even thousands of applicants for every scholarship."

"What about deadlines?"

"The deadlines vary, but some are as early as September or October. It pays to keep your eyes open and start early."

"Any other advice?"

"Don't count on finding a pot of gold. Most corporate or civic scholarships are small—in the five hundred to two thousand dollar range. Then again, every little bit helps."

Summer between Junior and Senior Year

Like many of his fellow applicants, Dave and his family take a summer college tour that includes many of the eastern schools where he wants to apply. When Dave has his admissions interviews, his parents take the opportunity to meet with financial aid officials at several stops along the way. The officials are sympathetic to his father's medical problem and ask that the family outline the particulars of his condition in a letter to accompany the financial aid application. They also suggest a letter from his physician. Though the financial aid officers make no guarantees, Dave's parents are reassured that they will be given a fair hearing.

> **Money Isn't Everything (But It Helps)**
>
> To check out a college's ability to provide need-based aid, examine its endowment per student. The higher it is, the more likely the school provides generous aid packages. A typical selective private college has about $100,000 per student.

Fall, Senior Year

Dave returns from summer vacation with a healthy tan and a head of steam to finish out his college search. Throughout the preceding months, he has toyed with the idea of applying early decision to Princeton. But Dave was turned off by his tour guide (too "stuck up") and by the aura he felt when visiting a dining hall. On a rainy day, the Gothic architecture seemed cold and forbidding. So much for Princeton. Without a clear first choice, Dave makes peace with the fact that he will not apply early decision to any college as many of his friends are doing. From a financial aid standpoint, his decision is a sensible one. As a potential merit scholarship candidate, his best move is to wait until all the offers are on the table before making a commitment.

As application time draws near, Dave hones his strategy for hitting financial pay dirt. All the schools on his list reflect his preference for a small liberal arts college in or near a city. But in making his final selections, he is careful to include choices in each of three categories:

1. prestigious colleges likely to provide the best need-based aid
2. less-selective private colleges where he might get a merit scholarship
3. leading public colleges that combine quality programs with low tuition

In early November, Dave completes the online registration for the CSS/Financial Aid PROFILE, which generates a personalized copy of the form with supplemental questions specified by each of Dave's colleges. Since his earliest financial aid deadline is not until February 1, he will wait and let his parents file the FAFSA and PROFILE together in January.

Tips for Filing the PROFILE and FAFSA

- Be sure your full legal name, social security number, and date of birth are correct. Errors on these important items can cause delays in processing.
- FAFSA filers should request a PIN at least two weeks before they plan to file the form. Both students and parents need a PIN.
- Do a dry run with a paper worksheet and then transfer data to the online form.
- If you are filling out both the FAFSA and PROFILE, make sure the figures match.
- Input your electronic signature and SAVE COPIES OF EVERYTHING.

Throughout the fall, Dave continues his search for outside scholarships. He locates a promising one for members of the Lutheran Church and files it in time for the November 15 deadline. He also finds several for students who intend to study history and another sponsored by the local Rotary Club. But he also decides not to apply for several national scholarships that require long essays. Even a financial aid whiz kid like Dave has his limits.

Winter, Senior Year

In early December, Dave's counselor announces that FAFSA worksheets have arrived from the Department of Education. Even though Dave will file electronically, he is among the first to come to the guidance office to get one. That evening, Dave sits down with his parents to review the timetable. The form should be filed after January 1, but before the deadlines specified by the colleges. Since the earliest of the latter (for both the FAFSA and PROFILE) is February 1, the family has a one-month window at the beginning of the new year to gather its tax information and file the forms.

It will be a tight squeeze. Though Dave's parents can estimate their income from salaries and capital gains, the 1099 forms detailing the latter are yet to arrive (even after multiple phone calls to speed the process). By mid-January, they have a dilemma. They can file the FAFSA and PROFILE using income estimates or they can wait to file until after completing their tax return and risk missing a deadline. Uncertain of how to proceed, Dave calls the financial aid office at the college with the earliest deadline. The representative advises the family to file the FAFSA before the deadline and to use estimated figures if necessary.

Filing with income estimates poses a slight problem because it often triggers the Verification process.

Filing with income estimates poses a slight problem because it often triggers the Verification process, in which the government requires submission of copies of tax forms to verify that the estimated figures are accurate. If discrepancies arise totaling more than four hundred dollars, the aid award must be calculated again. Though Verification is not as bad as getting hauled in by the IRS, it is a process to be avoided if possible. (A smaller proportion of applicants who file on the basis of completed tax returns are also selected for Verification.)

Fortunately, the deadline problem for Dave and his family solves itself. The final 1099 arrives on January 21, allowing them to complete the aid forms before the deadline with an official tax return. The process of filing via www.fafsa.ed.gov and www.collegeboard.com is quick and easy, in part because Dave and his parents have spent time reviewing paper worksheets from FAFSA and College Board. They take care to follow the directions to the letter, printing and saving where prompted and entering their PINs for an electronic signature.

The final element in the application process is a crucial one for Dave and his family: communication directly with the colleges. Several of them require submission of their own institutional form; all want copies of relevant tax documents. In addition, Dave's father has drafted a letter to each outlining his medical condition to send with a letter from his doctor.

With both forms submitted, Dave breathes a sigh of relief. But there is still work to be done. From the FAFSA processor comes a Student Aid Report (SAR) calculating his EFC based on the Federal Methodology. In response to submission of the CSS PROFILE, the family gets an acknowledgment listing the colleges to which his information has been sent along with a Data Confirmation Report. The family carefully scrutinizes everything to make sure that the information is accurate. (In the event that corrections were necessary, the family would promptly send them back according to the instructions on the respective forms.)

Spring, Senior Year

Life as a second-semester senior treats Dave well. After fifteen months in the college admissions torture chamber, Dave begins to relax. The color comes back to his complexion. He goes to parties with friends on the weekends and even asks a girl from his French class to the prom.

Early April puts an extra bounce in his step when he is accepted at five of the seven colleges to which he applied. Though he does not win any of the outside scholarship competitions, Dave enjoys a menu of awards from the colleges to which he applied. Below is the list of the ones that accepted him by category, along with the all-important offers of financial aid.

Category No.1: Prestigious Private Colleges

	Elite U.	Ivy U.
Sticker price:	$48,000	$51,000
Aid total:	$29,000	$26,000
Grant:	$22,500	$20,000
Loan:	$4,500	$4,000
Work-study:	$2,000	$2,000
Total Dave's family must pay:	$19,000	$25,000

Comments

Though Ivy and Elite both gave Dave need-based aid, only Elite made an adjustment for his father's illness. Ivy used its standard institutional methodology to calculate a twenty-five thousand dollar Expected Family Contribution. At Elite, the financial-aid office used what is called "professional judgment" to lessen the EFC by six thousand dollars. The issue is highly subjective because Dave's dad is still working.

Category No. 2: Less Selective Private Colleges

	Almost Ivy U.	Up-and-Coming U.
Sticker total:	$43,000	$41,000
Aid total:	$21,500	$34,500
Merit award:	$0	$34,500
Grant:	$20,000	
Loan:	$0	
Work study:	$1,500	
Total Dave's family must pay:	$21,500	$6,500

Comments

Dave hit the jackpot at Up-and-Coming with a four-year, full tuition Founder's Scholarship. He also made the final cut at Almost Ivy for a Presidential Merit Award, but was nosed out by a concert violinist who is also a junior-level rodeo champion. Since he is one of Almost Ivy's strongest applicants, the university is nonetheless very interested in enrolling him. Like Elite, they have made an allowance in their need-based formula for his father's illness, though not quite as large. They also used differential packaging to substitute a five thousand dollar Alumni Scholarship for what would normally be the loan component of Dave's aid package. His combination of strong credentials and high EFC made him an ideal choice for a discount. Little did they know that their offer would be dwarfed by Up-and-Coming.

Category No. 3: Public Liberal Arts College

	Public Liberal Arts College	State U.
Sticker Price:	$29,000 (out of state)	$15,000 (in state)
Aid total:	$2,000	$2,000
Merit award:	$2,000	$2,000
Total Dave's family must pay:	$27,000	$13,000

Comments

At Public Liberal Arts, need-based aid is limited primarily to government programs and major merit scholarships are earmarked for state residents. Dave does, however, get a two thousand dollar President's Leadership Award.

State U. never captured Dave's fancy, but it is inexpensive. The two thousand dollar merit award comes by virtue of Dave's acceptance into State U.'s honors program.

All in all, Dave has done well. As an excellent student with relatively strong financial resources, he has avoided being gapped by any of his colleges. Not all gave the family everything it wanted, but Dave feels the satisfaction of a job well done. As icing on the cake, he wins a five hundred dollar award from the Lutheran Church scholarship contest.

Despite all the good news, his father is miffed that Ivy U. did not make a better offer. (Ivy had always been his dad's first choice.) After fretting for a week, Dave's father suggests calling to appeal for more aid. He is sure that Ivy will beef up its package when it learns what archrival Elite has offered. Dave demurs. He has made his decision. Up-and-Coming is the school that really wants him—so that's where he'll go. The history department there is nationally known and he liked everything about the school when he visited. As Dave sees it, the primary difference between Ivy and Up-and-Coming will be the decal in the family car's back window. For a savings of nearly eighty thousand dollars across four years, that's a decal he can do without.

Part Four:

A Time
to Reflect

20. Fat Letters and Thin

A quick glance is all you need to tell whether an admissions office letter carries tidings of joy or cause for depression. Meaty envelopes have cordial letters of acceptance and information about enrollment and housing. Skinny envelopes hold nothing more than a "Dear John" letter or notification that you have been placed on a waitlist. Many of today's applicants don't bother to wait for the mailman. Colleges still send decision letters, but most also allow students to learn their fate online the day those letters are mailed.

Either way, the build-up to decision day can be excruciating. Your high school buzzes with gossip of who was accepted or rejected. Your relatives call to see if you've heard any news yet. The tension mounts. Your nerves become frazzled. You begin to believe your destiny is hanging in the balance. And you're certain that if the "best" school rejects you, your life will never be the same.

Before you fling yourself off the Golden Gate Bridge, get a grip. If you've followed the advice of this book, you haven't put all your hopes and dreams into one admissions basket. There is no such thing as the perfect college, but there are dozens—probably hundreds—of schools where you will fit in and get a good education. After a few weeks at your new alma mater, you'll probably forget that you ever applied anywhere else.

Can I Appeal a Denial?

In most cases, the answer is no. But if you are genuinely shocked at being denied admission, ask your counselor to call and inquire as to why. Occasionally, high school transcripts can be misinterpreted, scores lost, and so on. If the phone call yields a glimmer of hope or if you still can't put the matter to rest, ask your counselor for the name of the admissions representative assigned to your school. Write him or her a letter expressing your sincere disappointment and outlining why you still believe that this is the right school for you. Your appeal will have a better chance if you can include new information about your accomplishments or motivation. About a week after mailing the letter, call the admissions officer yourself to make your case. No matter what his reaction, be polite. Ranting and raving from either you or your parents are guaranteed to do no good.

Though the odds of a successful appeal are about the same as winning the lottery, there are occasional success stories, such as the applicant to Wabash College who was denied admission because of his less-than-impressive academic record. This young man reapplied and asked that he be interviewed by several faculty as well as members of the admissions committee. Against all odds, he sold them in person and was admitted.

Handling the Waitlist

Prospects for students on the waitlist are brighter, though far from sunny. Along with all the acceptances and denials, most colleges put at least several hundred students on the waitlist every year. Why? Because they are not sure how many of the ones they *Think hard about whether* accept will actually enroll. As *pursuing the waitlist is worth* more and more students submit *the time, effort, and agony.* multiple applications, colleges' yields have become more unpredictable. The waitlist is their margin of safety. The number of these who are ultimately accepted can vary widely. One year, a few hundred might ultimately get in; the next year, none at all. The odds of any individual student being accepted from a waitlist are less than fifty/fifty, but by no means minuscule.

If you find yourself on a waitlist, your first move should be to send a deposit to your first choice among the colleges that accepted you. You don't need to tell this college that you are pursuing the waitlist somewhere else; all of them know that a percentage of those who say yes in April will end up elsewhere in September.

Next, think hard about whether pursuing the waitlist is worth the time, effort, and agony. Though most waitlist activity occurs by the end of May, sometimes applicants are left dangling throughout the summer. Even if you hang in there and do everything right, success is far from assured.

The waitlist is an all-or-nothing proposition. To give yourself a chance, you'll need to mount a well-orchestrated campaign, enlisting the support of your teachers and counselors. "Calculated persistence and repeated statements of interest can pay off," says David Erdmann of Rollins College. "Don't be afraid to show your stuff."

To begin, fill out the postcard to express interest in pursuing the waitlist and send it in. Next, consider doing some or all of the following:

- Send a letter ASAP to the admissions director emphasizing your unyielding desire to attend. State specifically why you think the match is a good one and highlight new information.
- Call to see if you can arrange a campus interview. "Students who have been offered regular admission waitlist status are well advised to pay a visit by mid-April, perhaps with a set of recent grades in hand!" says Peter Van Buskirk, former Dean of Admissions at Franklin and Marshall.
- Send examples of impressive work. This is particularly relevant if you have an area of special talent or if you have produced new work of which you are especially proud.
- Ask a current teacher to write a recommendation

highlighting your recent achievements. Ask teachers who wrote letters for you previously to send updates.

- Ask your guidance counselor to write or call and see that the admissions office is kept up to date with your grades and other achievements.

Unfortunately, ability to pay also intrudes into the waitlist process. Most colleges have little or no financial aid remaining when they get to the waitlist and, as a result, high-need students rarely make it. Those with little or no need have the best chance and your odds will improve if you can assure the college that you plan to attend with or without aid.

Through it all, be a model of politeness. If you get testy or try to use pressure tactics, the game is over. Colleges use spots on the waitlist to make dreams come true for a lucky handful who have clearly communicated their wishes.

Onward and Upward

If you're agonizing over a waitlist decision that is still dangling—or maybe down in the dumps because First Choice U. didn't come through with an acceptance—take a moment to remind yourself of the big picture. The college selection process has a lot in common with finding a boyfriend or girlfriend: it is easy to fall in love and a rejection can seem like the end of the world. But soon enough, the reality dawns that there are others who could be just as good a match as the one that got away.

If you've experienced a disappointment, think again about the colleges where you did get in. Chances are, they'll offer just as many interesting courses and top professors and their student bodies will include just as many bright and interesting new people to meet. A world of opportunity will unfold no matter where you attend and your ultimate success may hinge less on which college you choose than on what you make of it once you are there.

The real value of college lies in what it does for you as a person—in expanding your horizons, challenging your beliefs, honing your skills, and exposing you to the broadest possible cross section of people and ideas. You've got four of the most invigorating and rewarding years of your life just ahead. Make the most of them.

21. Some Thoughts for Parents

Being the parent of a college applicant can be a white-knuckle experience. Like the basketball coach who sits helplessly as his team launches a last-second shot, parents can do little more than cheer from the sidelines as their child aims for Dream U. As many parents know from experience, the pressure of the big game is often more intense for those who watch than those who play.

Basketball analogies aside, there are things parents can do to help assure a successful college search. This chapter will cover a number of them, but one stands out: the ability to maintain perspective. Parents have seen more of life than their children: they've wept tears of joy in hospital delivery rooms and tears of sorrow beside open caskets. When college admission begins to seem like life or death in the eyes of an eighteen-year-old, parents must be there to help restore perspective.

Different applicants have different needs. Some students need a nudge to get motivated, others need reassurance to avoid paralyzing fear. Some need encouragement to aim higher, others need to know that attending a less prestigious school doesn't make them a lesser person. Many applicants simply need space to explore. You know your child better than anyone. Try to maintain enough perspective to provide what he or she needs.

The task is by no means easy. Psychologists know that major separation events can cause dysfunctional behaviors. One of the most common is denial. If your son or daughter has trouble focusing on the college search—or actively refuses to think about it—the reason may not be indifference. Many students use such tactics to avoid confronting a reality that scares them. If your student is in denial, stay calm. When students drag their feet, parents often feel an exaggerated sense of urgency. Resist the temptation to deliver ultimatums—or worse, take over the college search yourself. Such overreactions cause resentment and reinforce your child's dependence. Instead, help your child get unstuck with steady encouragement. For those with patience, the college search usually has a way of working out.

As graduation and college decision time draw near, many families experience an upsurge in conflict. The approach of college often intensifies arguments about curfews and duties. Students act out resentment toward parents, who in turn may show a heightened desire to hang on or seize a last chance to impart wisdom or values. If you feel such a spiral coming on, help your child take a step back. The amount of familial conflict at this time of life is often proportional to the amount of love.

Amid all the tumult, good parents will constantly seek ways to move the process forward. Here are some tips.

Communicate

One of the most important things that parents can do is encourage their sons and daughters to think through the basic questions. Why do you want to go to college? What are your most important needs and goals? What kind of college will best serve you? Communicating with an adolescent is not always easy, but look for the moments that present themselves. Being available to talk when your child has a question or wants to express an idea or feeling is one of the most important things you can do.

Set Financial Parameters

Paying for college is the area where parents have veto power. Try to reach an understanding early in the process as to how much each party is expected to pay (before hopes get pinned on a college that may be financially out of reach). If you haven't already done so, read the two chapters on financial aid. Then sit down with your child to formulate guidelines for the search.

Be Realistic

Don't set your child up for failure by encouraging unrealistic applications. Look honestly at your child's academic record. Then study the admissions profiles of the colleges that show up on your lists. If he or she is not Stanford material, don't swing by Palo Alto on your college tour. Make it your task to be sure that your son or daughter applies to at least two colleges

If he or she is not Stanford material, don't swing by Palo Alto on your college tour.

where he or she will definitely be accepted. Then even the worst-case scenario will still result in a productive college experience.

Think Broadly

The United States has the best and most diverse system of higher education anywhere in the world. As we've said many times, there are scores of colleges that would be a good match for every student. You are probably in a better position than your son or daughter to understand this and help discourage fixation on a single "dream" school (that may be highly selective). Some of the best colleges for your child may be ones that neither of you has ever heard of.

Let the Student Take Center Stage

In the college search, nothing is worse than a parent who steals the spotlight. Many parents, especially successful ones, are accustomed to manipulating the system to make it work for them. Resist the temptation. The admissions process is the time for teenagers to stand on their own. Parental attempts at marketing or influence peddling often do more harm than good.

Don't Live through Your Child

Many parents subconsciously relive their own hopes and dreams through their children. Some want children to follow in their footsteps, others want them to achieve things that they themselves never could. Still other parents see college admissions as their shot at an *A+* in parenting. Having hopes for your children is natural, but try to spare them the burden of expectations. One of the greatest gifts you can give your child is the freedom to follow his or her own dreams.

Be Supportive

As the process unfolds, remind your children that they will be accepted at a good school—one where they will make friends, have fun, be challenged, and get the education they deserve. When the decisions come in, redouble your efforts on this score and, if necessary, remind them of the fickle nature of the whole selection process.

We close with a message to parents delivered by the counselors at Weston High School in Connecticut. Though written many years ago, the sentiments are as timely now as the day they were written:

> We should help [our children] understand that we love and care for them no matter what a given college decides. We need to make it clear to them that college admission decisions are not evaluations of them either as students or as valuable human beings. Let them know that no matter what, you believe they are unique individuals whom you love and respect.

Appendix I
What to Do When

The following pages offer a chronological overview of the college search. For a more detailed guide to all the dates and deadlines of the college search, look for *Fiske Countdown to College: 41 To-Do Lists and a Plan for Every Year of High School.*

Freshman Year
Take challenging courses and join activities that may be pursued to levels of distinction or leadership. Advanced students may consider taking SAT Subject Tests in June. (Biology is the most frequent choice.)

Sophomore Year
Continue with challenging courses and make plans for honors and/or AP work in grades eleven and twelve. Take the PSAT in October if it is offered for sophomores at your school. Advanced students may consider taking SAT Subject Tests in June. (Chemistry and Math are the most frequent choices.) In early summer, begin looking ahead to the PSAT to be administered in October of eleventh grade and consider how to prepare. If the student is ready to begin the college search, consider visiting colleges.

Junior Year
Keep working hard! Your chances for admission or a scholarship will depend largely on your academic record.

September–November
Begin sizing up your college needs. Read college guides and/or use an online search. Meet with guidance counselor. Take the PSAT.

December–February
Prepare to take the SAT and register for the January, March, and/or May administration of the SAT. Do the same for ACT and register for the February or April dates. Talk to parents, teachers, older friends, and guidance counselors about colleges. Discuss finances and the college selection process with parents.

March–April
Sift through college mail. Begin preliminary winnowing. Meet with your guidance counselor to discuss a list of ten to twenty colleges. Begin visiting colleges and/or plan summer visits. Take the SAT or ACT if scheduled. Register for June administration of SAT Subject Tests or ACT.

May
Settle on a working list of ten to twelve colleges and continue scheduling visits. Take the SAT Subject Tests or AP tests if scheduled.

June
Take SAT Subject Tests or ACT if scheduled. Relax and enjoy the end of school.

July–August
Go on summer visits. Fine-tune your list of colleges. Talk to friends about the ones they are interested in. Begin work on college essays. Prepare for fall standardized tests.

Senior Year
September
Continue college visits. Meet with your counselor. Consider early decision or early action. Get application forms from the colleges. Arrange to take the SAT, Subject Tests, and/or ACT in October, November, and December, where applicable. Ask

teachers to write recommendations and provide them with the necessary forms and envelopes. Continue scholarship search. If applying for early decision/action, register for the CSS/Financial Aid PROFILE at www.collegeboard.com.

October

Continue college visits, and file early decision or action applications if applicable. Settle on a final list of schools to apply to. Get a copy of your transcript and check it over. Talk with your counselor about the logistics of the application process. Continue distributing teacher recommendation forms. Double-check deadlines for admission, housing, and financial aid. Take the SAT, Subject Tests, or ACT if scheduled. (Last date for first round early decision or action.) If applying early decision or action, file the CSS/Financial Aid PROFILE.

November

File applications with December deadlines. Continue distributing teacher recommendation forms. Continue working on applications. Take the SAT or Subject Tests if scheduled.

December

File applications with January deadlines. Politely check with teachers and the counselor to make sure that recommendations and your transcript have been sent. Register for the CSS/Financial Aid PROFILE at www.collegeboard.com. Get the paper worksheet for the Free Application for Federal Student Aid (FAFSA) from the guidance office and ask your parents to begin collecting tax information from the year that is ending. Take the SAT, Subject Tests, or ACT. (Last date for January or February application deadlines.)

January–February

Continue to file applications. Call admissions offices to

verify that the applications are complete. File the FAFSA and PROFILE using paper forms or at www.fafsa.ed.gov and www.collegeboard.com. Watch for follow-up mail addressed to the student. Mail necessary financial aid documentation directly to the colleges. Take your final SAT, Subject Tests, or ACT.

March–April
Receive decision letters. Scrutinize financial aid offers and call the colleges if you have concerns. If you are waitlisted, follow up with a letter and additional recommendations. Schedule last-minute visits to colleges where accepted or waitlisted. Make the final decision and send in a deposit.

May
Take AP tests if applicable. Give yourself a pat on the back. You did it!

Appendix II
Glossary

The language of college admissions is replete with arcane acronyms and obscure terms. Here are some definitions.

ACT. A nonprofit organization that administers the standardized test that bears its name. Most colleges allow students to submit results from either the ACT or the SAT to satisfy the standardized testing requirement. ACT is not affiliated with the College Board or ETS.

College Board. Also known as the College Entrance Examination Board, the College Board produces the Preliminary SAT (PSAT) and the SAT and Subject Tests. The College Board also runs the Advanced Placement (AP) Program and one of its subdivisions, the College Scholarship Service, is the maker of the CSS/Financial Aid PROFILE. See also: **Educational Testing Service**.

Common Application. A standard application form that is accepted by about three hundred selective colleges in lieu of their own form. Available at www.commonapp.org.

consortium. A group of colleges or universities that offer joint programs or allow students from one institution to take courses at another.

CSS/Financial Aid PROFILE. A financial aid form produced by the College Board that is required for students seeking aid at approximately 10 percent of the nation's four-year colleges (including most highly selective institutions).

deferral. The term applied to applications for early action or early decision that are deferred for consideration with the regular application pool.

demonstrated need. The difference between the Expected Family Contribution (EFC) and the total cost of attendance at a particular institution.

early action. A program whereby students receive an early admission decision, but are not obligated to enroll if admitted. Also known as **early notification**.

early decision. A program that gives students an early admission decision with the obligation to enroll if admitted and to withdraw applications from other institutions.

Educational Testing Service (ETS). A nonprofit organization that designs and administers the SAT and Subject Tests through a contractual arrangement with the College Board.

federal methodology (FM). The method of calculating the Expected Family Contribution (EFC) that rests solely on the data submitted in the Free Application for Federal Student Aid (FAFSA) and the federal aid formula.

financial aid package. The bundle of aid awarded by a particular college that may include grants, loans, and a work-study job.

Free Application for Federal Student Aid (FAFSA). A financial aid form produced by the federal government that is required for students seeking aid by nearly all colleges and universities.

institutional methodology (IM). A method of calculating Expected Family Contribution (EFC) that varies by college and may depend on data submitted in the Free Application for Federal Student Aid (FAFSA), the CSS/Financial Aid PROFILE, and the college's own aid form.

National Merit Scholarship Program. A scholarship and recognition program based primarily on scores from the Preliminary SAT (PSAT). More than seventy-five hundred students each year receive scholarships based on National Merit status, ranging from several hundred dollars to the full costs of attendance. Separate programs honor African American and Hispanic students.

need-blind admissions. The term that applies to colleges that make admissions decisions without regard to the financial circumstances of the applicants. Colleges with need-blind admissions do not necessarily offer aid to meet the full need of all accepted applicants.

Preliminary SAT (PSAT). A test produced by the College Board that is administered by high schools to eleventh graders and some tenth graders. The PSAT is the qualifying test for consideration in the National Merit Scholarship Program.

preferential packaging. A method of awarding financial aid in which colleges offer the best aid packages to their most desired applicants.

rolling admission. The term describing admissions without fixed application deadlines. Applications are evaluated as they are received until the class is full.

SAT. The SAT is a three-hour and forty-five minute test that has historically consisted of verbal and math sections. It was revised in 2005 to include Writing, Critical Reading, and Math. The writing section includes a 25-minute essay.

SAT Subject Tests. Formerly known as Achievement Tests, SAT Subject Tests are one-hour tests available in 18 subjects. Required only by the most selective colleges.

self–help. A term that describes the portion of a financial aid package consisting of loans and wages from a work-study job.

Student Aid Report (SAR). A form sent to families in response to submission of the Free Application for Federal Student Aid (FAFSA) that includes the Expected Family Contribution (EFC), a figure that may be modified at colleges that use institutional methodology (IM).

waiting list (or waitlist). A list of applicants to a particular college who are not admitted in the regular decision pool, but who may be considered if space is still available after admitted students have indicated whether or not they will attend.

work study. A federally funded program wherein students are given campus jobs with the wages calculated as part of their financial aid package.

yield. The percentage of accepted applicants at a particular college who choose to enroll.

Acknowledgments

We are grateful to many people for help in the preparation of this book. First and foremost, we would like to thank the scores of college admissions and financial aid professionals who gave us an inside look at how the system really works. We appreciate the ongoing advice of our College Counselors Advisory Group, which was particularly helpful in revising the One-Hour College Finder. We remain grateful to those who offered comments on portions of the first edition of the book, including Valerie R. Bell, Wynne Curry, Guy Hammond, Pam Fay-Williams, Donald J. Heider, Betsy Hughes, Whitney Lloyd, Gary Sabourin, and Susan Sour. We are deeply indebted to David Miller, director of financial aid at the College of Wooster, for his help in navigating the labyrinth of college financial aid. Julie Fiske Hogan stepped in with efficiency and good cheer to help verify quotes and check facts. Our editors, Todd Stocke, Peter Lynch, and Stephen O'Rear are a delight to work with, and we are grateful to everyone at Sourcebooks for their enthusiasm and support for this project. The efforts of all are much appreciated, but responsibility for the final product is ours alone.

College Counselors Advisory Group

Marilyn Albarelli, Moravian Academy (PA)

Scott Anderson, St. George's Independent School (TN)

Christine Asmussen, St. Andrew's-Sewanee School (TN)

Bruce Bailey, Lakeside School (WA)

Amy E. Belstra, Cherry Creek H.S. (CO)

Greg Birk, Kinkaid School (TX)

Susan T. Bisson, Advocates for Human Potential (MA)

Francine E. Block, American College Admissions Consultants (PA)

Robin Boren, Education Consultant (CO)

Clarice Boring, Cody H.S. (WY)

John B. Boshoven, Community High School & Jewish Academy of Metro Detroit (MI)

Mimi Bradley, St. Andrew's Episcopal School (MS)

Claire Cafaro, Clear Directions (NJ)

Nancy Caine, St. Augustine H.S. (CA)

Jane M. Catanzaro, College Advising Services (CT)

Mary Chapman, St. Catherine's School (VA)

Anthony L. Clay, Carolina Friends School (NC)

Kathy Cleaver, Durham Academy (NC)

Jimmie Lee Cogburn, Independent Counselor (GA)

Alison Cotten, Cypress Falls H.S. (TX)

Alice Cotti, Polytechnic School (CA)

Rod Cox, St. Johns Country Day School (FL)

Kim Crockard, Crockard College Counseling (AL)

Carroll K. Davis, North Central H.S. (IN)

Mary Jo Dawson, Academy of the Sacred Heart (MI)

Lexi Eagles, Greensboro Country Day School (NC)

Dan Feldhaus, Iolani School (HI)

Ralph S. Figueroa, Albuquerque Academy (NM)

Emily E. FitzHugh, The Gunnery (CT)

Larry Fletcher, Salesianum School (DE)

Nancy Fomby, Episcopal School of Dallas (TX)

Daniel Franklin, Education Consultant (CO)

Laura Johnson Frey, Vermont Academy (VT)

Phyllis Gill, Providence Day School (NC)

H. Scotte Gordon, Moses Brown School (RI)

Freida Gottsegen, Education Consultant (GA)

Molly Gotwals, Suffield Academy (CT)

Kathleen Barnes Grant, The Catlin Gabel School (OR)

Madelyn Gray, John Burroughs School (MO)

Amy Grieger, Northfield Mount Hermon School (MA)

Mimi Grossman, St. Mary's Episcopal School (TN)

Elizabeth Hall, Education Consulting Services (TX)

Andrea L. Hays, Education Consultant (GA)

Darnell Heywood, Columbus Academy (OH)

Bruce Hunter, Rowland Hall-St. Mark's School (UT)

Deanna L. Hunter, Shawnee Mission East H.S. (KS)

Linda King, College Connections (NY)

Sharon Koenings, Brookfield Academy (WI)

Joan Jacobson, Shawnee Mission South H.S. (KS)

Diane Johnson, Lawrence Public Schools (NY)

Gerimae Kleinman, Shaker Heights H.S. (OH)

Laurie Leftwich, Brother Martin High School (LA)

MaryJane London, Los Angeles Center for Enriched Studies (CA)

Martha Lyman, Deerfield Academy (MA)

Brad MacGowan, Newton North H.S. (MA)

Robert S. MacLellan, Jr., Hebron Academy (ME)

Susan Marrs, The Seven Hills School (OH)

Karen A. Mason, Germantown Academy (PA)

Lynne McConnell, Rumson-Fair Haven Regional H.S. (NJ)

Lisa Micele, University of Illinois Laboratory H.S. (IL)

Corky Miller-Strong, The Culver Academies (IN)

Janet Miranda, Prestonwood Christian Academy (TX)

Joyce Vining Morgan, White Mountain School (NH)

Gunnar W. Olson, Indian Springs School (AL)

Stuart Oremus, Wellington School (OH)

Deborah Robinson, Mandarin H.S. (FL)

Julie Rollins, Episcopal H.S. (TX)

Heidi Rose, Crystal Springs Uplands School (CA)

William C. Rowe, Thomas Jefferson School (MO)

Bruce Scher, Chicagoland Jewish H.S. (IL)

David Schindel, Sandia Preparatory School (NM)

Kathy Z. Schmidt, St. Mary's Hall (TX)

Barbara Simmons, Notre Dame High School (CA)

Joe Stehno, Bishop Brady H.S. (NH)

Bruce Stempien, Weston H.S. (CT)

Paul M. Stoneham, The Key School (MD)

Ted de Villafranca, Peddie School (NJ)

Scott White, Montclair H.S. (NJ)

Linda Zimring, Los Angeles United School District (CA)

One-Hour College Finder Index

Hobart and William Smith Colleges: architecture, 146; environmental studies, 132; small colleges, 94

Hofstra University: film/television, 165; learning disabilities programs, 136

Hollins University: art and design, 154; dance, 160; film/television, 165; women's colleges, 112

Holy Cross, College of the: Roman Catholic schools, 119

Hope College: conservative colleges, 124

Houghton College: conservative colleges, 124

Howard University: architecture, 146; business, 149; dance, 160; historically black institutions, 115

I

Idaho, College of: best-kept secrets, 109

Illinois–Urbana-Champaign, University of: architecture, 146; budget Ivy League, 79; business, 150; communications/ journalism, 162; engineering, 143; honors programs, 87

Illinois Institute of Technology: technical institutes, 141

Illinois Wesleyan University: best-kept secrets, 109; music, 158

Indiana University: business, 150; communications/journalism, 162; dance, 160; drama, 158; music, 157

Iowa, University of: budget Ivy League, 79; dance, 160; drama, 159

Iowa State University: engineering, 143

Ithaca College: business, 149; communications/journalism, 162; drama, 159; film/television, 164; music, 157; well-known universities, 102

J

James Madison University: business, 150

John Carroll University: Roman Catholic schools, 119

The Johns Hopkins University: engineering, 142; international studies, 133; top colleges, 75

Julliard School: dance, 160; drama, 159; music conservatories, 156

K

Kalamazoo College: innovative curriculums, 131; international studies, 133; study-abroad programs, 134

Kansas, University of: architecture, 146; budget Ivy League, 79; business, 150; communications/ journalism, 163; engineering, 143; film/television, 164

Kansas City Art Institute: art and design, 153

Kansas State University: architecture, 146

Keene State College: small-college bargains, 83

Kenyon College: art and design, 155; dance, 160; drama, 159; top colleges, 75

Knox College: best-kept secrets, 109; music, 158

L

Lafayette College: business, 151; engineering, 144; small colleges, 94

Lake Forest College: art and design, 155; business, 151; small colleges, 95

Landmark College: learning disabilities programs, 137

Lawrence University: drama, 159; music, 158; small colleges, 95

Lehigh University: architecture, 146; business, 149, 151; engineering, 144; well-known universities, 102

Lesley University: learning disabilities programs, 137

Lewis and Clark College: art and design, 155; business, 151; international studies, 133;

Mitchell College: learning disabilities programs, 137
Montana Technological University: technical institutes, 141
Moore College of Art and Design: art and design, 153
Morehouse College: business, 151; historically black institutions, 116; small-college bargains, 85
Morgan State University: historically black institutions, 116
Mount Holyoke College: international studies, 133; women's colleges, 113
Muhlenberg College: business, 151; dance, 161; drama, 159; small colleges, 95
music, 158
Muskingum College: learning disabilities programs, 137

N
Nebraska, University of: architecture, 146; communications/journalism, 163
Nebraska–Lincoln, University of: music, 157
New College of Florida: nonconformist colleges, 129; small-college bargains, 84
New England, University of: learning disabilities programs, 137
New England College: learning disabilities programs, 137
New Hampshire, University of: engineering, 143; environmental studies, 132; well-known universities, 104
New Jersey, College of: budget Ivy League, 80; engineering, 143
New Jersey Institute of Technology: architecture, 146; technical institutes, 141
New Mexico, University of: environmental studies, 132
New Mexico Institute of Mining and Technology: technical institutes, 141

New York, State University of. *see* SUNY
New York University: art and design, 154; business, 149; dance, 160; drama, 159; film/television, 165; music, 157; rising stars, 71
North Carolina, University of: rising stars, 73
North Carolina–Asheville, University of: environmental studies, 132; small-college bargains, 84
North Carolina–Chapel Hill, University of: budget Ivy League, 80; business, 150; communications/journalism, 163; drama, 159; honors programs, 87
North Carolina–Greensboro, University of: art and design, 155; environmental studies, 132
North Carolina School of the Arts: art and design, 153; dance, 161; music conservatories, 156
North Carolina State University: engineering, 143
Northeastern University: architecture, 146; engineering, 142; learning disabilities programs, 136; well-known universities, 104
Northwestern University: communications/journalism, 163; drama, 159; engineering, 142; film/television, 165; music, 157; rising stars, 72
Notre Dame, University of: architecture, 146; business, 149; engineering, 142; Roman Catholic schools, 119

O
Oberlin College: environmental studies, 132; music, 158; nonconformist colleges, 129; top colleges, 75
Occidental College: drama, 159; film/television, 165; international studies, 133;

General Index

About the Authors

In 1980, when he was Education editor of the *New York Times*, **Edward B. Fiske** sensed that college-bound students and their families needed better information on which to base their educational choices. Thus was born the *Fiske Guide to Colleges*. A graduate of Wesleyan University, Fiske did graduate work at Columbia University and assorted other bastions of higher learning. He left the *Times* in 1991 to pursue a variety of educational and journalistic interests, which included writing a book on school reform, *Smart Schools, Smart Kids*. When not visiting colleges, he can be found playing tennis, sailing, or doing research on the educational problems of Third World countries for UNESCO and other international organizations. Ted lives in Durham, North Carolina, near the campus Duke University, where his wife is a member of the faculty. They are coauthors of *When Schools Compete: A Cautionary Tale* and *Elusive Equity: Education Reform in Post Apartheid South Africa*.

Since entering Yale in the early 1980s, **Bruce G. Hammond** has devoted much of his time to counseling others about college admissions. At Yale, Hammond was editor-in-chief of *The Insider's Guide to the Colleges*. He subsequently served as managing editor of the *Fiske Guide to Colleges*. He has been quoted in numerous national publications including the *New York Times*, the *Wall Street Journal*, *USA Today*, the *Washington Post*, *Newsweek*, *U.S. News & World Report*, *Business Week*, and *Money Magazine*. Bruce is now director of college counseling at Dipont Education Management, a Chinese company dedicated to bringing American-style college counseling to students in Chinese public schools who wish to attend institutions in the Western world.

Notes

Notes

Notes

Notes

Notes

Notes